TOYNBEE: REAPPRAISALS

TOYNBEE

Reappraisals

Edited by

C.T. McIntire
Marvin Perry

UNIVERSITY OF TORONTO PRESS
Toronto Buffalo London

© University of Toronto Press 1989
Toronto Buffalo London
Printed in Canada
Reprinted in 2018
ISBN 0-8020-5785-3
ISBN 978-1-4875-7873-2 (paper)

Canadian Cataloguing in Publication Data

Main entry under title:

Toynbee: reappraisals

ISBN 0-8020-5785-3

1. Toynbee, Arnold J., 1889–1975.   2. Historiography.
I. McIntire, C. T.   II. Perry, Marvin.

CB18.T65A7 1989   907'.2024   C89-093830-X

Contents

PREFACE vii

C.T. MCINTIRE AND MARVIN PERRY
Toynbee's Achievement 3

WILLIAM H. MCNEILL
Toynbee's Life and Thought: Some Unresolved Questions 32

CHRISTIAN B. PEPER
Toynbee: An Historian's Conscience 50

C.T. MCINTIRE
Toynbee's Philosophy of History: His Christian Period 63

MARVIN PERRY
Toynbee and the Meaning of Athens and Jerusalem 93

THOMAS W. AFRICA
Toynbee: The Time Traveller 105

W. WARREN WAGAR
Toynbee as a Prophet of World Civilization 127

ROLAND N. STROMBERG
A Study of History and a World at War: Toynbee's Two Great Enterprises 141

BERNICE GLATZER ROSENTHAL
Toynbee's Interpretation of Russian History 160

EDWARD PESSEN
Toynbee on the United States 180

FREDERICK M. SCHWEITZER
Toynbee and Jewish History 195

THEODORE H. VON LAUE
Toynbee Amended and Updated 227

JANE CAPLAN
Working with Toynbee: A Personal Reminiscence 243

CONTRIBUTORS 253

Preface

1989 is the centenary of the birth of Arnold J. Toynbee (1889–1975), probably the best known, the most widely reviewed, and the most awesome historian of the twentieth century. His greatest work, *A Study of History* (12 vols, 1934–61; one vol. 1972), offered an interpretation of the history of every civilization and religion that has ever existed, and combined the methods and vision of history, religion, philosophy, and literature. His was an all-encompassing mind. The magnitude of his proposals and the audacity of his rhetoric can be overwhelming.

The authors of the essays in this volume are a group of historians who, having encountered so colossal a figure, make no attempt to examine his thought comprehensively. We have in mind the more accessible enterprise of reopening critical consideration of Toynbee now that his work is complete, and of asking our colleagues in the academic world and the world of public affairs to think freshly about his extraordinary achievement. We would like to begin a process of reinterpretation and reappraisal of Toynbee. Though we are well aware of the difficulties associated with a collection of essays by many authors, we are prepared to argue that Toynbee provides a prime case of the need for a veritable team of historians to engage in such a task. No one person has the knowledge or scope to accomplish the task alone. We are also well aware of the apparently devastating criticisms that have been made against Toynbee, but we are convinced that Toynbee's amplitude and creativity are such that no once-and-for-all dismissal of him is possible. We may expect historians, philosophers, and religion scholars to reconsider Toynbee from time to time for many generations to come.

All of us have had a long-standing interest in Toynbee. The topics that we have chosen to examine are ones that, upon reflection and in consultation with the editors, we have felt are important for opening the re-examination of his work. The essays discuss selectively a wide range of topics – his person, his religion, his historical thought, his vision of past and future, his surveys of international affairs, his treatment of specific themes, his global vision. We devote most attention to *A Study of History* and topics radiating from it. His most distinctive themes and categories show up in one form or another in nearly all the essays. In order to help people approach Toynbee more effectively and to read the essays with most benefit, the editors have provided an introduction to Toynbee and his achievement. We have included there a discussion of what kind of historian he was, an analysis of what his sources and method were in *A Study of History*, a characterization of his important concepts, and a comment about where the essays take us and what the ongoing merit of Toynbee might be.

We would like this book to be associated with two other books by two of our number. The first is Christian B. Peper's edition of Toynbee's forty-year correspondence with Columba Cary-Elwes, *An Historian's Conscience* (1986). The second is the biography of Toynbee by William H. McNeill (1989). We give our special thanks to Baruch College, City University of New York, who enabled the authors to meet together to hear and comment on each other's essays, and who provided a subvention for the publication of the book. We recommend S. Fiona Morton, *A Bibliography of Arnold J. Toynbee* (New York: Oxford University Press 1980) to all who wish to pursue further a study of Toynbee.

THE EDITORS

TOYNBEE: REAPPRAISALS

Toynbee's Achievement

C.T. McIntire and Marvin Perry

THE PHENOMENON

Toynbee's achievement and reputation depend primarily upon his most stunning work, to which he gave the unpretentious name *A Study of History*. The main body of *Study* included ten volumes published between 1934 and 1954. He extended this work to twelve volumes with the addition of an atlas in 1959 and a volume called *Reconsiderations* in 1961.[1] The first volume of a two-volume abridged edition appeared in 1947 and the second in 1957, and he eventually published a one-volume, fully illustrated, revised edition in 1972. Even the shortest volumes of *Study* ran to more than four hundred pages and most came to well over seven hundred pages each.[2] Counting from the day in 1921 when, according to his testimony, he began planning the book, until the moment he published the one-volume revision, Toynbee laboured on what he regarded as one book for fifty years. He had contemplated the problem of comparative history underlying the book even longer – since August 1914 and the outbreak of the First World War.[3] *A Study of History* is the most comprehensive attempt to understand the recurrent processes of universal history ever produced. Surrounding this magnum opus was an output of other books, articles, and reviews so prodigious that another book is required to name them all.[4] Toynbee's name has entered the short list of thinkers about history that every generation feels compelled to encounter – Thucydides, Polybius, Eusebius, Augustine, Machiavelli, Calvin, Vico, Voltaire, Hegel, Marx, Spengler, and perhaps a few others.

Oxford University Press put its own reputation and world-wide marketing facilities behind Toynbee and published *Study* and every other major book and nearly all the smaller books he ever wrote. They arranged for the Book-of-the-Month Club to feature the two-volume edition, and the circulation figures for that compact version mounted into the hundreds of thousands. Even today it is hard to find a historian over forty without it, and second-hand bookstores can still be depended upon to have at least one set on hand. Oxford keeps the two-volume paperback edition in print. As a result of invitations to lecture at virtually every important university and college in the world that was politically accessible to him, Toynbee met in person with a high proportion of two generations of history scholars. When *Time* magazine featured him on the cover of its 18 October 1954 issue, his name became a household word among the North American middle classes. His renown spread widely, although it is not certain that his readership increased.

Toynbee's reputation has gone through phases. When the first three volumes of *A Study of History* appeared in 1934 and the second three in 1939 he was on the whole well received by the academic community. Although they raised many criticisms, reviewers tended to acknowledge that he offered an intriguing theory of history that warranted serious consideration, and many scholars and community leaders called him a great historian.[5] After 1954, when volumes seven to ten appeared to complete his argument, and after *Time* and the Book-of-the-Month Club discovered him, he received accolades from an admiring public. In the United States this popular reputation was due, no doubt, to effective marketing, but it was also unmistakable that many people emerging from the disasters of world war, capitalist depression, and Nazi and Stalinist totalitarianism felt that he helped explain the experiences of their generation. They saw in Toynbee one who may have uncovered basic laws accounting for the growth and decline of civilizations, who offered the consolations of religion in a time of troubles, and who seemed to approve a large role for America in the world.

Among scholars Toynbee's reception after 1954 was very different. An avalanche of extraordinarily bad reviews fell upon him and, even though he continued to receive invitations to lecture on university campuses, his reputation among historians virtually dissipated.[6] The criticisms that were wholly negative were generally of three types. One kind of complaint came from specialists who repeated endlessly that Toynbee's work rested on a weak, or false, empirical basis – he got his details wrong, he created interpretations ex nihilo unheard of among specialists, he passed over what did not fit his theses. Another kind of criticism rejected the whole project as wrong or even impossible. Critics dismissed as misguided Toynbee's attempt to discover the laws that regulate the course of history, counted as trivial his indications of sample laws, or accused him of bending history to fit an arbitrary and rigid a priori framework. A third kind of attack rejected the religious content of his theory that became unmistakable in the 1954 volumes, and classified Toynbee as a theologian or prophet or mystic – almost anything except historian. Added to all these criticisms were many lesser ones, even from those who found redeeming qualities in his work.[7]

A devastating avalanche it was. Toynbee patiently collected the criticisms and, amazingly, wrote a full-scale reply that became volume twelve of *Study* (1961). He reaffirmed the basic character, the main theses, and the merit of his project, but on point after point he changed his mind, absorbing his critics here and dismissing them there. He blended his old and new conceptions into the one-volume synthesis published eleven years later (1972). In spite of his comprehensive replies, historians in Europe and North America generally took little notice and did not bother to read the revised Toynbee or think about the significance of his revisions, even if they had read Toynbee years before.

Meanwhile, Toynbee's reputation entered a new phase and carried on with vitality elsewhere – in the third world. Scholars there liked the way he gave recognition to the cultures past and present of Asia, Central and South America, and eventually Africa. For more than a decade, beginning in 1956, and amid great acclaim, he lectured often during journeys through the Middle East, South Asia, the Far East, Latin America, Africa, and Australasia, with repeated visits especially to Japan.

HISTORIAN

Toynbee made no more insistent claim about himself than that he wrote as a historian and he resisted no charge from his critics more vehemently than that his work was not empirical. We may perhaps best understand what he meant if we consider what kind of things he wrote.

We find that his professional work fell into three primary areas of scholarship.[8] The first was classical studies and the history of ancient Greece and Rome. His education as a youth at Winchester College, a private English boarding-school, was, in keeping with his upper-bourgeois class at that time, entirely classical. He learned to think and write in Greek and Latin and came to know thoroughly the thought and literature of Greece and Rome. He continued in classics at Balliol College, Oxford, in 1907, finishing his degree in 1911. After a year in Greece he took his first position as fellow and tutor in ancient history at Balliol. Coming out of the First World War, he extended his professional interest in Greece to the modern period, holding the appointment as the first Koraes Professor of Byzantine and Modern Greek Language, Literature, and History in the University of London from 1919 to 1924. Throughout his long career he published books, texts, and articles on Greece and Rome, notably *Greek Historical Thought from Homer to the Age of Heraclitus* (1924), *Greek Civilization and Character* (1924), *Hellenism* (1959), *Hannibal's Legacy: The Hannibalic War's Effects on Roman Life* (two volumes, 1965), and *An Ekistical Study of the Hellenic City State* (1972). *Hannibal's Legacy* was a formidable work of historical scholarship based on minute and exhaustive research into every available piece of evidence. *Hellenism* was a concise synthesis of Greek and Roman history, much of which he wrote from memory while on board ship sailing from Panama to New Zealand. It is not always clear which was his first cultural world – London, in which he was born and lived for most of his life, except for brief or seasonal periods in Oxford and Yorkshire, or ancient Greece and Rome.

When he resigned the Koraes chair under pressure from its Greek endowers, who detested his criticism of Greek atrocities against Turks, Toynbee entered his second professional field, international relations. His official position from 1924 until his formal retirement in 1955, the one from which he received his primary income, was as director of studies and non-teaching researcher in international affairs at the Royal Institute of International Affairs at Chatham House, St James Square, London. He also held the position of a research professor in the University of London as the Stevenson Professor of International Affairs. During both world wars he worked on international affairs in intelligence service for the British government. Between 1915 and 1932 he wrote several works on current world affairs, including *Nationality and the War* (1915) and *The World after the Peace Conference* (1925). Between 1925 and 1938 he wrote most of the monumental, annual volumes of the *Survey of International Affairs* as part of his job at Chatham House. He was associated with later volumes of the *Survey* into the 1950s. As part of this work he edited and wrote much of a multi-volume political history of the Second World War. The volumes of the *Survey* were detailed studies of current international history that supplied information and analysis of world politics year by year. They could be regarded as a creative addition to the tradition of annals and the historical chronicle, and were based largely on government reports, published documents, and newspaper accounts from around the world. There were scholars who depended on Toynbee's *Survey* for their own work in international affairs and who knew little of his contributions to ancient history or historical thought. His book *Democracy in the Atomic Age* (1957) became an influential analysis of international relations under the threat of the bomb.

Toynbee's third area of professional work was his writing about general history and historical thought. *A Study of History* belongs to this aspect of his career. It is important to remember that, formally speaking, Toynbee wrote the *Study* as a sideline during his Chatham House years, and the revisions after his retirement. Before the war Chatham House, with funding from the Rockefeller Foundation, allowed him to leave London for Yorkshire as soon as he finished his duties of writing the annual *Survey*. He spoke of how he valued this rhythm of spending half the year in the city on current international history and the other half in the country on the history of all the world's past civilizations. After the war Chatham House arranged with the Rockefeller Foundation to release Toynbee to work at least half-time on *Study* for several years, which enabled him to complete all ten volumes of the main body of the work before his retirement. After his retirement the Rockefeller Foundation again stepped in to finance his world travels with the aim of assisting his review of his own work. The results became *Reconsiderations* (1961) and the one-volume revised edition of 1972.[9]

While engaged in *Study* Toynbee followed the inner logic of his inquiry into what could almost be counted as a fourth area of work

– the study of the history of the world's religions – but which actually formed part of his work on general history. As a result of religious accents in the household of his youth and in his schooling at Winchester, he had absorbed the Bible and the Book of Common Prayer and made religion an inescapable element in his consciousness. Religion appeared in all of the first six volumes of *Study* and became a major subject in the final ones. Toynbee wrote as well other works on religion, including *An Historian's Approach to Religion* (1956) and *Christianity among the World Religions* (1957).

Toynbee considered *A Study of History* to be a synthetic and interpretive work, in contrast with a fact-finding work, even though he attached monographic annexes to each of the first ten volumes. He consciously pursued generalization rather than particulars, recurrence rather than uniqueness. He presented a general study about history and not a historical study of some subject. In other words, his volumes do not comprise a history of ancient Greece and Rome integrated with histories of China, the Mayans, and so on. Strictly speaking, *Study* is not a history of the world. Toynbee eventually did write a one-volume narrative history of the world, *Mankind and Mother Earth*, which appeared posthumously in 1976 and incorporated his thinking about civilizations. Toynbee called *Study* a comparative examination of the species of society known as civilizations.[10] He attempted to identify all the civilizations that have ever existed in the history of the world, and then to analyse their histories comparatively and philosophically, rather than to relate them in a chronological narrative.

What emerged was a theory about the typical life-history of civilizations, based on the detection of recurrent events and phenomena in their histories. Toynbee proposed that civilizations may be seen to experience a common rhythm in four beats – genesis, growth, breakdown, and disintegration. It was a variation on the elemental course of the history of anything there is – becoming, being, and ceasing-to-be.[11] In volumes one through six he analysed this recurrent rhythm and sought to understand and explain why civilizations began and why other societies with apparent prospects of civilization miscarried, why some grew and others failed to grow, why almost all that grew proceeded to break down, and why all that broke down either had disintegrated or were now in the process of disintegration. In volumes seven through nine Toynbee extended, in effect, his examination of the phase of disintegration, by analysing at length the three phenomena that he found typically appeared when civilizations began to disintegrate – universal states, universal churches, and external barbarian societies. In his discussion of universal churches he came to attribute an exceedingly prominent responsibility to religion in general history. In the same volumes he explored at length encounters between civilizations and the 'species of historical events known as renaissances.' He closed his comparative study of civilizations with a long discourse in volumes nine and ten on law and freedom in history and on his epistemology of historical study.

Our survey of the whole range of Toynbee's writings discloses that he produced three very different genres of professional work. The first was ancient history, the second was contemporary history, and the third was a melange of comparative history, philosophy of history, and eventually theology of history. The first spoke to ancient historians and classicists, the second to political scientists, historians of international affairs, and foreign-policy makers and analysts, and the third to historians interested in the larger questions, theologians, public leaders, and the general public. The first and second looked primarily at particulars, while the third self-consciously shifted attention to regularities and recurrences.[12] The first two genres rested on various kinds of research into large amounts of specific details about his subjects, past or current, while the third depended on his reading of history books about each of the many civilizations he identified.

In the light of his own life-history and this variety of writing we can venture two observations. First, Toynbee's claim to be a historian and to think like a historian is well-founded, whatever else he may also have been. We shall have to add that he was the kind of historian who took up the philosophy and the theology of history. He was socialized as a historian, not as a philosopher or theologian. His primary community of discourse was historians, and secondly philosophers and theologians. In all his work he kept before him the common theme of understanding history. When he entered into philosophical or theological themes, he did so as a historian and with the interests that historians typically have in the hows and whys of the processes of history.

Second, Toynbee's claim to be empirical is also well-founded, with the meaning of empirical varying according to the three genres of his work. In his monographic work, like *Hannibal's Legacy*, and in the *Survey of International Affairs* he worked critically with evidence and information in ways that historians of any school of thought could recognize as empirical, varying according to the constraints and interests of the study of past history as contrasted with current history. It is another matter to decide by critical investigation whether his procedures were suitable and his results valid or at least plausible. His work in *Study* was empirical in a different sense. Here he examined all the known cases of the phenomenon he called a civilization. Then he sought to generalize about their life-histories in a comparative manner, an act that took him far from the usual habits of historians. None the less, his theory was based upon evidence for the existence and histories of the many civilizations as mediated by the historical studies he consulted. The criteria appropriate for understanding the empirical character of *Study* are those that belong to the comparative study of civilizations and to the construction of a theory about their life-histories, not those applicable merely to the historical study of particular subjects. Again, whether Toynbee's procedures are well-done and his results valid or plausible can be assessed by critical discussion. In other words, both monographic and synthetic history are empirical, but in different ways, and both can be assessed critically within the community of scholars.

Toynbee devoted himself to his historical work as if he were on a mission, and this, too, disturbed his critics. He looked on himself as a chance survivor of the First World War, in which so many of his Oxford contemporaries were killed, and he believed that he was obliged to justify the unmerited extension of life he enjoyed, almost to compensate for the wastage of his colleagues' lives. He commenced *Study* in the 1920s as a quest to understand the mystery of the rise and fall of civilizations. As his sense of the troubles of Western civilization intensified in the 1930s he longed to use his study of history to influence the course of history, especially to encourage the creation of a viable political world order. Slowly this desire converted into his wish to contribute to the salvation of his own civilization, and his quest transformed almost imperceptibly into a spiritual journey.[13] After the Second World War, in lectures and publications in the 1940s and 1950s, Toynbee considered at length the prospects of the West. He stressed the reality of human freedom in history, and urged his hearers to reach for spiritual renewal as the means of defeating the breakdown of their civilization. He began to observe more and more that the West was creating the means by which the world experienced unity. It was a short next step to convert his *Study* into an appeal for world unity in which the West took its seat along with all the other civilizations in a world federal union. But the transmutation of his mission did not end there. In *Reconsiderations* Toynbee called for the transferral of all local and national loyalties to 'mankind as a whole.' In the final revision of his work in the edition of 1972 his eyes beheld a coming 'new ecumenical civilization' blended from the contributions of all the civilizations of the world. He hoped that *Mankind and Mother Earth* would contribute to the promotion of human unity and human solidarity with the 'biosphere.' Throughout these many redirections in his mission as a historian Toynbee displayed continuously the moral passions of a man who wanted his *Study* to work against oppression, war, and self-centredness.[14]

SOURCES AND METHOD

Toynbee readily revealed the sources and the influences that lay behind *A Study of History*. He named the works he consulted in his text and footnotes and appended a long 'Acknowledgements and Thanks' to volume ten.[15] First of all, in sheer quantity of citations, was the Bible in the King James Version. Next would come the classical myths, like that of Prometheus, and large numbers of classical authors, particularly Thucydides, Polybius, and Aeschylus. And then Goethe's *Faust*. Behind everything was his mother, who encouraged his interest in history. He named Edward Gibbon and *The History of the Decline and Fall of the Roman Empire* as his perpetual 'cynosure.' With Gibbon in his head and prompted by the experience of the First World War, Toynbee had begun his life-work in order to understand analogues he perceived between the rise and fall of the ancient Greek and Roman world and the course of his own.[16] He thought the poetry of Robert Browning provided him, via osmosis, with what became his most characteristic notion, the concept of challenge and response. Henri Bergson, especially *L'Évolution Créatrice* (24th ed., 1921) and *Les Deux Sources de la Morale et de la Religion* (1932), served him in his understanding of life as the subject of historical study, of the *élan vital* and the growth of civilizations, and of the link between the brotherhood of 'man' and the fatherhood of God. J.C. Smuts's *Holism and Evolution* (2nd ed., 1927) was essential to his statement about the genesis of civilizations and appears again in the volume on growth. Karl Marx led him to think about social schism and conflict, which he believed were evidences of disintegration in the social body of a civilization. As his sense of the crisis of his own society intensified, Toynbee began to rely on St Augustine as an inspiration for understanding breakdown and disintegration, and on Augustine's notion of the City of God for his image of the goal of history in the final volumes. Carl Jung's *Psychological Types* (1923) gave him the understanding of the soul and the higher religions he needed in volume seven. He called Oswald Spengler the leading practitioner of the philosophy of history of the previous generation, but opposed his organic determinism and utilized him as a foil in all phases of his theory. He was attracted later to Philip Bagby's *Culture and History: Prolegomena to the Comparative Study of Civilizations* (1958), which he counted as compatible with his own in genre and attitude.

For the vast body of his work Toynbee depended upon a lengthy list of historians. In the first six volumes he tended to cite general histories and surveys of each nation or civilization or religion he included. For example, he used V.A. Smith, *The Early History of India* (1903), Friedrich Hirth, *The Ancient History of China* (1908), P.A. Means, *Ancient Civilizations of the Andes* (1931), T. Gann and J.E. Thompson, *The History of the Maya* (1931), and J. Murdoch, *A History of Japan* (1926). Throughout most of the volumes he cited Eduard Meyer, *Geschichte des Altertums* (3 vols, 1901, and later eds). After World War Two he continued the same practice of citing general histories in volumes seven and eight. He used Charles Eliot, *Hinduism and Buddhism* (1921), and J.G. Frazer's *The Golden Bough: Adonis, Attis, Orisis: Studies in the History of Oriental Religion* (2nd ed., 1907). Only occasionally in the ten volumes did he cite works of research, like H.L. Hoskins, *British Routes to India* (1928), or P.E. Moseley, *Russian Diplomacy and the Opening of the Eastern Question in 1838 and 1839* (1934). In all the volumes Toynbee relied primarily on works published in the 1920s and the early 1930s or before, many going well back into the nineteenth century, although in the last four volumes he added some titles from the 1940s and 1950s. He acknowledged that he completed most of his reading for all ten volumes well before the second war, and that he wrote the final four main volumes largely from old notes that were stored in New York during the war.[17] However, it is evident from *Reconsiderations* (1961) and the revised edition of 1972 that he read freshly and widely again after his retirement. In this later reading he continued to depend on general histories, works like Basil Davidson, *The Africans* (1969).

This review of the major influences on Toynbee's thought and the kinds of items in his bibliography reveals the predominance of two classes of works and instructs us about the empirical level on which he worked. The first group included sacred scriptures, mythology, drama, poetry, philosophy, religion – writings he classed as imaginative. To these he would add his imaginative experiences while travelling, his close association with the Benedictine monks of Ampleforth Abbey, and his religious and mystical experiences, including his experiences of time-travel. The second group consisted of history books – the books he would class as empirical and products of the intellect. To these he would add atlases and his examination of the geography of the areas in which he travelled.[18]

It is hard to think of what he might add to the first group to increase the range of his imagination. The second group, however, has two huge lacunae, historical sources and historical monographs. *Study* was not based on the primary sources of historical study, the documents, the artefacts, the various remains of bygone peoples, or on the monographs of historical research. It was based on general histories. Toynbee did use some general histories of special themes, like J.L. Strachan-Davidson, *Problems of the Roman Criminal Law* (1912), or Samuel Dill, *Roman Society in Gaul in the Merovingian Age* (1926), but on the whole his list skewed towards works themselves already the products of survey, like N. Jorga, *Geschichte des Osmanischen Reiches* (5 vols, 1908–13), or C.P. Fitzgerald, *China: A Short Cultural History* (1935). In other words, Toynbee worked three or four steps removed from historical research, at a distance dependent on multiple levels of prior generalization. While thinking at so remote a distance from historical research does not render his work unempirical, it does allow ample opportunities for mistakes and misunderstandings to intervene, and it takes him a long way from the specialists in any one of his civilizations today. He was deliberate in his decision to use general histories.

He confessed in volume ten that he felt a drive towards acquiring omniscient knowledge about every civilization, and only general histories were comprehensive enough to satisfy him. At the same time, he opposed in principle the expectation that historians should be merely specialists, even though he fit the description of a specialist in certain aspects of Greek and Roman history. He had resolved 'never to allow himself to be coralled in a specialist's pound' and to devote himself instead to the 'catholicity' of historical interests. His inclination towards general histories as the source of his empirical information about the many civilizations melded naturally with his attraction to scriptures, myths, literature, and philosophy. Indeed, he recognized structural similarities between 'a scholar in quest of intellectual omniscience' and 'a soul in quest of spiritual perfection.'[19]

The two classes of readings behind Toynbee's thought paralleled the two major components of his method: imagination and historical analysis. He spoke often and deliberately about his method, especially in volumes one, seven, eight, ten, and twelve. He was, in volume one, very conscious of distinguishing his method from that of the natural sciences, on the one hand, and from narrowly empirical history, on the other. Following Bergson, he insisted that an appropriate historical method required a feeling for life and life as a whole, for actions and ideas, and necessitated a break with methods constructed for dealing with inanimate nature. Because his subject was living creatures he felt compelled to range beyond 'the formulae of Science' and to entertain for a moment 'the language of Mythology.' This did not mean that he denied analogies between historical method and scientific method. As he carried on with his study he found himself more and more using the language of 'law' to indicate regularities in human affairs, even though he felt discomfited by the connotation of 'inexorable' that came with it. He eventually changed the title of part XI in volume nine from the less scientific sounding 'Rhythms in the Histories of Civilization' to 'Law and Freedom in History' and argued strongly for the notion of natural laws in human affairs. Years later, in *Reconsiderations*, he further muted his statement of the difference between his historical method and that of the natural sciences, and acknowledged that his method of analysis and classification was basically like that in the sciences.[20]

Analysis and classification of civilizations were where Toynbee started in volume one, and he sounded like a biologist naming genera and species or exploring genetics, growth, and generations. His first step was to identify the largest social unit in space and time of which he could say that other social units were parts. His answer was 'a Society.' He thought about Great Britain and reasoned that his 'nation' had a kinship relation with others, like France, and that their common social ancestry took them back to the Roman Empire. Then Gibbon came to mind. In a significant intellectual move, following Eduard Meyer, Toynbee determined that Greek and Roman history were united as the history of 'Hellenic Society.' The unit containing Great Britain would be 'Western Society,' which he then reckoned began with the end of the Roman Empire, but which sustained an affiliated relationship with the earlier Hellenic unit. He testified later that 'once I had identified one civilization, twenty other societies of the same species came into focus, one after another, in my field of historical vision.' Actually he did not name them civilizations right away. He waited until he spoke about the Todas of the Nilgiri Hills in south India within the British Empire, and then distinguished civilizations from primitive societies. On first count he found 21 civilizations (for instance, Egyptiac, Indic, Western) and at least 650 primitive societies (for example, Todas).[21]

Toynbee constructed his thought rigorously in volume one, but logic was not his only instrument. He also worked with an extraordinarily active imagination. He claimed that Plato had taught him that 'when in a mental voyage, I found myself at the upper limit of the atmosphere accessible to Reason, not to hesitate to let my imagination carry me on up into the stratosphere on the wings of a myth.'[22] He rode his imagination often, and at crucial moments in his thinking, moments that are worth noting.

To begin with, he claimed that the whole plan of his giant project came to him in an act of imagination at the end of a day riding on the Orient Express through Greece in 1921, a day spent ruminating on ancient sites and modern experiences. Volumes one, four, and seven came out much as he thought that day. Imagination also gave him the clues to both the genesis and the growth of civilizations.[23] We have already mentioned Toynbee's reference to the poetry of Robert Browning as the probable well-spring of his idea of challenge and response. After a lengthy empirical discussion of the inadequacy of using race or physical environment to explain why civilizations come into existence, he turned to mythology for inspiration. He found in Job and Goethe's *Faust* what he called the 'encounter between two superhuman personalities,' and there he discovered 'that creation is the outcome of an encounter, or – to re-translate the imagery of myths into the terminology of Science – that genesis is a function of interaction.' This process he named 'challenge and response.' The challenges are invariably either physical, such as the cold of the Arctic and the chaotic flooding of the Nile river, or social, such as the mass migration of an alien people into the homeland of another people. The responses are what affected societies do about the physical or social challenges. At the end of volume one and in volume two Toynbee looked for cycles of challenge and response in his twenty-one civilizations using the many general histories in his bibliography. He sought to determine what the challenges were and how successful responses put these twenty-one societies on the path of civilization, while the responses of three or four others failed, turning them into 'abortive civilizations' (for instance, the Scandinavian).

In volume three Toynbee turned to mythology again for a clue to why there was no assurance that a civilization, once born, will grow. His initial inquiries had shown him that twenty-one societies that had become civilizations had also entered on a process of growth, while five other societies failed to grow, becoming instead 'arrested civilizations' (for example, Eskimo, Nomadic). He saw in Aeschylus and the Prometheus myth a suggestion of the answer in the form of creative personalities. Creative leaders, provided they attract the following of the masses, may set in motion a process of dynamic change and growth that moves a society from a static Yin state into a burst of Yang activity. As long as the leadership of the society sustains the same creativity that generated its birth as a civilization, the process continues according to a recurrent rhythm of challenge, successful response, new challenge, new successful response. Toynbee again traversed his list of civilizations and consulted his bibliography of general histories to determine how the process worked in detail. Thus he suggested that the people who constructed the irrigation system around the Nile responded well to the physical challenge, but that the frigid Arctic arrested the social growth of the Eskimo. He repeated his procedure of reflection on myth and comparative analysis of general histories when he reached the phases of breakdown and disintegration in volumes four to six. Here his consideration of myth guided him in his discussion of nemesis, idolatry, schism in the soul, and regeneration (palingenesia).[24] He was able to identify the approximate moment of the breakdown of a civilization by reference to the appearance of Universal States (for example, Roman Empire, Mongol Empire) Indeed it is probable that he used the presence of a universal state as the pivot of his whole system of indicating the existence of a civilization and elaborating its four-beat rhythm. He decided by means of his moral imagination that universal states were instruments of oppression, and hence evidences of decline and not of glory. He then would move comparatively across and chronologically through his civilizations to elucidate their phases of breakdown and disintegration.[25] He observed that most civilizations were now dead (for instance, Minoan, Mayan), but that seven civilizations were still alive today. He concluded that six of these were unmistakably in disintegration (for example, Islamic, Hindu). The remaining one (Western) exhibited signs of breakdown. In addition, he discovered seven 'fossilized relics of societies' (for instance, Jews as fossil of Syriac, Parsees as fossil of Indic).[26] Toynbee's intensive concentration on religion in volumes seven, eight, and ten was yet another product of his long-standing deference to imagination as an important component of his historical method. By the time he wrote volume ten he was prepared to articulate at length his conviction that historical study was both necessarily empirical and dependent on imaginative elements like curiosity, a feeling for the poetry in the details of history, and a desire to discover the meaning of history.

Toynbee's comparative method presupposed what he called the philosophical contemporaneity of the civilizations. The civilizations were contemporary in two ways. In one sense, on the enormous time-scale of the history of the earth and of human habitation of the earth, all the civilizations he named were clustered together at the recent end of the scale, and belonged to the same civilizational period of human history. In another sense, in terms of social classification, all the civilizations were members of a class of societies having in common 'an element of regularity and recurrence,' and could be analysed as if the courses of their histories were parallel. He defended his method as a corrective to the essentially linear method that he regarded as supportive of a self-serving interpretation of Western civilization as the epitome of civilization and the destination of all previous history.[27] He admitted that his theory could look deterministic, but in spite of the heavy death toll, and near-death toll, he insisted that civilizations were not bound to die. He invariably attributed breakdown and disintegration to human weaknesses that people have the capacity to remedy.[28]

CIVILIZATIONS AND OTHER CONCEPTS

Toynbee's whole theory of comparative history stood on his concept of civilizations. He was reticent to define his term in advance, because he wanted to allow the specifics to emerge in his usage. Over the years, however, he expended much thought on his concept, and showed a remarkable willingness to adapt to criticism. The problem he faced was that the specification of what counted as a civilization was not as simple as he first believed.

In his initial discussion of civilizations Toynbee referred to social units that were relatively self-contained, and that had internal affairs and external relations. He seemed to be thinking by analogy with nation-states that have members, boundaries, and insides and outsides. Yet he disliked nation-states and sought in civilizations a wider 'intelligible field of study' that included nations as parts. He also disliked the conventional pairing of the term civilization with the concept of barbarism and the attendant notion that human beings had progressed from barbarism to civilization, and he tried to uncouple the connection. To do so he adopted the term 'society' as his comprehensive category, and suggested in volumes one to six that societies came in two kinds, which he named Civilizations and Primitive Societies. Compared to primitive societies, civilizations are less plentiful, larger in population and geographical range, and supposedly longer-lived. In spite of his misgivings about the idea of progress from barbarian to civilized life, Toynbee reckoned civilizations to be a stage of human history succeeding primitive societies, and regarded primitive societies alive today as static leftovers of a previous epoch. He thought of civilizations as dynamic and often used the phrase 'Man in process of civilization' to describe the age of civilizations that began perhaps six thousand years ago. He retained the word barbarian in the term Barbarian War-Bands (for instance, the Franks), but did not clarify whether they were primitive societies, arrested civilizations (for example, Nomadic), or some other form of society. His social classification could seem almost haphazard.[29]

Early in volume one Toynbee designated two criteria for identifying civilizations and distinguishing them from each other. The first was the religion of the civilization (for instance, Hinduism, Islam), and the second was geographical extent. As he proceeded, however, he became unhappy with this understanding of the relationship between civilizations and religions. Finally, in volume seven he magnified the role of religion and reversed his theory. He came to the conclusion that the social units he called Universal Churches were not best accounted for as parts of civilizations or as symptoms of the disintegration of a civilization. They should be classed as a third kind of society of the same rank as civilizations and primitive societies. He now called them Higher Religions (for example, Hinduism, Christianity), and proposed to think of their appearance as marking generally a third age in human history succeeding the other two societies. Higher religions were not the religions of primitive societies or even of civilizations, but were a new kind of society based on love, compassion, and selflessness. They were a legacy of the entire previous history of humanity. In volume twelve Toynbee placed even greater stress on his belief that the emergence of the higher religions created a break with all previous history. In the higher religions human beings for the first time came into direct communion as individuals with 'absolute spiritual Reality,' the name Toynbee now gave to what he used to name as God. In the same volume, to match his new interpretation of history as spiritual progress, he revised his depiction of civilizations. Civilizations were 'an endeavour to create a state of society in which the whole of mankind will be able to live together in harmony, as members of an all-inclusive family' – the kind of life envisioned by the prophets of the higher religions.[30]

Toynbee's understanding of Universal States paralleled his concept of Universal Churches, and underwent a comparable, but less dramatic change. In his theory a universal state replaced a multitude of separate states some time after breakdown began, and was the product of the Dominant Minority, one of three classes of people that appeared during breakdown. The dominant minority, once the creative leadership impelling the growth of the civilization, now attempted to prevent the disintegration of the civilization, and thus to preserve their inherited dominance. They constructed the apparatus of the universal state, the effect of which was to oppress the majority of the population. The masses, who previously had accepted their leadership, but who had already begun to withdraw their support from this uninspired minority, rejected the new oppression and converted into an Internal Proletariat, a class struggling against the state. Disinherited, uprooted, and alienated, the internal proletariat demonstrated their own creativity by founding a universal church. At the same time, on the borders of the civilization the barbarian war-bands appeared as an External Proletariat, the third class involved in the breakdown, which contributed to the process of disintegration, and even occasionally served as instruments in establishing the universal state (for instance, Mogul Empire in India). From volume seven onward Toynbee considered universal states to be a form of idolatry and accentuated their importance as means in the emergence of the higher religions.[31]

The inspiration for much of this part of his theory – class struggle, oppression, alienation, the emergence of proletariats – came from Marx, but Toynbee transmuted Marx's economic interpretation into political and religious categories.[32] His normal practice throughout his thought was to give only a small role to economic factors. The primary role belonged to physical, political, and religious factors. He discoursed at length on the effects of geography and climate, the impact of war, empire, and religious change, and the influence of great individuals in church and state. He even included ample reference to science, technology, literature, and art, but he paid small attention to commerce, industry, or the control of the means of production. All the major social units in his theory were religious or political – states, churches, war-bands, even civilizations and primitive societies, and not markets, factories, cities, social classes, or families. Toynbee's explanations for the movement of civilizations through the four beats of the recurrent rhythm were predominantly religious, political, and physical. The relation between what he called Macrocosm and Microcosm in volumes one to six was the relation between social or physical factors and spiritual factors, between what he thought of as the external and the internal worlds of a civilization or an individual. In every case when he sought an explanation for growth, breakdown, and disintegration of civilizations he found it not in the macrocosm, but in the microcosm. The criterion of growth was the response in the form of inward self-determination to challenges arising from within, while the criterion of disintegration was the appearance of schism in the soul and not merely in political and religious institutions.[33] At issue in all of this, Toynbee thought, was an understanding of human freedom and an appreciation of human beings as responsible for their own history, for good or for ill. His reflections in volume nine on law in history and human freedom led him to affirm both law and freedom and to resolve any apparent tensions between the two by identifying freedom in its highest form with the fulfilment of God's law of love.[34]

It would be interesting to speculate about what would have happened to Toynbee's theory of civilizations if he had incorporated a lengthy analysis of market relations. As he discovered with religions, markets have had a way of spreading beyond political units and assuming a social existence all their own. They have not confined themselves merely to the 'internal' life of civilizations. If Toynbee pursued this line of thought, analogous to his reconsideration of universal churches, would he need to belittle civilizations even further, and treat something like Universal Markets as a distinct species of society next to civilizations, primitive societies, and higher religions? And what would happen to his theory of the four-beat rhythm of the history of civilizations if he worked economic factors into his thought systematically? Economic factors became even more remote from Toynbee's theory as he moved through his volumes and amplified his stress on religious factors. By the time he reached volume ten he was prepared to subsume all factors in human history under religious meanings. History was, he confessed, 'a vision of God's creation on the move, from God as its source towards God as its goal.' He made the sublimation of economic-technological factors to spiritual meanings complete towards the end of *Study* and in *An Historian's Approach to Religion* (1956) and *America and the World Revolution* (1962) when he interpreted the attitudes towards technology and its accomplishments within modern industrial capitalism and America as idolatry, much as he had treated universal states in his theory earlier. In *Reconsiderations*, looking back over his thought, he wrote, 'In general, I minimize the effects of material factors of all kinds, economic and technical as well as military, and I magnify the effects of spiritual factors.'[35]

The eventual effect of the advent of universal churches, universal states, and barbarian war-bands in history, at least as Toynbee conceived it in volume one, was the dissolution of one civilization and the genesis of a succeeding civilization. He styled this relationship 'apparentation and affiliation,' and spoke of generations of civilizations. He detected two civilizations with no offspring (Egyptiac and Andean), but the rest had some generational connection with at least one other civilization. There were a few cases of three consecutive generations extending from the beginning of the age of civilizations to the present (for instance, Minoan-Hellenic-Western, Minoan-Syriac-Islamic). After Toynbee inverted the relation between civilizations and higher religions, the three ages that then appeared in his theory, when conjoined with his generational proposal, became, in effect, seven ages: primitive societies, primary civilizations, rudimentary higher religions (for instance, Osiris and Isis worship), secondary civilizations, higher religions, tertiary civilizations, secondary higher religions (for example, Baha'i).[36]

In the light of further reading and the multitude of critical comments on his proposals, Toynbee abided by his own understanding of the empirical character of his method and changed his mind on the number, the identities, and the generational relations between civilizations. Inadvertently, he admitted the extreme fragility of his primary concept. In *Reconsiderations* (1961) he drastically reduced the number of independent civilizations from twenty-one to thirteen by simplification (for instance, Middle American covered three others, Sinic absorbed all of Chinese history), but he created a class named 'satellite civilizations' (for example, Mississippian as satellite to Middle American) that included fifteen members and allowed him to rearrange some and add new ones to his list. Thus he raised his total number to twenty-eight, plus six abortive civilizations. He carried his revisions even further for the one-volume edition in 1972, finally adding an African civilization. This brought the number of independent civilizations to fourteen, while raising the satellite number to seventeen, for a total of thirty-one, plus the six abortive ones. Presumably the arrested civilizations and the fossils of civilizations were still on his list.[37]

Toynbee showed the same flexibility in changing his mind about the historical model he used in his reflections. He frankly acknowledged that he took the Greco-Roman world and the European world and their relationship as the basis for every important element in his entire theory of civilizations. In response to the empirical arguments of his critics, he rethought his Hellenic-Western model and tried out both a Chinese model and a Jewish model. He tried a fourth model as well, a combination of the Hellenic-Western and the Chinese models, and concluded that it would serve best as a new standard for a revised theory. He only barely hinted at the monumental revisions of his theory that a switch of his prime model would require.[38]

THE ESSAYS

Toynbee's theory raises a thousand questions, any one of which is worth an essay. The essays presented here are beginnings, gateways into Toynbee's personal and social world and his historical thought. Each adds to our interpretation of Toynbee as historian and to our critical understanding of his proposals.

The first two essays, written by people who knew him well, provide an opening for new knowledge of Toynbee's life in relation to his historical study. William McNeill, the author of the first biography of Toynbee, considers the problem of writing the biography of a man of such complexity. He selects three difficult issues that all interpreters of Toynbee face and that McNeill himself had to handle in preparing the biography – the impact of Spengler, the effect of Toynbee's mystical experiences on his interpretation of history, and his relation to his first wife, Rosalind. McNeill does not argue that these are the three most crucial matters for interpreting Toynbee, but he shows none the less that if they can be settled satisfactorily we will have come far in our comprehension of him. McNeill's speculations make use of Toynbee's poetry in a way no other commentator has before. He leaves us with a strong feeling for the interweaving of Toynbee's personal affairs with his thinking and decisions as a historian.

For forty years Toynbee carried on an extensive and utterly compelling personal correspondence with Father Columba, a Roman Catholic monk of Ampleforth Abbey in Yorkshire. Christian Peper, the editor of the published edition of that exchange, carefully examines the letters and shows how they disclose the changes in Toynbee's religion and conscience. Peper emphasizes Toynbee's struggle against the classic doctrine of Christianity about the uniqueness of Jesus Christ as Saviour, and documents how Toynbee worked out his arguments in the letters with Columba long before he brought them to the public in his writings. The image that appears in the letters from the 1930s and 1940s is of a historian already famous in Great Britain agonizing over the great spiritual matters of life as posed by Christianity. The Christianity he met came in the form of a very loving and intellectual younger monk who helped him to perceive the merits of the Roman Catholic church. He drew very near to that church, but did not convert to it. Towards Rome Toynbee remained a 'philo-Catholic.' After the Second World War he carried on an intense correspondence with Columba about all the world religions, as both the historian and the monk experienced spiritual changes.

Innumerable commentators have discussed Toynbee's stress on religion in his published historical writings. C.T. McIntire asks us to ponder the question in a new light and examines in detail the relationship between Toynbee's religion and his philosophy of history. McIntire investigates Toynbee's public statements in all forms, including *A Study of History* as well as the occasional articles and lectures. Collating these with the Columba correspondence and the evidence for Toynbee's participation in the church, McIntire proposes a two-step solution to the problem of religion in Toynbee's thought. First, he identifies the changes in Toynbee's religious orientation, suggesting in particular that during the height of his career he resumed the Anglican orientation of his youth, but in a new mode that incorporated the experiences and knowledge of the mature historian. Second, he analyses closely how Toynbee introduced this Christian orientation into the composition of his philosophy of history, adopting the outlook of the Christian tradition of historical interpretation, and for a time according a priority to Jesus Christ as the highest revelation of the divine. McIntire suggests that the years from about 1937 to about 1957 are the Christian period of Toynbee's philosophy of history. This treatment of Toynbee's historical thought confirms that his religion structures the very contents of his historical theory, and that his historical thought demands an understanding of his religion.

If it is true that religion, particularly Christianity, was decisive for Toynbee's thought, what happens to the secular tradition of rationality? The usual view has claimed that Toynbee's stress on religion was a defeat for secularity and rationality, and has accused him of wantonly dismissing the rational and humanist tradition in Western civilization. Marvin Perry disputes that potent criticism and argues that Toynbee brought the Greek and the Enlightenment appreciation of reason into his synthesis, along with the heritage of Christianity and the input of other world religions. In fact, Perry points out, Toynbee rejected many Christian dogmas, including the orthodox view of the divinity and resurrection of Jesus Christ, because they conflicted with reason. At the same time, Toynbee held that if reason is not guided by prophetic values, it will degrade the individual and corrupt social relations. In this way, contends Perry, Toynbee compels us to rethink the rational-humanist tradition and to embrace what elevates the human spirit and reject what distorts it.

Toynbee's union of intellectual modes of knowledge with imaginative modes baffled his critics repeatedly. And some of his imaginative experiences seemed to defy explanation. For instance, what do we make of his almost matter-of-fact comments about his travels in time? He does not *feel* like he is in Teanun in 80 BC witnessing a suicide. He is actually *present* at the suicide. Thomas Africa analyses every case of time-travel that Toynbee divulges, and makes surprising discoveries. On one level, the episodes accentuate Toynbee's identity as a historian, as one who lives intimately with the people and happenings of the past. At a deeper level, however, they disclose his communion with his mother, the one, Africa suggests, who sustained him as a historian deep within his psyche. In other words, even his mystical experiences confirm his vocation as historian. The Toynbee who attached himself to Jung could feel at home with Africa's interpretation.

Toynbee as historian was devoted to the past, but as historian he was also an explorer of the future. Awareness of this trait of Toynbee as prophet has led critics to dismiss him as historian. Warren Wagar is not as impressed as he used to be with Toynbee's suggestions about the future, but he still thinks that there may be something worthwhile in them. What marks Toynbee's discussions about the future is that they depend on his occupation as historian and on his theory of civilizations. He assumes that history is the process of past, present, and future, and founds his projections on his vast knowledge of the past. On the basis of his discernment of the recurrent dynamics of human history Toynbee ventures estimates of the future. Through it all he remains a modified believer in net general progress in history.

Wagar pays most attention to Toynbee's picture of a coming ecumenical civilization and the outline of a world government, whether in dictatorial or democratic format.

We know that Toynbee appreciated his personal rhythm of moving between *A Study of History* and the *Survey of International Affairs*, but no one has seriously examined the two works together. Roland Stromberg underlines the need to read the two in tandem. Notably, he shows how Toynbee used the two works to fructify each other. For example, his work on *Survey* for 1931 gave him the detailed analysis of crisis that he later employed in building his theory of breakdown and disintegration in volumes four to six of *Study*. His assessment in the *Survey* for 1933 of Hitler's advent to power rested on his theory of nation-states that he defined in the early volumes of *Study*. Toynbee vehemently opposed Hitler from the start. Stromberg judges Toynbee to be at the height of his powers in the 1930s, and reasons that the full range of his talents is revealed by reading both works side by side. For example, if *Study* in the late 1930s discloses Toynbee becoming the saint, the volumes of *Survey* in the same years reveal Toynbee remaining the analyst of power. In any case, the *Survey* in those years represents an entrancing political history of the world between the wars as the history was happening. Toynbee's style and insights in those volumes match what emerges in *Study*.

Specialists have invariably found Toynbee deficient in his treatment of their subjects, even though they may marvel that he seems to know enough to debate with them in their own areas of specialization. Bernice Glatzer Rosenthal tests his interpretation of Russian history and arrives at a mixed conclusion. She finds many serious misinterpretations and omissions, especially of social and economic factors, and many idiosyncratic interpretations whose virtue seems to be that they fit his theory. But she also notes that Toynbee's idea of challenge and response does work for Russia in some ways. For example, early challenges from nomadic peoples from the steppes and later challenges from Europe through Westernization were real and did evoke responses that were significant for Russian history. Rosenthal also points out, however, that an assessment of Toynbee depends in part on the beliefs and ideologies of the interpreters as much as it does on anything else. She observes that Toynbee's classification of Russia as an offshoot civilization of the main Byzantine Orthodox civilization parallels both the nineteenth-century Slavophile and the twentieth-century neo-Slavophile interpretation of Russian history. She speculates that Toynbee may owe much to Nicholas Berdyaev, the Russian Orthodox philosopher, for his view of Russia as well as of Communism.

If Toynbee counted Russia as a civilization, or at least a satellite civilization, he considered the United States of America to be no more than one nation-state out of many. In consequence, he pays relatively little attention to America in *Study*. Later Toynbee said more on the subject in a separate series of lectures. Edward Pessen looks at a few of Toynbee's interpretations of America and finds them simplistic and mono-causal. But he also finds them interesting. Above all Toynbee understood the United States to be materialistic and imperialistic, a nation opposed to Russian Communism out of reaction to a perceived threat to American wealth and power. Pessen notes that Toynbee was deficient in the sources he used and in the narrowness of the explanation he offered. At the same time, Toynbee's comments could make one pause to reflect. Ironically, in contrast with his ordinary lack of consideration of economic affairs, Toynbee's treatment of America hangs on his understanding of economics and wealth in America. While not a Marxist view, his view of America has socialist tendencies. Once again we are reminded that ideology is a factor in how Toynbee interprets history and how the critics interpret Toynbee.

None of Toynbee's classifications has evoked more outright hostile response than his identification of the Jews as a 'fossil' of ancient Syriac civilization. Indeed, even when Toynbee tries to soften the impact of his term, as he does in *Reconsiderations*, and even when he tries out a Jewish model for his theory of civilizations, he still manages to provoke antagonism. Frederick M. Schweitzer conducts a detailed review of Toynbee's handling of Jewish history and walks away with nothing good to say about it. Toynbee's interpretation of the Jews may be the nadir of his historical thought. Schweitzer documents how, in point after point, Toynbee takes a negative view of the Jews. Toynbee was disturbed by what he believed was the ancient Jewish claim to be 'God's chosen people,' and by the military and apocalyptic aggressiveness he believed he found in the Hebrew scriptures. In reaction, he follows an age-old prejudice against the Jews as having no significant history after the advent of Christianity. Schweitzer suggests that Fernand Braudel's classification of the Jews as a 'civilization of the diaspora type' would be fairer to the vitality and course of Jewish history.

Toynbee's trademark as historian is the theme of the necessity of comparative thinking and global history. Theodore Von Laue applauds his world-embracing proposals, but argues that he did not carry them far enough. Toynbee's concentration on civilizations and his assumption that they were self-contained social units led him into a serious misunderstanding of the twentieth century. In both Toynbee's time and our own the possibility of perceiving boundaries between civilizations has vanished before what Von Laue calls 'the world revolution of Westernization.' The important 'intelligible field of study' today is the whole world and the entire framework of the interaction of the peoples of the world. The effective units within the world system are now states and what counts are their relations of power. While criticizing the concept of civilizations on which Toynbee's theory rests, Von Laue none the less suggests a way to extend what he believes is Toynbee's undoubted insight into the world character of history.

Critics have consistently felt that Toynbee was rigid in his theory and have allowed the pronouncement quality of some of his rhetoric to close their minds to his ideas. Jane Caplan's memoir gives us another picture of the man. Caplan collaborated for two years with Toynbee on the one-volume revision of *Study* (1972) and got inside the process of the revision of his ideas of history. She acknowledges that Toynbee can sound rigid, but she attributes that to his feeling of self-confidence in his undertaking and to his historical vision. She helps us understand that changing his mind was part of his method, and that his systematic thinking was not rigid or predetermined, but expressive of an elasticity that belonged to the original conception of *Study*. She lets us inside his adoption of Africa into the list of civilizations and the abandonment of a whole section of his argument on disintegration from volume six. She draws a very appealing picture of the man, his work, and his thought, and helps to restore balance to our perceptions. Caplan also undermines impressions that Toynbee was nothing more than an abstract mind. The effect of her essay is to allow us to conclude our reconsiderations of Toynbee with the realization that the author of one of the most imposing works of our time was a humane person with a devotion to truth.

The essays, taken together, offer striking reinterpretations and reassessments of Toynbee, proposals that substantially alter our understanding of his work and thought. The authors have not intentionally come to any agreement about Toynbee's achievement, and we do not propose to make a common statement. Upon reflection, however, we might suggest in the context of this introductory essay some observations concerning Toynbee's ongoing merit.

It would not seem possible to perpetuate Toynbee as a system, for only Toynbee could do that, and it is unclear whether any of his distinctive features, like challenge and response, is worth pursuing. His value for understanding specific cases is mixed, depending on the subject, while in at least one case his views seem destructive. His neglect of economic and social history is hardly excusable as is his neglect of historical monographs. His attempts to theorize about recurrence as well as the ongoing process of things in history are worthy, and perhaps more approachable today because of the impact of the social sciences on historians. His encounter with the grand themes of history and human existence can inspire, even when one disagrees with him, and his capacity to envision a spiritual interpretation of history can connect the religiously minded with the ultimate concerns of life. In any case, Toynbee continues as a source of arresting juxtapositions and authentic insights into history. His insistence on comparative history should become an imperative for the community of historians. Whatever we finally think about the concept of civilizations, the notion at least raises the historical experience of whole peoples as a totality, and that needs to be done. In his efforts to achieve a synthetic interpretation and a comprehensive embrace of history Toynbee can be the teacher of us all.

Above all, Toynbee's global vision of the history of all the peoples, cultures, and religions of the world moves us beyond our self-centredness and our numberless parochialisms and overspecializations. It is this sense of the global history of humanity that propels us past even our most substantial criticisms of his work. This is the feature of his thought that has appealed to scholars in India, Japan, Argentina, and elsewhere throughout the world, and that ought to make him newly interesting today to scholars in Europe and North America. In our own time many weighty factors equip us to think freshly about world history and to draw Toynbee from his day into ours. We need only mention global migration, war and revolution, world markets and manufacture, famine, global communications, the nuclear threat, and global ecology. The time is opportune for us to learn from Toynbee.

We have not spoken the last word on Arnold Toynbee. We would count our volume of essays successful if we encouraged others to think anew about Toynbee and world history.

NOTES

1 Toynbee, *A Study of History* (London and New York: Oxford University Press 1934–61); hereafter, *Study*
2 Toynbee, *A Study of History*, abridgment by D.C. Somervell, 2 vols (New York and London: Oxford University Press 1947, 1957); Toynbee, *A Study of History*, new edition revised and abridged by the author and Jane Caplan (London: Oxford University Press 1972); hereafter, *Study* (one vol.)
3 Toynbee, *Study*, 7: ix–x; *Experiences* (New York and London: Oxford University Press, 1969); *Study* (one vol.), 11, 13
4 S. Fiona Morton, *A Bibliography of Arnold J. Toynbee* (New York: Oxford University Press 1980)
5 For example, see Pitirim A. Sorokin, 'Toynbee's Philosophy of History,' in Pieter Geyl, A. Toynbee, and Pitirim A. Sorokin, *The Pattern of the Past: Can We Determine It?* (Boston: Beacon Press 1949), 95–126; and see the comment on Toynbee by the Anglican bishop of London, J.W.C. Wand, in Foreword to *Man at Work in God's World*, ed. Canon G.E. DeMille (New York and London: Longmans, Green 1956), v.
6 A small collection of the reviews was published in *Toynbee and History: Critical Essays and Reviews*, ed. M.F. Ashley Montagu (Boston: Porter Sargent 1956).
7 Toynbee listed all the reviews he knew of in *Reconsiderations*, *Study*, 12: 680–90. Morton's *Bibliography* lists many more.
8 Much information about Toynbee's activities can be learned from *An Historian's Conscience: The Correspondence of Arnold J. Toynbee and Columba Cary-Elwes, Monk of Ampleforth*, ed. Christian B. Peper (Boston: Beacon Press 1986); from Toynbee, *Experiences*; and from references scattered throughout many of his other writings.
9 *Experiences*, 86–7; *Study*, 7: viii–ix, 10: 227–8, and 12: v
10 *Study*, 1: 49–52
11 See C.T. McIntire, 'Historical Study and the Historical Dimension of Our World,' in McIntire and Ronald A. Wells, *Historical and Historical Understanding* (Grand Rapids: Eerdmans 1984), 19–41.

12 *Study*, 12: 13
13 Ibid., 1: 37; 4: 3–4, 318–22; 6: 319–26
14 Section entitled 'The Prospects of the Western Civilization,' *Study*, 9: 406–644, especially 528–9, and 619; *Study* (one vol.), 543
15 *Study*, 10: 213–42
16 Ibid., 7: ix–x
17 Ibid., 10: 237
18 See especially *Study*, 10: 228
19 *Historian's Conscience, passim*; *Study*, 10: 24–32
20 Ibid., 1: 7–9, 271; 7: viii; and 12: 12
21 Ibid., 1: part I, especially 41–3, 147–9, and 10: 233
22 Ibid., 10: 228
23 Ibid., 7: ix–x
24 Ibid., 1: 270–2, 299–300, 3: 112, 119–20; see 4: 7–39, 245–62, and 5: 13–14, 16, 23–7, 376.
25 Ibid., 1: 52–4; and see table I, *Study*, 6: 327, and the table, 12: 559.
26 Ibid., 1: 51, 133, 2: 322, 340, 369, 388; 3: 1–2, 134, 4: 1–2. Toynbee counted either five or seven civilizations still alive today.
27 Ibid., 1: 148–81; 10: 233
28 Ibid., 4: 1–4, 12–13
29 Ibid., 16, 51–2, 147–60
30 Ibid., 1: 129–33; 6: 325–6; 7: 420–3; 12: 279, 307–8
31 Ibid., 5: 20–7, 52–4; 7: 1–6; 12: 308–13
32 Ibid., 5: 25–8
33 Ibid., 3: 128, 187, 192; 5: 21, 376
34 Ibid., 9: 338–9, 395, 404–5
35 Ibid., 10: 3; Toynbee, *An Historian's Approach to Religion* (London: Oxford University Press 1956), chap. 17; *Study*, 12: 609
36 *Study* 1: 130–2, 172–3; 7: 421–2, and table IV after 7: 772
37 Ibid., 12: 559–61; *Study* (one vol.), 70–2
38 *Study*, 1: 44–6, 51–4; 5: 18–19; 12: 170–217

Toynbee's Life and Thought:
Some Unresolved Questions

William H. McNeill

Each of us is an island and no effort of the imagination can close the gap between one person and another entirely. On top of that, time, with its subtle transmutations, now begins to separate Arnold Toynbee's life from our own; and an American has the further problem of trying to understand what it was like to be English, particularly in the years before the First World War, when Toynbee's most fundamental commitments and ambitions took shape. To be sure, Toynbee left several autobiographical fragments behind and even wrote a short essay 'My View of History' that purports to tell how notions about the rise and fall of civilizations arose in his mind.[1] Most historians are more secretive and anyone interested in asking how Toynbee's life acted and interacted on his thought across the decades of his life must be grateful for the autobiographical information he made public.

But on some matters Toynbee was unwilling or unable to express himself freely, at least in public. What his private papers may reveal is something I hope to find out in the future, for I have agreed to undertake a book-length biography and will have access to whatever records his surviving son, Lawrence Toynbee, has in his possession. In the meantime, three questions about the interrelation of Toynbee's life and thought seem important to me based entirely on what he said in print – and what remains unsaid, or barely hinted at.

OSWALD SPENGLER

First is the question of his relation to Oswald Spengler. Toynbee explained in 1948 how Lewis Namier induced him to read Spengler's *Untergang des Abendlandes* in the summer of 1920 with the result that he 'wondered at first whether my whole inquiry had been disposed of by Spengler before even the questions, not to speak of the answers, had fully taken shape in my own mind ... But when I looked in Spengler's book for an answer to my question about the geneses of civilizations, I saw that there was still work for me to do, for on this point Spengler was, it seemed to me, most unilluminatingly dogmatic and deterministic.'[2]

If Toynbee 'wondered at first whether my whole inquiry had been disposed of,' surely on first reading Spengler he found much to admire and agree with. Yet if one searches the surprisingly few references to Spengler in *A Study of History*, one finds that the German is quoted only to be refuted, and achieves two passing references – no more. What then really happened in the summer of 1920? What kind of encounter was it between the two scholars whose names are now so commonly linked together as modern pioneers of the cyclical, civilizational view of history?

What I suspect is the following: before reading Spengler, Toynbee had thought very little about civilizations and peoples other than the ancient Greeks and Romans on the one hand and modern Europeans on the other. In Greek and Roman history he had already discerned the pattern of genesis, growth, breakdown, and dissolution that he later applied to all civilizations. This fact is attested by a truly remarkable lecture 'The Tragedy of Greece' that Toynbee delivered at Oxford in the spring of 1920, *before* reading Spengler. The tragic form he there applied to ancient Mediterranean history was itself borrowed from the Greeks; and the centrality of Thucydides' history, and of the moral change during the Peloponnesian War that Thucydides and Toynbee both took to be symptomatic of 'breakdown,' is unmistakable.[3]

Clearly, most of what Toynbee was later to apply to other peoples in other times and places had already taken shape, as far as what he later called Hellenic civilization was concerned, in the spring of 1920. But I know of no evidence that he had seriously thought about the rest of the world before reading Spengler. He had been aware of the ancient oriental background of Greek history from childhood; and as an undergraduate at Oxford had looked into the early history of India and China.[4] But I do not think the notion had occurred to him that the histories of these peoples, too, could be made conformable to the tragic pattern he had discerned at the heart of classical historical experience.

Toynbee tells us that he first began to explore 'The Mystery of Man' in the form of a commentary on a chorus of Sophocles' *Antigone* in the summer of 1920, but found that approach 'unpromising' and 'a false move.'[5] If the manuscript of this false start survives it will allow an easy check on guesswork. But in the absence of clear evidence, I suspect that some part of what made the commentary on Sophocles unsatisfactory was Toynbee's realization, thanks to Spengler, that there were other civilizations to be considered, together with peoples who never attained civilization, before his ambition to decipher 'The Mystery of Man' could be achieved.

If I am right in this hypothesis, one may ask why Toynbee was so sparing in acknowledging the debt, for his references to Spengler in *A Study of History* are either casual or critical. Moreover, Spengler's name is conspicuously missing from the litany of persons and places whose help he acknowledges with thanks at the close of *A Study of History*.[6]

Perhaps the reason is that Spengler frightened Toynbee by making the ambitious young historian wonder whether his 'whole inquiry had been disposed of' already, and then burdened him with the recognition that there was far more to be done in acquainting himself with the histories of Asian, African, and Amerindian peoples than Toynbee had previously imagined or supposed. Active composition of the great work, attempted in 1920, had to be postponed until 1930, as a matter of fact, when Toynbee again began to address the 'mystery of man' under the (doubtless deliberately) modest title *A Study of History*.[7] Other factors intervened of course; in particular, the necessity of earning a living by writing annual volumes on international affairs. But I suspect that Spengler's formidable figure also had a good deal to do with the delay. Only by coming to grips with as much, and more, empirical material as Spengler had ever looked at could Toynbee hope to enter the lists on even terms and become able to explain 'the mystery of man' more adequately and less dogmatically than the German had done.

If Toynbee was measuring himself against Spengler from 1920 until sometime in the 1940s, when his reputation suddenly eclipsed that of his German rival and predecessor, at least in the English-speaking world, perhaps his spare references and belittling remarks about Spengler are to be understood as a kind of self-protection – a way of standing on his own feet, and avoiding the reduction of his own work to the status of a commentary upon or dialogue with his predecessor. I did much the same in writing my own magnum opus. Toynbee taught me what Spengler may have first taught him: the simple and fundamental notion of the historicity of non-Western peoples. But no one can tell from reading what I wrote in *The Rise of the West* that I owed such a debt. It was too fundamental to footnote. Perhaps the same was true of Toynbee's debt to Spengler.

MYSTIC EXPERIENCES

A second question about Toynbee's life and thought that needs further illumination is the role of his mystic experiences in altering his view of the relative importance of secular and religious affairs. When Toynbee planned *A Study of History* and when he wrote the first three volumes of that work (1930–4), he viewed civilization as humanity's supreme work of art. Religion had a subordinate place: its main function was to act as a chrysalis whereby a decaying civilization could transmit a precious freight of knowledge and skill to its successor. But once the new civilization began to arise, knowledge and skills transmitted to it through religious institutions entered into new, secular contexts, and flowered in new ways as challenge and response worked their rhythms of growth.

By the time the second group of three volumes appeared (1939) Toynbee had changed his mind, and now believed that religion was far more important than he had thought before. But a close examination of volumes four to six shows, I think, that the passages in which Toynbee speaks of God are set into longer passages in which the secular tone and outlook of his earlier years remained unaltered. It looks to me, therefore, as though the passages expressing his 'conversion' may all have been added to an existing text in the course of final revision of the manuscript for the printer. If so, one is justified in thinking that Toynbee's change of views may have come in 1939; and perhaps after and as a consequence of the second of two mystic experiences that he described long afterwards as follows:

How are we to picture to ourselves a god who is spiritually higher than the highest human spiritual flights, yet is at the same time, in one of his aspects, a person like enough to a human person for communication, person to person, to be possible between God and a human being? I find this incomprehensible intellectually. The nearest that I have come to understanding the mystery has been in two experiences that were not acts of thought but that felt as if they were flashes of insight or revelation. Each experience came to me at a moment of very great spiritual stress. The earlier one came when I was in a moral conflict between the better and the worse side of myself, and this at a moment when the better side was fighting with its back to the wall. The second experience came at the moment of the death – a tragic death – of a fellow human being with whose life mine was intimately bound up. On the first occasion it felt as if a transcendant spiritual presence, standing for righteousness beyond my reach, had come down to my rescue and had given to my inadequate human righteousness the aid without which it could not have won its desperate battle. On the second occasion it felt as if the same transcendant spiritual presence, standing for love beyond my, or my dying fellow human being's capacity, had pulled aside at that awful moment the veil that ordinarily makes us unaware of God's perpetual closeness to us. God had revealed himself for an instant to give an unmistakable assurance of his mercy and forgiveness.[8]

The first of these encounters with God occurred in China in 1929, as is evident from two of Toynbee's dated poems in Greek titled 'Grammatikos Minotauros' (that is, Scholar Bull-man) and 'Agnostoi Theoi' (The Unknown God), grouped together under the heading 'Agōnia' – Agony. Toynbee travelled through Asia in 1929 to attend a conference incidental to the establishment of the Institute of Pacific Relations. In China he met Eileen Power, to whom he was powerfully attracted. But as his own translation of the two poems says,

> Alone, I face, with naked breast,
> The rampant black primaeval beast.

And then,

> Left desolate by all my gods,
> A god unknown stood by me. Then
> My strength was as the strength of ten.
> With naked hand I smote: and, lo,
> The beast fell prone at one brave blow.[9]

The literary and moral conventions in these poems seem archaic today, but beneath the rhetoric one can still recognize a genuinely tortured human being – tortured by his inability to control his emotions and to bring them into conformity with the sexual code to which he had been brought up. The further fact that by 1929 his relationship with his wife had probably begun to unravel must have intensified the whole experience. None the less, this encounter with 'an unknown god' remained in lower case; and does not seem to have altered his worldview in any fundamental fashion.

It was otherwise in 1939 when the second of his encounters with 'transcendental reality' occurred. The occasion was the suicide of his eldest son, occasioned by disappointment in love. This family disaster coincided with the approach of the Second World War, that is, with the failure of Toynbee's effort to so inform the public about international relations that a reprise of 1914 would become impossible. That had been his professional purpose since 1924 when his work at Chatham House began. He certainly seemed to have failed in that endeavour by 1939; and the suicide of his eldest son, in whose future Toynbee had set great store,[10] added another, far heavier burden. By this time, too, relations with his wife were distant, and the suicide did not bring them closer together – at least not for long.

Clearly the intense pressures Toynbee found himself under in 1939 heightened the intensity of this second encounter with what he soon began confidently to refer to as God, in the singular and capitalized. Its enduring imprint on his outlook is not, therefore, surprising, if, indeed, it *was* this momentary experience that decisively altered his view of the meaning of history and the relationship between secular and religious affairs. I am inclined to believe that it *was* decisive, but do not know for sure. Toynbee never says as much; and his account of the experience, quoted above, introduces the subject casually, as a way of explaining how he approached the intellectually insoluble mystery of how God could be enough like a person to be capable of communicating with individual human beings. In personal conversation he was reticent about these experiences; indeed the surprising thing is that he confessed as much as he did in the passage I quoted. He was, after all, aware of Freudian and Jungian psychology; and he says himself:

Evidently these two experiences are open to more than one interpretation ... The visual images that these non-visual experiences have left in my mind are manifestly derived from traditional Christian mythology. In the first image of the two, God makes his epiphany in the guise of St George; in the second he makes it in the likeness of Michelangelo's vision of the Creator giving life to Adam. A rationalist might suggest that, in the first image, I was externalizing what was in reality a wholly internal psychic conflict, and that, in the second image, I was consoling myself with a fallacious assurance of the fulfillment of a wish that I could not bear to see disappointed. I cannot disprove these demythologizations; I cannot give a different explanation of my experiences that is cogent, even to myself. All I can say is that, in these experiences, I have come the nearest that I have ever come, so far, to what has felt like an immediate encounter with the godhead to whom our human prayers are addressed.[11]

Two other circumstances need to be considered in any effort to assess the importance of these mystic encounters. First, in 1939 Toynbee was under pressure to imitate his wife in converting to Roman Catholicism. Her acceptance of that faith in 1932 inaugurated a long and intimate association with monks of Ampleforth Abbey, Yorkshire, among whom the most important for Toynbee was Father Columba. We can now read their correspondence over a period of forty years in *An Historian's Conscience*.[12] I will say no more about this relationship now. My point is merely to emphasize that the change in Toynbee's view of the relative importance of religion and civilization that took place in 1939 was nourished and sustained by more than a single, momentary mystic experience, however important that moment may have been in convincing him of the real existence of a personal God, capable of communicating with human beings.

After his own personal encounter with God in 1939, the scepticism that had blocked Toynbee's faith in such a possibility ceased to matter. Instead he felt free, indeed obligated, to put God back into history whence Enlightenment thinkers of the eighteenth century had banished Him. In doing so, Toynbee did not become a Christian. Nevertheless, his childhood indoctrination into biblical lore by his 'Uncle Harry,' into whose London house his parents had moved when Uncle Harry's wife died, welled forth in the pages of volumes seven to ten of the *Study*, while classical references, the staple of his schooling, took second place. Toynbee called himself a 'Post Christian,' but, as such, his Christian heritage overtook and in large part eclipsed his classical heritage, while both were modified by his continuing awareness of the claims of non-Western societies and civilizations to equal status with the Western world. Multiple paths to God and multiple revelations of God — an idea completely familiar in the religions of India — seemed to Toynbee the only adequate view of the facts. His growing admiration for Buddhism, and in particular its Mahayana form, reflected this conviction; but he explored the literature of Buddhism too late in life for it to enter deeply into his personality in the way both biblical and classical thought patterns and literary traditions had done.

A second circumstance makes Toynbee's mystical experiences of 1929 and 1939 more nearly comprehensible and less surprising than they would have been for other, less imaginative individuals. His powers of imagination were vast, vivacious, and freely exercised so as frequently to carry him beyond ordinary states of consciousness. A literary passage or the sight of some famous place was enough to put his mind into communion with vanished persons and peoples, permitting him to imagine old battles and ancient personal tragedies with all the poignancy of the original. We know of these experiences because at the end of his great work, under the rubric 'The Inspiration of Historians,' he listed a number of occasions when the ordinary state of his consciousness had been interrupted by imaginative transport of the kind others feel only in the theatre or when reading a novel and identifying themselves with fictional characters. But Toynbee's practised imagination permitted him to identify himself with historical figures, with great events, and even with a collectivity as abstract as the whole of humanity. At any rate, such an identification occurred on one climactic occasion, which he reports as follows:

In London in the southern section of the Buckingham Palace Road, walking southward along the pavement skirting the west wall of Victoria Station, the writer, once, one afternoon not long after the end of the first World War – he had failed to record the exact date – had found himself in communion, not just with this or that episode in History, but with all that had been, and was, and was to come. In that instant he was directly aware of the passage of History gently flowing through him in a mighty current, and of his own life welling like a wave in the flow of this vast tide.[13]

This extraordinary experience, obviously, was a secular, this-worldly equivalent of his two later encounters, first with an unknown god and then with God Himself. The first experience (c. 1919) validated his secular vision of the human condition, as the last of them (1939) validated the theocentric vision of his later years; while the intermediate experience of 1929 affected his judgments about human affairs only retrospectively when assimilated to his experience of 1939.

Toynbee's soaring imagination, tuned to sympathy with the drama of past human suffering and struggles against fate, obviously chafed at the restraints of everyday consciousness, and occasionally left ordinary reasoning far behind. Biblical prophets loomed large in his earliest years, and the poet as inspired seer was, after all, a commonplace of the Greco-Roman culture, in which Toynbee's schooling had steeped him. He was also brought up to admire the sovereignty of the creative imagination as expressed in English and German romantic poetry. With such cultural sanction Toynbee's imagination was accordingly able to give vent to his powerful, and some thought recklessly overweening, ambition (even in his youth)[14] to know everything and put it all together into a comprehensible whole.

It seems clear, therefore, that the fierce emotional drives that fed his imagination came together with extraordinary powers of memory and association to shape Toynbee's personal and professional life. The central drama of that life, I suspect, beneath a conventionally successful career, was the evolving patterns of combat and co-operation between Toynbee's unusual emotional reach and his no less unusual intellectual control over the mingling of pride, ambition, love, and fear that fuelled his inmost personal life. Beginning in childhood he managed to harness extraordinary diligence to his vaulting imagination; but harnessing his emotions was more difficult. Perhaps he never achieved an inward peace of mind, if only because relations with the members of his immediate family always remained tense enough to threaten new or renewed disruption of his routine of work and life.

ROSALIND

This brings me to the third question about Toynbee's life and thought upon which more information and insight is needed. Toynbee's published autobiographical remarks say next to nothing about his father, Harry V. Toynbee. There is a reason for this reticence. Harry Toynbee was committed to an insane asylum when Toynbee was an undergraduate at Oxford. Mental illness was surrounded by fears and taboos in Edwardian England, and was commonly believed to be hereditary. Consequently, for years and years Toynbee dreaded following his father into some sort of mental derangement. The two crises of 1929 and 1939, which we have already glanced at, were probably heightened by this fear.

His father had lived under the shadow of a brilliant elder brother, Arnold, after whom his son was named. That son also had to compete with the shadow of his namesake, the first and for a long time the really famous Arnold Toynbee. The uncle had been a historian and social worker in the 1880s. As historian he invented the concept of an 'industrial revolution' in eighteenth-century Britain; and as social worker he pioneered efforts to do something to improve the conditions of the London poor. Partly because of the circumstances of his death, the first settlement house in the world was named after him. For Arnold Toynbee's brilliant promise was cut off in youth by a fatal disease he contracted in London's East End. His death occurred six years before Arnold J. Toynbee was born, and meant that the baby's name was not fully his own – a fact borne in upon him when he published a first book in 1916 and was reprimanded by relatives for omitting his middle initial and thus usurping his uncle's name. Thereafter he was Arnold J. Toynbee in print until near the end of his life, when he reverted to Arnold Toynbee, having by then won the right to the preferred form of his own name.[15]

His uncle's early and dramatic death, followed by his father's descent into a sort of living death, was reinforced and recapitulated by the deaths of a great many of his own contemporaries in the First World War. Toynbee himself was judged ineligible for military service owing to dysentery he had contracted in Greece in 1911 – a stroke of chance that assumed extraordinary significance as the carnage of the war continued to destroy his friends and fellow scholars. It was easy for him to believe that he had been spared the fate of his uncle, father, and contemporaries for some special reason. Or, put another way, that he was under special obligation to accomplish something great in order to deserve the gift of a long and, at least outwardly, comfortable life. Toynbee's prophetic sense of having been chosen to correct and enlarge received views of the past, which Trevor-Roper lampooned so cruelly in 1957,[16] fed on this sort of anxiety.

Equally or more important in Toynbee's personal life was his troubled relationship with Rosalind Murray, his first wife and great love. Rosalind's side of the story is hidden from me; so is most of Toynbee's. Yet there are glimpses, especially in his published poetry. Three years before he married her he wrote four lines in Greek, titled 'Epiphany,' which translate as follows: 'As I toil strenuously in the darkness you suddenly show your heavenly light, Rosalind. I shall do great deeds; through deeds I might approach you; and if I fail, I shall do still greater deeds.' A few months later, another poem reads (in part): 'I do not know whether you love me, nor how much you love me – I know clearly this one thing alone: I love you, Rosalind, with all my heart.'[17] In 1913 Rosalind did marry him, perhaps in part because her father, Gilbert Murray, liked and respected the young Oxford don and budding classicist and thought his daughter ought to settle down to the routine of an academic's wife.

But it did not turn out that way, for the war of 1914–18 interrupted Toynbee's Oxford career. Afterwards he settled in London, where he had been born and spent his childhood. Three sons came in swift succession, and Toynbee found it hard to earn enough money to maintain the household at a level that would satisfy Rosalind's aristocratic heritage and expectations.[18]

Toynbee admired his wife extravagantly and wanted to work, no less extravagantly. How else could he satisfy his own ambitions, earn a living, and meet those anxieties concerning his mission? How matters worked out in practice I do not know, but I suspect that Rosalind found herself left to attend the children and manage the household with very little help from her husband. But, as I say, the domestic reality remained veiled: only their divorce, after thirty years of marriage, was public knowledge until his letters with Father Columba revealed his own agonies over her.

Rosalind had literary ambitions of her own, and indeed published five novels, the first when she was only seventeen years of age. They met with only mediocre success, however, and the tasks of raising three sons and looking after the household must have taken a good deal of her attention in the 1920s. An important stage in her life came in 1932 when she was formally received into the Roman Catholic church. Rosalind thereupon launched a new literary career as pamphleteer and apologist for Catholic truth. Her championship of Catholicism won considerable notice, and she made successful lecture tours in the United States and elsewhere on the 'Catholic circuit.' Toynbee's flirtation with Catholicism but continued resistance to conversion, recorded in some detail in the Toynbee-Columba correspondence, must be understood against this background of his wife's example. But, however much he regretted it, Rosalind and he pulled apart, intellectually and emotionally. It was a prolonged and painful tragedy, at least for him; but when and how it began remains entirely hidden from me by the reticence of the two principals. The breakup of his marriage was too important and too painful for Toynbee to speak about in public.

His emotions must have been complicated by the fact that at Chatham House, from 1925 onwards, he collaborated with the woman who became his second wife in 1946, after divorce from Rosalind had been finalized. Veronica Boulter was a polar opposite from Rosalind in many respects. Diligent, punctilious, and reliable, she admired Toynbee, and delighted to help him with his writing. Of middle-class background, she was, like him, careful with money. Perhaps one may say that in the 1920s and 1930s he served Rosalind, while Veronica served him; with the difference that Veronica served Toynbee wholeheartedly, whereas he served Rosalind only with a divided mind. Remember those remarkable words of his in the poem of 1910: 'I shall do great deeds; through deeds I might approach you; and if I fail, I shall do still greater deeds.' The great deeds whereby he wrote a stout volume on international affairs every year (and in some years came out with two) while also preparing to write and then writing the initial volumes of *A Study of History* may well have had the effect not of allowing him to approach Rosalind by winning her admiration, but rather of sidelining her; and the more he fell short of basking in her 'heavenly light,' the more the second half of the prophecy took over: 'and if I fail, I shall do still greater deeds' – that is, work even harder and more unintermittently, leaving less and less time for his sons and his wife as the great work came ever closer to realization.

All this is mere speculation. It is a fact, none the less, that Toynbee prefaced the first three volumes of the *Study* with another Greek poem which he wrote in 1910 and revised in 1927. It is entitled 'Writer's Life' and as a poetical autobiography is remarkable enough to deserve full translation here.

> Goddesses of death, no matter how many of you oppress me,
>   not by having yielded to you will I myself voluntarily
>   incur the charge of cowardice.
> No, by the great oath of the god, who swore that I
>   would not die in vain, having once seen the glorious
>   light of the sun,
> having accomplished labours among men,
>   trusting in him I am no longer a slave to them;
> but I will go, for it is the right moment. O shadowy avengers
>   begone! I have found the protective ones. Give way!
>
> Gentle, merciful Muses, you came to me
>   on a stormy sea in a shuddering boat
> in a winter storm of pain. The force of the winds
>   struck me hard, terribly, and no end of the evil was visible.
> Eternal toil follows, and it had reached as far as the eye
>   could see
> and there was murky air and inhospitable surging waves.
> From these things then, protectors, you freed me
>   and once again I pass over the dismal seas with a
>   straight keel.
>
> I will sing the Muses as far as steady thought can follow,

Some Unresolved Questions 45

I will serve the Muses with the entire strength of my hand,
and I will fail the Muses only on that day when you fail me,
   dearest of shortlived mortals – don't pity me.

I love; but the Muses call me. You stay far from men,
  Muses, far, dwellers on Helicon.
You have springs there, and wooded Tempe,
  and the path, being rough, inspires eager rivalry in the foot,
and a great peak, the end of the journey, stands before
  and the heavenly, glittering, conspicuous – would that
    I might touch it – snow.

Love was no longer a companion: indeed, that one possesses
  the gentle works of men; but, bewitched, having been turned
towards the mountains, I abandon him. But I love you.
  Hold me, dear, throwing your arms around my shoulders.

You held me when I was in great anguish, and he, departing
  turned around, charmed by your hand, not gone after all – Love.
He himself followed, a third traveller – and not only a third,
  for with him he led the band of Muses.
'Greetings, mistresses leaving the shining peak, Helicon.'
  Gracious Calliope laughed and said, 'Children
Let us walk the same path, whose end is certainly
  not Helicon, nor the peak nor the snow.
We won't live far away – that hasty word escaped
  the fence of your teeth – and this one is our common guide.'
For I see you coming, you who bring to an end, you who end care
  for all mortals, now the right time for me: Death.
Farewell from me, not then having lived in vain, to whom
  Rosalind was mate, the Muses priestesses, and Love guide.[19]

Translated in this almost literal way, the poem may be more puzzling than elegant. Its allusiveness is of course deliberate: Toynbee set out to say and not to say those things that mattered most. But let me attempt a gloss, clumsy and only partly informed, in the hope that some of the meanings will come clear to persons like ourselves who are not steeped in classical conventions.

The first and second stanzas express Toynbee's sense of mission: 'The great oath of the god, who swore that I would not die in vain ... having accomplished labours among men.' It also exorcises 'goddesses of death' – the goddesses who had engulfed his father and uncle at the time the first version of this poem was written. Instead, the Muses take over: Toynbee's 'protective ones.'

The next stanza introduces a conflict between his dedication to the Muses and to love. Then comes the crux: 'Love was no longer a companion ... I abandon him. But I love you.' You, surely, in this case refers to Rosalind. Her magic, then, in the next stanza reconciles love and the Muses: she even makes the Muses the obedient followers of Love, persuading them to abandon Helicon and its snows for some place close by!

Toynbee in short is celebrating the banishment of his youthful fears of death and madness, and a triumphant reconciliation of his literary ambitions with his love for Rosalind, as worked out in 1927; and in the final lines he foresees a completed life, with death coming, eventually, after his work has been accomplished, to a man who could congratulate himself on 'not having lived in vain, to whom Rosalind was mate, the Muses priestesses, and Love guide.' A great boast indeed; and an act of hubris too, as it turned out, when Rosalind's love went sour. By 1944, in still another poem, this one in Latin, he could say:

> Having rejoiced in youth to describe the turning-points of my life
>   I had myself dared to survey my fate.
> I saw a triple harmony – of propitiously-leading love,
>   of the company of the Muses, of my wife –
> I was insane who, wandering, traversing the plains of the vast sea,
>   did not look out for your thunder bolt, savage storm.
> Not again will I speak oracles about myself: you
>   saved my fate, you who know me, God.[20]

This poem scarcely needs comment, since it recapitulates and retracts by referring directly to the poem of 1927. Still, the use of the word 'insane' is striking; this is the spectre that had haunted Toynbee's mind from undergraduate years, and to call his former confidence in being able to combine life with work 'insane' is a striking peripeteia of meanings, even for a classicist like Toynbee.

By 1965, when the pain of his divorce from Rosalind had subsided, when his literary ambitions had been abundantly fulfilled, and when his second wife's patient help and support had soothed his private life for twenty years, Toynbee could write a Greek distich playing on the literal meaning of Veronica's name, as follows:

An Act of Faith

To what victor, indeed, did Victory-bearer [Veronica] bring victory?
This Victor – Love. Who then is this? God.[21]

Veronica, then, brought him love, too, in the end; and her love helped instead of hindered his literary achievement. But the real victor he declared was Love, and Love was God. This Toynbee believed in his old age to be the central meaning of human existence; and it was his private life rather than his study of history, I suggest, that led him to that quasi-Christian conclusion.

NOTES

1 Reprinted in Toynbee, *Civilization on Trial* (New York: Oxford University Press 1948), 3–15
2 *Civilization on Trial*, 9–10
3 A subordinate question, well worth pursuing, is how much the young Toynbee owed to Francis Cornford, *Thucydides Mythistoricus* (London: Edward Arnold 1907). This book argued that Thucydides' record of the Peloponnesian War was made to conform to the tragic mould because the historian came to see Athens's eventual defeat as a case of heroic hubris bringing an appropriate punishment. In so far as Toynbee accepted Cornford's idea, he had a very distinguished predecessor in resorting to a tragic mould for the writing of history. In a sense, Toynbee simply affirmed Thucydides' vision, projecting it across the centuries from 900 BC to AD 600, thereby putting the Peloponnesian War into a far larger framework, running before and after anything the great Greek historian could possibly know in his own lifetime.

I once asked Toynbee what he thought of Cornford. He replied that he held him in high esteem; and when I asked further why Cornford had never persuaded most of his fellow classicists of the validity of his ideas about Thucydides, Toynbee gave me no distinct answer. Cornford was at Cambridge, and thus belonged to a different and rival tradition of learning. To turn admiringly to Cambridge was, perhaps, mildly heretical at Oxford in 1907, when Toynbee was an undergraduate and must have read and discussed Cornford's new book. None the less, Cornford is among those Toynbee acknowledges as having helped to shape his mind (*A Study of History* [London, New York, and Toronto: Oxford University Press 1954–61], 10: 230–1), but what Toynbee there attributes to Cornford – the use of an abstract noun with its initial letter printed as a capital' as a way to symbolize 'psychic principalities and powers' and 'emanations from a subconscious abyss of the Psyche – was, I believe, a small part of what he actually owed to the elder scholar's thought.

4 Toynbee dates his investigation of early India to 1907 and of ancient China to 1908; *A Study of History* (London, New York, and Toronto: Oxford University Press 1954), 10: 221–2.
5 *Study*, 10: 323
6 Ibid., 10: 213–42
7 Perhaps it is worth mentioning that in family circles the great work was regularly referred to as 'The Nonsense Book'; though whether this camouflage title was invented by Toynbee or someone else I do not know.
8 *Experiences* (New York and London: Oxford University Press 1969), 176
9 *Experiences*, 389–91
10 *Acquaintances* (London: Oxford University Press 1967), 262–6
11 *Experiences*, 176–7
12 *An Historian's Conscience*, ed. Christian B. Peper (Boston: Beacon Press 1986)
13 *Study*, 10: 139
14 *Study*, 10: 28–9, where Toynbee tells how in 1906 he rejected his uncle's advice 'to make your choice of some single subject and to concentrate hereafter on that.'
15 *Acquaintances*, 33–5
16 Hugh Trevor-Roper, 'Arnold Toynbee's Millennium,' *Encounter* 8 (June 1957): 122–4
17 Translated by Arthur Adkins
18 She was related to the Earl of Carlisle on her mother's side, and the Murrays,

before emigrating to Australia, had enjoyed at least quasi-aristocratic rank in Ireland.
19 Translated by Elizabeth Meyer
20 Translated by Elizabeth Meyer
21 Translated by Elizabeth Meyer

Toynbee:
An Historian's Conscience
Christian B. Peper

A concern with the Absolute Reality behind the phenomena is ubiquitous throughout Arnold J. Toynbee's published work. His imagination is so fecund, his religious positions so apparently protean, that it is often difficult to trace a clear and consistent pattern of belief. We are in need of a thread of Ariadne as a guide in the labyrinthine ways of his conscience. Such a thread perhaps now may be found in the recently published correspondence between Toynbee and Columba Cary-Elwes, a monk of Ampleforth Abbey.[1]

In these letters we may observe the testing and forging of Arnold Toynbee's religious concepts, many of which appear formally in the published works; here is a revelation of his diurnal life, the personal and family milieu in which he moved; through the letters we may now for the first time see how a constant and pervasive concern with religion informed his daily life; that Toynbee was deeply religious readily appears from a perusal of his published works; but the depth of his piety (in the larger sense of *pietas*) and the warmth of his love of God and man only now are clearly revealed. Accordingly, the letters will serve as a *vade mecum* in this discussion of the historian's conscience, taken in its broadest sense as his in-wit, his awareness of his relation to God.

RELIGIO HISTORICI[2]

Toynbee had an ordinary Anglican upbringing at home and at school; at Winchester, among other compulsory services, every Saturday brought a liturgy in honour of the Theotokos (Mother of God). But about the time he went up as an undergraduate to Oxford in 1907 he drifted 'by infinitesmally gradual stages' into a state of disbelief in the existence of any 'transcendental reality, life or personality.'[3] In 1913 he married Rosalind Murray, the daughter of doctrinaire post-Christians; she had not been baptized; the wedding was in a registry office.

The historian's recovery of a belief in God in 1930 'came through an experience of help in withstanding a very strong temptation. But the change precipitated by this experience had probably been long in preparation.'[4] The (perhaps mystical) experience is described in *Experiences*,[5] the temptation and its defeat in his two Greek poems (with an English pony) entitled 'Ἀγωνία.'[6] The nature of the ordeal is now revealed in notes to the letters.[7]

Rosalind Toynbee entered the Catholic Church in 1932, an act that 'produced disquiet and foreboding' in the historian.[8] Their youngest son, Lawrence, was sent to Ampleforth College, conducted by the Benedictine monks of Ampleforth Abbey.

THE LETTERS BEGIN

It was at Ampleforth in 1936 that Arnold Toynbee met Columba Cary-Elwes; and the mature historian and the younger monk, both *nel mezzo del cammin*, commenced a friendship and correspondence that extended to Toynbee's death thirty-nine years later. The younger monk revered the older historian as a distinguished scholar; Arnold with characteristic humility regarded Columba as a spiritual counsellor: 'You are my most direct door to God.'[9] Columba attempted to bring Arnold into the Church as a latter-day St Augustine. Arnold refused to abandon his 'intellectual freedom'; but the correspondence remained an exchange among equals: a deepening friendship transcended the conceptual theological differences; and the influence of each upon the other is revealed in their use of an increasingly similar terminology.

THE APOLOGIA

Early in the correspondence, in 1938, Toynbee wrote the elaborate *apologia pro religione sua*, which constitutes a new *locus classicus* for any study of his religious positions. In the *apologia* Toynbee traced his journey from belief to disbelief and back to belief, and described the obstacles in the way of his passing from his then present (1938) belief in the existence of God to an acceptance of the doctrines of 'either the Christian churches in general or of the Roman Church in particular.'[10] Under the category of 'intellectual obstacles' he found (1) that the propagation and survival of religion and Catholicism have been 'contingent upon mundane historical causes: some trivial, some unedifying, all natural'; (2) that 'the mode of operation of Nature – Spiritual as well as Physical – is prodigality and manifoldness, not uniqueness, or economy'; and (3) that 'in an anthropologist's eye, it seems unlikely that God, in putting Mankind into communication with Himself,' would choose only one channel of grace. To these intellectual obstacles Toynbee added a professional obstacle: 'In so far as he [Toynbee] is conscious of having any religious or pastoral mission, this mission is to help his fellow pagan "intellectuals" to move' to a belief in God; even if his intellectual obstacles were to be surmounted, to move into Catholicism would be to bring his 'mission to the heathen' to an end, because he would be written off 'as a fellow who had "gone soft-headed" and was no longer to be taken seriously.' At this point he would have to make the choice, in Buddhist terms, of being a Bodhisattva or an Arhat; and his choice would be, as a Bodhisattva, to stop at the threshold of Nirvana and prolong his servitude to the 'Wheel of existence' for the sake of remaining in a position to help his fellows forward.[11]

During the remaining thirty-seven years of Toynbee's life there were many fluctuations and changes of emphasis in his religious beliefs. For example, to the obstacle of uniqueness he added a brooding awareness of the problem of evil. None the less the statement of 1938 remains that of his essential position until the time of his death.

A PHILO-CATHOLIC

The letters of the years from 1938 to 1947 show Toynbee at his nearest approach to traditional Christianity: 'I certainly am, and shall remain, a philo-Catholic.'[12] This also is apparent in volumes four through six of the *Study*: 'And now, as we stand and gaze with our eyes fixed upon the farther shore, a single figure rises from the flood and straightway fills the whole horizon. There is the Saviour.'[13] But throughout the correspondence there is evidence that certain basic conceptual barriers to his complete embrace of traditional Christianity remained and in later years became even more fixed.

A FOLLOWER OF SYMMACHUS

Toynbee valued symbols and was profoundly moved by archetypal phrases: among these was the reply that the fourth-century pagan orator Quintus Aurelius Symmachus made to the Christians as he urged restoration of the altar of Victory to the Senate House: *Uno itinere non potest perveniri ad tam grande secretum* ('the heart of so great a mystery can never be reached by following one road only' – AJT).[14] Toynbee insisted that no revelation was unique: 'If the revelation of the One True God is to be accessible to all men, it has to be diffracted.'[15] Toynbee's belief in the diversity of revelation remained an impenetrable obstacle to his acceptance of the unique role of Christianity; he acknowledges to Columba: 'Uniqueness, as you point out, is the stumbling block for me.'[16] He had a scrupulous fear that his own Christian indoctrination might prejudice his conclusions: 'Brought up as you and I have been, within the Christian circle, how can we know that the other religions are not alternative roads to a single god?'[17]

REVELATION, MYTHS, AND THEOLOGY

To Toynbee, Revelation comes, not through exclusive channels, not as 'a "release" by God of information telling the truth about Reality in some absolute sense.'[18] The spiritual presence in the universe manifests itself in many forms; and one is in myths, 'in which our human imagination penetrates perhaps farthest into the mystery of the Universe'[19]; and myths are an 'indispensable means for expressing as much as we can express of the ineffable.'[20] Toynbee praises C.G. Jung for restoring to honour in the Western World the 'subconscious wellspring of Poetry and Prophecy' long after Plato had used the myth to reconnoitre 'regions of the Spiritual Universe beyond the Reason's range.'[21] He concludes that the purpose of theology is to 'clarify the meaning of myths.'[22]

COSMIC REVELATION

These revelations may come through the gates of horn and not of ivory.[23] 'It is not in a waterspout but in a gentle shower that the golden rain pierces the brazen carapace of Danae's dungeon. And God's method of progressive revelation may be accurately described, in Newman's famous phrase, as "an economy of truth."'[24] The theme became almost explicitly Christian in an early letter to Columba (14 May 1940): 'About the reign of the mock king, I am diffident about offering any explanation of those anticipations, in history, of the Incarnation and the Passion which I have discussed in that Annex ['Christus Patiens,' *Study*, 6: 376–539]. For myself, I think the rationalists' explanation is, if at all true, only a part of the truth and that not the most important part. The simile in my mind is that of dawn before sunrise: the Light spreads over the sky before the Sun himself appears: but this is only an image.'[25]

Toynbee conceded that we may discern in the passions of Tammuz and Attis and Adonis and Osiris 'a foreshadowing of the Passion of Christ'[26] and that 'in the sacrifice of the Mass, Christians were still partaking of the sacrament of all the pagan mysteries.'[27] He concluded that 'an historian peering into the future in A.D. 1952' could imagine Christianity surviving 'as the heir of all the philosophies ... and of all the higher religions.'[28]

But Toynbee remained syncretistic to the end: 'My knee bows, like every Christian's knee, at the deed of self-sacrifice, done for love of us men and for our salvation, that is recited by Saint Paul to the Philippians. For me, the doer of this deed is one presence in more than one epiphany. It is Christ, and, because it is Christ, it is also the Buddha and the bodhisattvas.'[29] Ironically, Toynbee's clinging to Symmachus's dictum may have led Columba to arrive at an increased appreciation of cosmic revelation: 'God has left his imprint everywhere on the things He has made.'[30]

Despite Toynbee's interest in myth and cosmic revelation, the letters reveal him as lacking in sympathy with the sacramental aspects of religion. This becomes most apparent in the interesting exchange of letters in 1950 at the time of the definition of the dogma of the Assumption. In reading the dialogue between Arnold and Columba, one finds a curious and unexpected lack of understanding that makes the dialogue an oblique rather than direct exchange of thoughts. Columba even reproaches Arnold with the accusation that his attitude towards religion is '*Very Low Church* and spiritual.'[31]

THE NATURE OF THE ABSOLUTE

From June 1958 to October 1959, the correspondents carried on a deliberate discussion of the higher religions. It is of interest that during most of this time Toynbee was completing the *Reconsiderations* that constituted volume twelve of the *Study*. Toynbee here is concerned with the question whether the 'Absolute' is personal or impersonal; he concludes that 'Reality is in touch with all Its creations, and must have a facet with which each of them can communicate with It.' Thus Reality must have a personal facet looking towards persons, and other facets for 'animals, vegetables, minerals, gases.' The vision of Reality in our image as seen by the Judaic religions differs from that in the Indian tradition where 'the cable of personality was given up, for wireless communication with "It," at an early stage.'[32] In sum, Toynbee concludes that the Absolute is neither personal nor impersonal, though it is both, and all-embracing; nor is there a real difference between 'God' and 'the ground of being.'[33]

MARCION AND THE PROBLEM OF EVIL

The *Apologia* of August 1938 contains no reference to the problem of evil; but in later years his awareness of the problem became increasingly intrusive. Here the archetypal phrase was that of Lucretius, a poet who supplied more texts to the *Study* than did Vergil: the universe cannot have been divinely created for our benefit, *it is so loaded with fault* (*tanta stat praedita culpa*).[34] Arnold raises the question in writing about his estrangement from Rosalind: 'It is certainly an evil and therefore cannot, in itself, be God's will ... Does submitting to God's will mean acquiescing in something that cannot be God's will? This baffles me.'[35] At one time he found a reconciliation: 'This paradoxical truth that Love is inseparable from the Almighty Power put forth in Creation is visually portrayed in Medieval Western Christian *mappae mundi* in which the latent figure of Christ Crucified holds together and sustains the World.'[36] And again he found that God is 'Love as well as Omnipotence.'[37]

But in later years, Toynbee became increasingly sympathetic with Marcion, the second-century heretic, who held a dualistic view that the God of Power of the Old Testament was other than the 'stranger God' of Love of the New. In a late letter, which contains a summary of his religious positions, Arnold writes to Columba: 'I am also a Marcionite in believing that love is not omnipotent, whereas you are presumably a Irenaean. (I cannot reconcile omnipotence with beneficence.) I believe in the Agony in the Garden and in the Crucifixion, but not in the Resurrection. (I am using all these words in the symbolic sense.)'[38]

THE LIMITS OF BELIEF

These were the central concepts; but one should note that Toynbee's mythopoetic imagination was sensitive to the stimuli of a changing world, without and within. He frequently felt impelled to assay *jeux d'esprit* that surely should not be taken *au pied de la lettre*. Thus, in his concern for the biosphere he spoke with sympathy of the Byzantine neo-pagan George Yemistos Plethon's (c. 1360–1452) attempt to revive the Hellenic deities: 'The antidote to monotheism is a polytheism which recognizes that non-human Nature is divine and that consequently she has divine rights which Man violates at his peril.'[39]

We must remember the excursus 'The Roman Revolution from the flora's point of view' in *Hannibal's Legacy*,[40] and the chapter 'If Alexander the Great Had Lived on' in *Some Problems of Greek History*.[41] The great historian had a playful fancy and was not unwilling to challenge by shock. To attempt to incorporate all his obiter dicta into a basic pattern of belief is to attempt to 'draw out Leviathan with an hook.'[42] This may explain in part (but only in part) Toynbee's increasing disclaimers of orthodox Christian positions in his later published writings, and, indeed, in the letters themselves.

LE COEUR A SES RAISONS QUE LA RAISON NE CONNAÎT POINT

The letters cast an illuminating light not only upon the historian's formal (and protean) theological opinions, but even more arrestingly upon the workings of his heart; the reticences and veiled references of his public works are removed; in the letters the heart is revealed as that of an *anima naturaliter Christiana* in its prayerful response to suffering.

At the death of his son, Tony, a suicide: 'This time, as I was straining forward to do what I could for him, instead of finding myself up against Tony himself in the unhappy way which I knew so well, I felt myself come face to face with God, and realized that, from now on, I should be dealing about Tony with God, and not with Tony himself.'[43]

When Arnold writes Columba about his estrangement from Rosalind:

I have been able, by God's mercy, to pray to God more actively and fruitfully than I ever have since I was a child, and I believe this will remain with me. I am able to meditate on the first half of the Lord's Prayer ... I try to do three spiritual acts: –
First, to think and feel the comfort of the paradox in the combination of 'Father' with 'Heaven'. Where you might expect to find nothing but merciless unapproachable impersonal forces, you actually find a person who, while as formidable as the astronomical universe, is, again by paradox, not only formidable but also loving and tender: one can turn to Him.[44]

Thérèse of Lisieux was a favourite saint. During his ordeal, one day in Paris Arnold found himself, with Rosalind in mind, walking to the Sacré-Coeur, where he prayed before the statue of Ste Thérèse 'in very great agony,' that at the last moment Rosalind and he might be reconciled. This experience is recorded in a moving passage in his letter of 5 October 1947.[45]

Upon hearing of Rosalind's death, Arnold's basic belief that God is Love becomes a cry from the heart: 'Yes, I love Rosalind with all my heart, and I love Veronica, too, with all my heart, because the heart can give the whole of itself to more than one person; this is one of the things in which love is unique and in which the First Epistle General of Saint John speaks one of the ultimate truths when it identifies love with God.'[46]

Indeed, one of the most interesting disclosures of the letters is that of Arnold's life of prayer: his concern with the proper objects of prayer and the need for 'God's grace';[47] his analysis of the Lord's Prayer;[48] his use of the prayer of surrender to God's will (*suscipe, Domine, universam meam libertatem*) of St Ignatius Loyola.[49] In wakeful nights

Arnold would visualize the symbol of the Buddha, the blank circle of detachment; this he attempted to fill with a turning towards God and 'a transfer of one's focus from oneself to Him.'[50] The mingling of a Buddhist symbol with a Christian exercise of the will is vintage Toynbee.

A BODHISATTVA TO THE END

Arnold Toynbee throughout his life retained the role of the Bodhisattva that he had described in the *Apologia* of August 1938; perhaps with this role in mind, he held that 'the impulse of an ex-Christian on the run to find a hiding-place in Christ's riven side ran directly counter to the spirit and significance of Christ's incarnation.'[51] The intellectual obstacles remained in place. When Columba reports that he tells the monks that Arnold would be Catholic 'but for a deep fear of abandoning your liberty and too soft a place for eastern religions,' Arnold replies: 'Your description of me hits both nails on the head. I hold to my liberty to follow wherever the argument may lead me (and it may never stop keeping me on the move).'[52] This role was intensified by his belief in the value of suffering epitomized in Aeschylus's πάθει μάθος (learning through suffering): 'The attitude towards suffering is, for me, the acid test, and on this I am Christian, not Buddhist.'[53]

Thus, Toynbee remained without commitment, except perhaps that symbolized in his dream of 1936 in which he was 'clasping the foot of the crucifix hanging over the high altar of the Abbey of Ampleforth and was hearing a voice saying to him *Amplexus expecta* ("Cling and wait").'[54] Columba completely understood: 'You have followed truth as you see it – and, in my terms, God already loves you infinitely for that.'[55]

EPILOGUE

On 2–3 August 1974 Arnold Toynbee suffered a severe stroke; he lingered until 22 October 1975, in a state of frustration, unable to speak more than a few, occasional words; unable, after an attempt, to write intelligibly. The writer and his wife visited him, in the Purey Cust nursing home at York, in mid-September 1975. He greeted us with his cordial smile, and I spoke to him about our recent travels on the Continent; he made no answer, but appeared to be listening with his customary courtesy.

At this time Columba paid a farewell visit to Arnold and Veronica. Veronica recalled that Arnold, aware that Columba was going to Africa, had been depressed for several hours. Columba reports: 'During our last meeting ... during which he was incapable of clear speech or writing, suddenly he said very distinctly the words, "In the name of the Father and of the Son and of the Holy Ghost," and then fell back into silence.'[56]

This may bear several interpretations. Veronica Toynbee considered it an act of courtesy and love to Columba. To the writer it appears more likely that it was this, and more: by affirming the Trinity, Arnold Toynbee was saying, 'Yes, this is *one* aspect of the Ultimate Reality.' A less likely interpretation, which we cannot reject conclusively, is that Arnold was telling Columba that his mission was ended, and that he had doffed the role of Bodhisattva.

NOTES

1 *An Historian's Conscience: The Correspondence of Arnold J. Toynbee and Columba Cary-Elwes, Monk of Ampleforth*, ed. Christian B. Peper (Boston: Beacon Press 1986)
2 'Religion is Man's attempt to get into touch with an absolute spiritual Reality behind the phenomena of the Universe, and, having made contact with It, to live in harmony with It.' *A Study of History*, 12 vols. (London and New York: Oxford University Press 1934–61), 12: 663
3 *Historian's Conscience*, 19 and 15, where he refers to this state as one of 'Liberal rational paganism.'
4 Ibid., 19–20
5 London: Oxford University Press 1969, 176
6 Ibid., 389–91
7 *Historian's Conscience*, 21–2, n. 1
8 Ibid., 171, and cf. Rosalind's *The Good Pagan's Failure* (London: The Catholic Book Club 1939).
9 *Historian's Conscience*, 37
10 Ibid., 19
11 Ibid., 20–1
12 Ibid., 168

13 *Study*, 6: 278
14 Ibid., 7: 442; and cf. *Study*, 12: 625 and *Historian's Conscience*, 179, n. 3.
15 *Study*, 7: 443. Symmachus (c. 340–402), a leader of the Roman aristocracy, still in part pagan, was a man of letters and a statesman who attained the consulship; his plea to Valentinian II (*Relatio Tertia*) for restoration of the altar was resisted by St Ambrose and failed; but apparently relations between pagan and Christian were not marked by the *odium theologicum*: Symmachus's surviving letters to St Ambrose are written in the tone of friendship; and St Ambrose, in turn, respects Symmachus's zeal and eloquence. Cf. Samuel Dill, *Roman Society in the Last Century of the Western Empire*, 2nd ed. (London: Macmillan 1919), 22–3, 143–66.
16 *Historian's Conscience*, 400
17 Ibid., 242
18 *Study*, 12: 98, n. 2
19 Ibid., 12: 621
20 *An Historian's Approach to Religion* (London: Oxford University Press 1956), 280
21 *Study*, 10: 228; and see the extended discussion of Jung's categories in *Study*, 7: 716–36; the revelations contained in the higher religions are here discussed in terms of Jung's psychological types.
22 *Historian's Approach*, 281
23 Vergil, *Aeneid*, 6.893–6
24 *Study*, 6: 538; and cf. John Henry Newman, *An Essay on the Development of Christian Doctrine*, new ed. (New York: Longmans, Green and Co. 1949), 355–7 and *passim*; Avery Robert Dulles, *Models of Revelation* (New York: Doubleday & Co. 1983); AJT was prescient of modern theology in this field.
25 *Historian's Conscience*, 62
26 *Study*, 7: 423
27 Ibid., 7: 458
28 Ibid., 7: 107
29 Ibid., 12: 102; and see the 'Litany' 'after looking once more, this afternoon, at Fra Angelico's picture of the Beatific Vision' (*Study*, 10: 143–4).
30 *Historian's Conscience*, 393
31 Ibid., 268–74
32 Ibid., 387
33 Ibid., 398–9
34 Lucretius, *De Rerum Natura*, 5.199
35 *Historian's Conscience*, 157

36 *Study*, 9: 401
37 Ibid., 9: 382
38 *Historian's Conscience*, 537; the conflict between the concepts of Love and Omnipotence is discussed at length in *Experiences*, 146–69.
39 *The Greeks and Their Heritages* (New York: Oxford University Press 1981), 313; see Thomas W. Africa, 'The Final Vision of Arnold Toynbee,' *Historical Reflections/Réflexions historiques* 10, no. 2 (1983): 221–8.
40 2 vols (London: Oxford University Press 1965), 2: 585–99
41 London: Oxford University Press 1969, 441–86
42 Job 41:1. To this must be added Toynbee's humility and sympathy for others, which at times seem to colour his approach; in the posthumously published discussions with Daisaku Ikeda he concludes 'that the religion we need to embrace now is pantheism, as exemplified in Shinto, and that the religion we now need to discard is Judaic monotheism and the post-Christian nontheistic faith in scientific progress.' Toynbee and Daisaku Ikeda, *The Toynbee-Ikeda Dialogue: Man Himself Must Choose* (Tokyo: Kodansha 1976), 300. With this Ikeda, a Buddhist, disagreed, and Toynbee ended the dialogue by agreeing that 'a universal system of laws of life, such as is presented in Buddhism, is likely to be a less misleading representation of ultimate spiritual reality than either a pantheon – Zeus, Athena, and Apollo – or a unique god – Yahweh' (ibid., 303).
43 *Historian's Conscience*, 33
44 Ibid., 132
45 Ibid., 203
46 Ibid., 479
47 Ibid., 145
48 Ibid., 132–3
49 Ibid., 233; this prayer was copied in Rosalind's hand in Toynbee's unpublished notebook ('Farrago Toynbeiana') now in the writer's possession. The Farrago contains entries from 1907 to 1973.
50 *Historian's Conscience*, 357
51 *Study*, 9: 632
52 *Historian's Conscience*, 317–18
53 Ibid., 318
54 *Study*, 9: 634–5; *Historian's Conscience*, 37. In his 'Farrago Toynbeiana,' he recounts in its entirety a lengthy dream in which he was vainly struggling to board a transatlantic liner. The conclusion came: 'My distress became so great that I woke up; and then, as I woke, I found myself clasping the feet of the big crucifix ... and I heard ringing in my ears the words "Cling and

wait"'; it is interesting to note that these words were reported as heard in English, not in Latin.
55 Ibid., 536
56 Ibid., 587

Toynbee's Philosophy of History:
His Christian Period
C.T. McIntire

RELIGION AND TOYNBEE'S PHILOSOPHY OF HISTORY

When Arnold Toynbee published the last four volumes of *A Study of History* in 1954, he told the world that he had changed his mind on his major thesis. The higher religions were not, as he once thought, the handmaidens of civilizations with the function of helping civilizations rise to higher achievements. He now believed it was the other way around: civilizations came into existence and passed away in order to promote the spiritual progress of humanity by means of the creation of the higher religions.[1] Toynbee presented this reversal of his central thesis with all the earnestness of a prophet. He astonished many of his readers: Toynbee had found religion, it seemed. They recorded their alarm in reviews that now could cover the entire ten volumes of his magnum opus.

But had Toynbee found religion? If he had, what religion, or religions, had he found? And what did religion have to do with his study of history? Commentators over the years have not agreed among themselves, or with Toynbee, about Toynbee's religion. Overshadowing the discussions we have Toynbee's self-description about his religious journey. Until age eighteen he was an Anglican, baptized and confirmed in the Church of England and educated in an Anglican residential school, Winchester College. When he went up to Balliol College, Oxford, in 1907 he uneventfully slipped away from the Church. According to his own unequivocal testimony in his autobiography in 1969: 'When I was an undergraduate at Oxford, I became an agnostic ... Now, more than half a century later, I am still an agnostic, as the sequel will show.'[2] To reviewers in the 1950s, Toynbee hardly seemed agnostic – he was too committed and all too knowing in matters of religion. They disagreed vehemently over identifying what his religion was. On one side, the reviewer in the *Times Literary Supplement* called him 'the prophet of a new apocalypse, the evangelist of a syncretic higher "higher religion,"' A.J.P. Taylor proclaimed that 'Professor Toynbee is no longer a Christian,' but the apostle of a new 'mish-mash' religion. Evangelical Protestants then and later tended to agree.[3] By contrast, Linus Walker observed, 'It should be noted that Toynbee's own beliefs are almost all entirely Christian in inspiration,' even though it was clear that his beliefs would not meet the standards of orthodoxy. Martin Wight concurred, also noting Toynbee's unorthodox, but Christian, tendencies.[4] In any case, Pieter Geyl found Toynbee's religion so intrusive as to render him a prophet and not a historian. Later reviewers were calmer in their statements, but no less in disagreement. William McNeill, writing after 1969, accepted Toynbee's self-description as an agnostic. Roland Stromberg found his religion vague and sentimental. Edward Rochie Hardy was tempted to call his religion 'Toynbeeism.'[5] Whatever the religion, nearly everyone was inclined to treat it as an addendum and a distraction from Toynbee's work as a historian, except when the subject-matter was religion.

Toynbee the agnostic? the syncretist? the unorthodox Christian? And where does his religion fit into his professional work? To gain ground in the discussion, I propose that we not simply concentrate on his personal religious faith or on the orthodoxy of his religious beliefs according to ecclesiastical standards, but look specifically at what his writings on the study of history are appropriately able to reveal to us, namely his philosophy of history. If our interest is Toynbee as historian, the thing that matters about his religion and his thought about history is the impact of his religion on the character of his philosophy of history. It becomes clear that he did not keep his religion sequestered away from his professional work of thinking about history. He worked out his personal religious quest by means of his professional thought as well as by means of anything else that he encountered in the course of his daily life. Toynbee's own integrity requires that we ask our questions in ways that allow us to consider his religion and his historical work together.

The chief question then becomes: What *was* Toynbee's religion before and after the time of the writing of his last four volumes, and what effect did it have on *The Study of History*? To explore this question I will need to approach his religion and his philosophy of history historically, and follow the sequences of his articulation of religion within his philosophy of history. I will concentrate on his published academic writings, including *Study* and all his other books and articles that touch on religion and history, but I will also look at his references to his religion in his private correspondence and published personal reflections. We quickly detect that over the course of his career Toynbee changed his thought fundamentally more than once, rendering it impossible to treat his thought as one system.[6]

When we look at Toynbee's writings in the years before and after 1954, the religion that we primarily encounter is Christianity, but we also meet his experiences, or at least his awareness, of virtually every other religion, and attitude towards religion, in history. We will find that we meet the problem of interpreting Toynbee's relationship with Christianity, particularly the question of whether his thinking may at any time be classified within the tradition of a Christian philosophy of history. To help us, may I suggest that we employ these straightforward criteria for telling a Christian philosophy of history from other philosophies of history: a Christian philosophy of history is one whose basic inspiration and character are given by the ultimate meaning found in Jesus Christ; notions and categories not explicitly related to the symbol of Jesus Christ are counted as belonging to a Christian philosophy of history if they are, or have been, found within the Christian community of discourse about history.[7] With these criteria in mind we will embark on a detailed study of Toynbee's religion and its influence on his historical thought.

THE LATE 1930S: TOWARDS A CHRISTIAN VIEW

The 1954 volumes of *Study*, which raised publicly and dramatically the question of Toynbee's religion, were his third 'batch' of volumes, as he liked to call them. In the first three volumes from 1934, in which he discussed the themes of the genesis and growth of civilizations, he treated the scriptures and mythology of many civilizations as equivalent to each other and accorded no priority to Christianity. His use of the model of the relation between ancient Greek and Roman civilization and his own modern Western civilization came easily from his classical education and attachment to his own English culture. He interpreted the role of Christianity in history as that of a chrysalis that accomplished the transmutation from the Greco-Roman parent civilization to the Western offspring.[8] Christian figures like St Paul, St Benedict, and St Gregory the Great were important to his analysis, but they appeared as equals with a host of others like Mohammed and Solon, and Jesus Christ was not included.[9] Toynbee's approach was, indeed, noticeably agnostic about religion. We can none the less readily detect evidence of his Christian upbringing and his saturation in the Bible, and we find strong evidence of an appreciation of the superiority of spirituality over what he might regard as the materialism of Western civilization. Notably, he gave religion an important place in his thinking. Religion was one of two criteria that he used to identify distinct civilizations, and it was crucial to what he called 'etherialization,' the tendency of a civilization in the growth phase to pass, on many levels, from lower to higher states. In terms of religion he described this growth as 'a conversion of the soul from the World, the Flesh, and the Devil to the Kingdom of God.' The supreme expression of the principle he believed was found in the Christian Gospels, in Matthew 6:25–33: 'But seek ye first the Kingdom of God, and His righteousness.'[10]

In the second batch of three volumes from 1939, however, we notice an important change. In these volumes, which discussed the breakdown and disintegration of civilizations, Toynbee explicitly raised the matter of religion and gave evidence of beginning to work a Christian view of history into the exposition of his theory. This he did long before 1954. He confronted his readers with religion in his preface to the three new volumes, found in volume four and dated 31 March 1939. He testified that he experienced the present time as 'a moment of public anxiety and private grief.'[11] On the public horizon, just two weeks earlier Hitler and the Nazi army had annexed Czechoslovakia to Germany, intensifying the threat of a war that could make the previous great war of 1914–18 look secondary. For many years Toynbee had agonized over the barbarism of Nazism, the sufferings due to the Great Depression in Capitalism, and the totalitarian triumphs of Stalinism. Such happenings had heightened his sense of the breakdown of his own Western civilization. In the 1939 preface he testified that he found strength in recalling St Augustine and associated his own project with Augustine's magisterial work *The City of God*. He noted that both were large works that had taken many years to write, and that both were major studies of history prompted by profound crisis in civilization. Toynbee acknowledged that he felt attracted to Augustine's 'supra-mundane range of vision' that had managed to 'inspire the souls of Christians from that day to this.' He confessed: 'A glimpse of this vision is the boon for which the present writer is the most deeply grateful to the writer of *De Civitate Dei*.'[12]

The reference to private grief referred to the recent death of his mother, his closest confidante, and the suicide of his eldest son, Tony, two weeks before. This was when, he later confessed, he felt as if 'God had revealed himself for an instant to give an unmistakable assurance of his mercy and forgiveness.'[13]

Toynbee's 1939 experience of God came as part of what appears to be a gradual and increasingly intense personal re-encounter with God and with Christian religion in particular. Certainly he dates the beginning of the process from at least 1930, perhaps 1929, when he was 41 years of age.[14] His wife Rosalind's conversion to the Roman Catholic church in 1932, and his son Lawrence's enrolment as a pupil in the Roman Catholic school of Ampleforth Abbey in 1935 had brought him once again into communication with the organized church.[15] The remarkable friendship with Father Columba of Ampleforth from 1936 onward provided Toynbee with a spiritual partner and teacher whose influence in the late 1930s he readily acknowledged.[16] Bridget Reddin, his typist for the whole of *Study*, beginning in 1930, and a devout Roman Catholic, prayed without ceasing for his conversion to the Roman Catholic church.[17]

Evidence of Toynbee's movement towards Christianity appeared in his public statements as early as January 1937, when he was forty-eight, and is reflected in the very first letters exchanged between himself and Columba. No doubt aware in 1936 of his inclination towards Christianity, the organizers of the ecumenical Oxford Conference on Church, Community, and State, which would be convened in July 1937, invited Toynbee to participate with Sir Walter Moberly, T.S.

Eliot, and others in a preparatory series of lectures to be broadcast over the BBC, beginning in January 1937. The aim of the conference would be 'to pave the way for a restatement of the permanent beliefs of the Christian Churches.' The published version of Toynbee's lecture, as it appeared in *The Listener*, bore the title 'Post-War Paganism versus Christianity.' The new paganism was Fascism and Communism, both of which depended upon 'the idolatrous worship of organised human power.' Both movements, Toynbee charged, committed the fatal error identified by St Paul as the worship of the creature instead of the Creator. By contrast, he believed that Christianity had provided the means for people to lead a new life, exemplified in the lives of the saints, and had revealed new insight into God's purpose in the world. As a consequence we have new knowledge of 'the true home of Man' which is, he affirmed, the City of God.[18] Before very long, in his letters to Columba, he added modern Western liberalism to the list of paganisms.[19]

Toynbee's BBC lecture witnessed to his personal movement of faith towards Christianity and his willingness to co-operate with organized endeavours of Christian churches, but, more important for our purposes, it also disclosed his use of several major categories of historical analysis provided by the Christian tradition of discourse about history – notions of spiritual life, spiritual warfare, idolatry, community, the City or Kingdom of God, the purpose of human existence, and divine will.

We find these and other comparable categories beginning to appear in *A Study of History* as Toynbee moved forward in the writing of volumes four, five, and six. He composed these volumes between 1933 and 1939, during the very same time in which he experienced personal religious change. We can watch him transmute his personal transformation into new categories of historical analysis. In volume four, begun in 1933, he defined 'breakdown' in a civilization as 'failures in an audacious attempt to ascend from the level of a Primitive Humanity, living the life of a social animal, to the heights of some superhuman kind of being in a Communion of Saints.'[20] He borrowed the latter image from St Paul's metaphor for the Church as affirmed in the Apostles' Creed. In volume one, Toynbee had already spoken of history as progressive.[21] Now he could say that the goal of the progress of history was the achievement of a new spiritual being and spiritual community. Why did those failures occur? Toynbee's answer assigned responsibility to the loss of creative power in the human soul.[22] Can this nemesis of creativity be averted? Yes, he replied, through a 'spiritual rebirth.' Quoting words from the King James Version of the Bible attributed to Jesus, Toynbee continued: 'Except ye become as little children, ye shall not enter the Kingdom of God.'[23] In other words, breakdowns in civilizations could be averted by meeting the spiritual requirements of the Kingdom of God. What happened during the breakdowns? The creative leaders of a civilization lost their creativity by turning to idolatry and making idols out of an ephemeral self, or institution, or technique. Toynbee defined idolatry in Christian terms as 'an intellectually and morally purblind worship of the part instead of the whole, of the creature instead of the Creator, of Time instead of Eternity.'[24] We can understand how Toynbee's adoption of a Christian notion of idolatry influenced his analysis of history by observing a change that occurs in his treatment of nationalism. Whereas in volume one (1934) he expressed mild concern about occasional over-emphasis on nationality, now he wrote strongly against nationalism as the idolatry of nation and moved the discussion of nationalism to the centre of his explanation of why civilizations broke down.[25]

In volume five Toynbee's interpretive repertoire became even more explicitly Christian as he discussed the disintegration of civilizations. He theorized that disintegrations entail two schisms, one in the body social and one in the soul of a civilization.[26] He admitted that his assertion about soul was bound to be 'unpalatable to modern man,' but he believed that he needed such a category in order to penetrate to a deeper spiritual level and to understand how profound a crisis disintegration was. Using the imagery for the meaning of a sacrament in Christian churches, he described schism in the body social as 'the outward visible sign of an inward spiritual rift' in the soul.[27] In other words, Toynbee now believed that spiritual schism was basic, and that religious occurrences were central to the life of a civilization. He presented this claim in the form of an important observation about history and he did not press it as an urgent message. As for the goal of history, he affirmed that the goal of the Kingdom of Heaven as understood within Christianity – Augustine's City of God – was superior to the Buddhist goal of Nirvana or the Hellenist City of Zeus. Both of those non-Christian goals required the negation of this world, while the Christian goal embraced at once both this world and the world to come.[28] Indeed, Toynbee suggested that the Christian social ideal of community as advocated in Acts 4, which is based on human fellowship and achieved by spiritual transfiguration, could be translated into Christian socialism and become one earthly expression of the supramundane City of God.[29] The attainment of even the beginnings of the City of God in this world, he believed, would break the hold of what Christians call 'original sin' in our earthly life. Original sin, said Toynbee, is best understood as our hubris, our graceless self-centredness.[30]

Toynbee took himself much further still in volume six, which he wrote in 1937 and 1938.[31] It is fair to say that in volume six Toynbee argued his way to Jesus Christ. The theme of the volume was spiritual schism in the soul of civilization. Toynbee identified several types of response to such schism, including the attempts to return to the past, to leap to some ideal future, or to cultivate utter detachment. Superior to these, he asserted, was the response of transfiguration offered by Christianity. Transfiguration is an act of God expressed as love whereby a people are taken into the Kingdom of God. This Kingdom, or City of God, is held together by love and, he now confessed, led by Jesus Christ who manifested love above all. With St Augustine Toynbee recommended 'taking our departure from the City of Destruction' and 'enrolling ourselves as citizens of a *Civitas Dei* of which Christ Crucified is King.'[32] Toynbee advocated such transfiguration as the highest form of palingenesia – regeneration – the rebirth that Jesus revealed to Nicodemus and for which Jesus was born at Bethlehem as the king of the new Kingdom of God.[33] In a long section on saviours and an even longer annex, entitled 'Christus Patiens,' Toynbee critically reviewed the list of the world's proffered saviours – the demi-gods, the avatars, the bearers of the sword, the dei ex machina – and then he came to Jesus and John 3:16. In Jesus he found God incarnate who surpasses all would-be saviours, the single figure who 'rises from the flood and straightway fills the whole horizon.' For Toynbee, Jesus Christ stands above all as the one who suffered for love, Christus Patiens.[34]

In this way Toynbee, by 1938, brought himself to Jesus Christ in his historical thought, and he began to face what such a Christian orientation meant for understanding history. At the very end of volume six Toynbee compared history to a great garment or tapestry woven by a master weaver on the loom of Time. Looking back over the patterns of history that he had detected in his first six volumes, Toynbee let himself wonder what might hold the key to the meaning of the weaver's work. He introduced a telling metaphor. If the rise and fall of the many civilizations are the perpetual turning of a wheel, it is 'not a vain repetition if, at each revolution, it is carrying a vehicle that much nearer to its goal.' Toynbee continued: 'And if "palingenesia" signifies the birth of something new, and not just the rebirth of something that has lived and died any numbers of times already, then the Wheel of Existence is not just a devilish device for inflicting an everlasting torment on a damned Ixion.'[35] Toynbee had come far enough to believe that of the three phenomena that his theory led him to believe issued from the disintegration of civilizations – universal states, universal churches, and barbarian war-bands – at least one may not be a mere waste product. The key to the meaning of history, he proposed, may lie in understanding 'the destiny of the universal church in which every higher religion seeks to embody itself.' Toynbee brought volume six to an end with a suggestion of where he was headed in his analysis: he could not rest 'without trying to unlock the secret of this mystery.'[36] To Columba he wrote, 'Parts of my book will be in harmony with your outlook; other parts you may, I am afraid, feel discordant. I am in a kind of limbo or "no-man's-land" between two worlds, as you know.' He was, he admitted, feeling his way.[37]

1939 TO THE LATE 1950S: A CHRISTIAN PHILOSOPHY OF HISTORY

The war began in September 1939 when Hitler invaded Poland and Great Britain and France responded with a declaration of war on Germany. The winter of 1939–40, although a catastrophe for Europe, was a fruitful one for Toynbee's philosophy of history. He came rather quickly to the decision that the key to the meaning of history was indeed religion, specifically Christianity. Toynbee explicitly embraced a Christian understanding of history and began to rework his philosophy of history accordingly.

Along with the other staff of Chatham House, Toynbee moved to Oxford as soon as the war began in order to take up his war work as a researcher in service to the British government. He was based in

Balliol College, his old college. The anxieties he acknowledged in the 1939 preface to *Study* had not left him, particularly the agony caused by the war and the deaths of his mother and son Tony. His religious migration continued. He made it clear to Columba that he saw his war work as Christian service and that he saw the need of the hour to be a recovery of the spiritual dimension of Western civilization, notably in a recovery of Christianity. Toynbee interpreted the war as the blow that would bring the era of the nation-state to an end. He could imagine the destruction caused by the war as 'a preliminary external treatment to make it easier for the soul to do what only the soul and God together can do, that is, help the soul to find its way to God.[38]

In Oxford Toynbee prayed daily, began a regular program of contemplation and devotional reading, including St Augustine's *Confessions* and the Book of Common Prayer, gave his support to the *Christian News Letter* founded by J.H. Oldham, who had been the prime mover in the Oxford Conference of 1937, and led the reinstitution of worship in Balliol College chapel. His role in the worship services at Balliol shocked Columba, who considered Anglican worship as the pale light of the moon next to the bright sunlight of the Roman Catholic mass.[39] When Rosalind left Toynbee to settle back in London in October 1940, and then separated from him in 1942 and divorced him in 1946, he added a new agony to his experience of pain in the world, and he turned ever more to the consolation of religion.[40] He turned as well to Veronica Boulter, his long-time assistant, the daughter of a Church of England clergyman, and finally married her in 1946 with both civil and Anglican ceremonies.[41] He also read theology and found himself especially attracted to Reinhold Niebuhr's *Nature and Destiny of Man*.[42]

What all this added up to was that Toynbee had resumed his life as an Anglican, the life he had given up in 1907. Columba was happy with this religious move as far as it went, but he softly, yet consistently, pressed Toynbee to convert to the Roman Catholic church. It was in relation to his not entering that church that Toynbee described himself as a 'philo-Catholic' none the less. Columba and Ampleforth eventually broke relations with Toynbee in 1944 in order to avoid spiritually misleading him. Toynbee continued as an Anglican.[43]

The public forum in which Toynbee first made his renewed Christian expression evident was the Burge Memorial Lecture delivered at Oxford on 23 May 1940. The Germans had just invaded Belgium and then France and, even as he spoke, were pushing rapidly across northern France to trap the British at Dunkirk. Toynbee's theme was 'Christianity and Civilization.' The lecture is a classic case of how discourse on philosophy of history can have immediate practical value for an audience.[44] Toynbee reviewed the options for understanding the relation between Christianity and civilization. There was the view of Edward Gibbon and Sir J.G. Frazer that Christianity destroyed civilization. There was Toynbee's earlier view expressed in the plan for *A Study of History* that Christianity and the other religions were the chrysalis of civilizations to enable their rise, like the butterfly.[45] Then there was a third view, which Toynbee now adopted, that 'the successive rises and falls of civilizations may be subsidiary to the growth of religion.' He continued by expanding the metaphor he had briefly introduced at the end of volume six: 'If religion is a chariot, it looks as if the wheels on which it mounts towards Heaven may be the periodic downfalls of civilizations on Earth. It looks as if the movement of civilisations may be cyclic and recurrent, while the movement of religion may be on a single continuous line.'

In other words, if civilizations are cyclic, the history of religion reveals a progressive ascent towards a goal. Progress is the coming of the Kingdom of God, while the achievement of the goal is the realization of that kingdom, the salvation 'which is the true end of man and the true purpose of life on Earth.' Toynbee was ready to conclude that the highest manifestation of both progress and the destination has already been disclosed in Christ. All the other religions participated in that progress by partially revealing what Christ most fully revealed. Toynbee affirmed, 'The Passion of Christ was the culminating and crowning experience of the sufferings of human souls in successive failures in the enterprise of secular civilization.' While people in all times and cultures have had a sufficient means of salvation available to them, Christ has provided the brightest illumination and the most abundant grace for salvation. Along the way Christianity has brought 'an immeasurable improvement in the conditions of human social life on Earth' by combining love for God with love for neighbour.[46]

The Burge lecture at Oxford indicated that Toynbee had adopted the symbol of Jesus Christ as the ultimate referent for his philosophy of history. The key to Toynbee's new-found Christian view of history was the way in which Christ handled suffering. Unlike all previous saviours, Christ accepted death for the sake of the love of others. By his crucifixion as an act of love he bore their sufferings and thereby broke the power of evil that Toynbee, with the Christian tradition, called original sin. Toynbee believed that Christ exemplified most fully one of the greatest spiritual laws of the universe articulated long ago by Aeschylus: *pathei mathos*, 'it is through suffering that learning comes.' Toynbee claimed that the crucifixion of Jesus with its spiritual consequences remains the greatest new event in universal history. He expected that Christianity would not be superseded, but that it would endure past the possible disintegration of Western civilization and continue to spread world-wide. He prophesied: 'Christianity may be left as the spiritual heir of all the higher religions, from the post-Sumerian rudiment of one in the worship of Tammuz and Ishtar down to those that (today) are still living separate lives side by side with Christianity, and of all the philosophies from Ikhnaton's to Hegel's; while the Christian Church as an institution may be left as the social heir of all the other churches and all the civilizations.'[47] Toynbee repeated this prophecy in 1943 in the context of a book on the aftermath of the war.[48] He worked no more on *A Study of History* during the war, devoting himself to intelligence research at Balliol, but he had already achieved the essential insight into the meaning of history he had hoped for.

When the war ended he resumed his monumental *Study* with the general outline unchanged, but now guided by the reversal of his view about the relationship between religions and civilizations. Between 1946 and 1949 he accepted invitations to lecture in Great Britain and North America and introduced audiences to his ideas for each part of the remaining four volumes. He elaborated his philosophy of history in keeping with his Christian thesis.[49] On one of these occasions, in March 1947, he lectured at Union Theological Seminary in New York where Reinhold Niebuhr, Paul Tillich, and John C. Bennett had congregated. They published his lecture in their periodical *Christianity and Crisis* under the title 'The Meaning of History for the Soul.' Toynbee continued themes begun in his Oxford lecture in 1940. By means of the advance of religion culminating in Christianity, he argued, 'a cumulative increase in the means of grace' became available to each soul in this world. The result is that people today have the wherewithal to deny the age-old false polarity between this-worldly and other-worldly religion. While still in this world they can 'come to know God better and come to love Him more nearly in his own way.' In Christian terms, they can come to love God and neighbour without separating the two. As a consequence the world could become, as it were, one province of the Kingdom of God.[50]

Toynbee's publisher, Oxford University Press, collected many of his lectures and topical essays during these years into the book *Civilization on Trial*, published in 1948. In the preface, Toynbee described himself as a historian who seeks to apprehend the universe as a whole – 'souls and bodies, experiences and events' – and to gain 'some gleam of insight into the meaning of this mysterious spectacle.' He recalled that to achieve this knowledge he had felt driven many years ago to move from the accepted nationalist framework of historical study to the horizon of entire civilizations. Now he admitted experiencing even that horizon as too narrow. He needed to move outward to the universal scale of the higher religions that emerge from the encounter of civilizations. But he would have to go beyond even the higher religions: 'That is not, however, the end of the historian's quest, for no higher religion is intelligible in terms of this world only. The mundane history of the higher religions is one aspect of the life of a Kingdom of Heaven, of which this world is one province. So history passes over into Theology. "To Him return ye every one."'[51] From nation to civilization to higher religion to the Kingdom of God – there, in brief summary, Toynbee characterized the stages in the transformation of his philosophy of history.

With the war over and with the task of reconstruction at hand, he added the theme of saving Western civilization to his message. Western civilization was worth saving because it was the highest social product of Christianity, the religion in which all other religions culminated. Toynbee hoped that his own work of understanding history would be an instrument to help meet so great a need. He earnestly believed that Western civilization could turn off the path followed by so many earlier civilizations, the path of suicide. 'What shall we do to be saved?' he asked in an essay entitled 'Does History Repeat Itself?' published in the *New York Times* in 1947. He answered: in politics, establish a constitutional, co-operative system of world government; in economics, create a working compromise between free enterprise and socialism; and in the life of the spirit, put the civilization back onto religious foundations. Toynbee counted the religious task as by far the most important in the long run, necessitating nothing less than a spiritual rebirth. To save Western civilization spiritual rebirth would mean the revival of Christianity.[52] He made similar statements in an article in the *Yale Review* and in a two-part series on the BBC.[53] He pursued the theme at length in lectures at Columbia University in April 1948, later published as *The Prospects of Western Civilization*.

By now Toynbee was well aware that he had made some sweeping assertions on behalf of Christianity in world history and that he could be interpreted as belittling the spiritual validity of the other world religions. This was the moment when he began to see new meaning in the line about human access to the divine that he had come across years before, attributed to the pagan Roman senator Symmachus in the 380s AD: 'The heart of so great a mystery can never be reached by following one road only.' Toynbee placed the quotation on his Christmas card in 1946 to Columba, with whom he had recently restored relations. Toynbee and Columba entered a new period of their correspondence that dwelled for many years on themes concerning the encounter with the world religions.[54] Toynbee reflected the Symmachus quotation in his lectures at Columbia by testifying that he had come to believe 'that each of the higher religions, perhaps each in a different degree, represents a different aspect of one and the same truth about God and man's relation to God.' He envisioned worldwide co-operation among the higher religions. Yet, in spite of his explicit efforts to embrace the truth of all the world's religions, he none the less continued to rank Christianity highest on the scale of spiritual progress. Of all the religions, Toynbee said, the 'future in this world can only be found in a way of life inspired by the belief that God is love, the belief that inspires Christianity and is embodied in the life of Christ himself and in the life of Saint Francis of Assisi – the belief that God is a God who takes man's suffering on Himself.' Christ and the Christian manifestation of the truth securely occupied the highest position for him.[55]

Toynbee's reputation as an ecumenical and Anglican advocate of Christianity spread in church circles. While he worked on the writing and revision of the last four volumes of his *Study*, between 1947 and

1953, he accepted a number of church-related assignments: among others, he became a member of the Commission of the Churches on International Affairs of the World Council of Churches, shared in a forum with C.S. Lewis and Amos Wilder on 'Christian Hope' (the theme of the Council's forthcoming assembly), and participated in a series of Anglican discussions on Communism convened by George Bell, the Bishop of Chichester, in 1950. This latter activity yielded a book of essays by Anglican authors, edited by D.M. Mackinnon.[56] Toynbee's essay in the volume stands as perhaps the most concise statement of his Christian philosophy of history. Under the title 'The Christian Understanding of History' he sought to identify what made a Christian view unique. His spirit and procedure echoed his argument at the end of volume six of *Study* in which he led himself to see Jesus Christ as the highest saviour. What he now found to be uniquely Christian was Jesus as the Incarnation by which God out of love for his creatures voluntarily 'emptied Himself' (Philippians 2:5–8) to become human, sharing all the sufferings his creatures experienced. The Incarnation meant that the world was redeemable as a part of God's Kingdom, and that history had purpose as the process by which humans are saved from original sin and directed through Christ to communion with God. Through the Incarnation even suffering acquires meaning as a component in the way of salvation. Toynbee concluded: 'Christianity's last word will be that mankind has nevertheless been given a chance of salvation from the nemesis of its own sinful acts in being enabled, in virtue of Christ's passion, to seek this salvation by praying for God's grace.'[57]

Volumes seven to ten of *A Study of History* appeared in 1954 and Toynbee's great work was complete. He carried out his treatment of two of the three phenomena after the breakdown of a civilization – Universal States and Barbarian External Proletariats – more or less according to his original plan, but he completely reconceived his treatment of Universal Churches and his interpretation of the prospects of Western civilization. The second half of volume seven and much of volume eight contain an exhaustive statement of the reversal of Toynbee's theory of the relationship between civilizations and religions that he had first made public in 1940 in his Oxford lecture. His exposition pivoted on the by now familiar metaphor of the chariot of religion advancing upward on the wheels of the rise and fall of civilizations.⁵⁸ Volume nine presents his lengthy assessment of the prospects for Western civilization. Toynbee again employed his Pauline-inspired concept of idolatry to analyse the situation he believed people in Western civilization faced after the Second World War. The choice he believed they must make was not between religion or no religion, but between the religion of narcissistic human self-worship and the Christian religion. Toynbee thought that Western technological, scientific, and economic prowess, while rendering a return to Nature worship implausible, had made human self-worship appear attractive. There were two prominent versions of human self-worship available – the liberal Capitalist worship of individuality in pursuit of profit, and the Communist worship of the collectivity. He could not imagine that either of these held out any hope for genuine satisfaction of human spiritual need.⁵⁹ The best hope lay in Christianity, but not in the stultifying form presented by the ecclesiastical traditions of orthodox dogma and authority. After an exhaustive analysis filled with biblical quotations, Toynbee came to a conclusion about what a 'Western pilgrim' needed to be saved: 'What is required of him at this hour is to hold on his course and to trust in God's grace; and, if he prayed God to grant him a pilot for the perilous passage, he would find the bodhisattva psychopompus whom he was seeking in a Francesco Bernardone of Assisi, who was the most god-like soul that had been born into the Western World so far.' Toynbee himself was that pilgrim and he could envision his own spiritual journey as a symbol of the course of Western civilization. He could understand himself to be an agnostic when confronted with the traditions of church dogma and authority, but, in relation to authentic Christianity, a follower of St Francis as a follower of Christ.⁶⁰

The big new thing in Toynbee's theory was the centrality of religion, and Christianity in particular. He acknowledged that his new emphasis on religion in his philosophy of history was directly due to his experience of profound crisis in Western civilization and in his own inner world since the late 1930s.⁶¹ In the final four volumes he gathered together all the salient features of his Christian philosophy of history as he had come to believe them over the years: the understanding of human history as essentially spiritual, the appreciation of religion as perhaps the decisive historical factor, the interpretation of progress as the advance of spiritual opportunity and illumination, the accent on the Augustinian contrast between the love of God and self-love, the rejection of the idolatry of worshipping the creature rather than the Creator, the acceptance of Jesus Christ as the highest disclosure of God, the confession of the all-importance of Christ's act of suffering out of love for others, the recognition of Christianity as the means of combining this-worldly and other-worldly reality, and the desire to pursue the love of God and the love of neighbour in realizing the coming of the Kingdom of God. Toynbee had summarized his approach in a letter to Columba in 1948, while completing volume seven: 'I think history as all really spiritual history – when you strip the rind off the kernel. It is the history of people's relations with God and, through God, with each other.'[62]

Toynbee presented his Christian philosophy of history quite undogmatically, conveying the attitude that whatever he proposed was subject to change. He often used the third-person form – for example, 'a disciple of St Francis would' – when making his proposals. He openly admitted that he was struggling with the traditional Christian claim of the uniqueness of Christ as the one way of salvation for all humanity. This claim he called 'a crux for a historian brought up in a Christian tradition.' Now that he had reversed his understanding of the relation of religion and civilization he could claim that the new aim of his *Study*, in keeping with a long Christian tradition, was 'to see and present the flux of human life *sub specie aeternitatis*.' Toynbee acknowledged that he was no doubt bound to tell the story in terms of his ancestral Christian tradition. In doing so, however, he wanted his readers to know that he intended no claims of exclusivity for the Christian form of his vision. He had come to believe that the four leading higher religions that still aspired to world influence – Christianity, Mahayana Buddhism, Islam, and Hinduism – were 'four variations on a single theme.' He recalled a view expressed by Anglican Archbishop William Temple in 1939: 'All that is noble in the non-Christian systems of thought or conduct or worship is the work of Christ upon them and within them. By the Word of God – that is to say, by Jesus Christ – Isaiah and Plato and Zoroaster and (the) Buddha and Confucius conceived and uttered such truths as they declared.' Although commenting that a Buddhist, Muslim, or Hindu might be able to make the same point in the terms of his or her own religion, Toynbee accepted Temple's Christian version as his own.[63] He was satisfied that the essence of Christianity was also the essence of all the higher religions. What the world needed was for Christians and devotees of all the other higher religions to stress that common essence and to minimize the particularity of each religion. Toynbee did not venture to identify the essence, except to say that the higher religions all stood together in declaring that humans were not God and in rejecting human self-idolatry in modern times.[64] Even so, without denying that all religions revealed the divine, he wanted to acknowledge that he believed that Christianity and Mahayana Buddhism surpassed the other religions in doing so because of their emphasis on self-sacrifice, and that Christianity stood out as the highest expression in history of God's self-sacrifice out of love for the world's people.[65]

Toynbee concluded volume ten, the culmination of his extraordinary survey of history, with his version of a beatific vision, a glimpse of what he called 'a meaning behind the facts of history.' His spiritual pilgrimage as a historian, he confessed, had given him the experience of communion with other human beings throughout history and even with the whole of history, and he had come to experience the transfiguration of such a mundane brotherhood into a spiritual Communion of Saints. Then he began to utter an astonishing prayer modelled on the Great Litany he knew well from the Book of Common Prayer, punctuated by the line 'Christ, hear our prayer.' More than anything else, this prayer, found on the last two pages of his work, convinced commentators that Toynbee was a syncretist or a would-be creator of a new 'mish-mash' religion. He gave a place in the prayer to the spiritual figures of higher religions past and present – Tammuz, Buddha, Lucretius, Zarathustra, Mohammed, Confucius, and many, many more. At first glance it does exhibit all the appearances of hodgepodge. But a second look discloses the pre-eminence of Jesus Christ in the litany. Toynbee constructed the litany on the framework of Christ and the Christian saints, and he blessed all the other saviours according to their relation to Jesus Christ – as forerunners of the Saviour, disciples of Christ, and bearers of Christ's message of love and humility. Toynbee's litany was a Christian prayer that sought to absorb Archbishop Temple's interpretation of Christianity and the other religions. Toynbee tells us that after writing the litany and thereby bringing his long labours to a close he walked the short distance from

Chatham House to the National Gallery to look once more at Fra Angelico's 'Beatific Vision.'[66]

Soon after Toynbee completed the writing of *A Study of History* in 1952, he delivered the Gifford Lectures for 1952 and 1953 in Edinburgh. He published a book from the lectures in 1956 under the title *An Historian's Approach to Religion*. He used the lectures to return to the question of a common essence of all the higher religions, a task he left unfinished in volume seven of *Study*. He approached the subject by proposing a historical theory of religions and by discussing secularization and the future of religion in modern Western civilization. The Pauline notion of idolatry served as the basic category in Toynbee's analysis of the history of religions. There were, he suggested, three objects of worship in all the history of religions: nature, 'man,' and God (Absolute Reality).[67] Nature worship was the deepest and oldest form of religion. 'Man'-worship came next in three versions: worship of the local collective human power (for instance, Athene), of an ecumenical community (for example, Rome), and of a self-sufficient philosophy (for instance, the Stoics). Then came the higher religions, which directed human spirituality away from the nature and human self-worship towards the worship of Absolute Reality. In modern times in the West, Toynbee continued, Westerners, who became appalled by dogmatism, authoritarianism, and religious warfare within ecclesiastical Christianity, reverted to new and secularized forms of 'man'-worship. Chief among these are the worship of human reason, technique, and science, of individual profit and material goods, and of collective human power. In the context of Western secular civilization, whose influence now reached world-wide, Toynbee believed that the higher religions of the world possessed a new mission – to lead humanity once again away from self-centredness and towards Absolute Reality and human fellowship. In order to carry out their new mission the higher religions needed to emphasize their common essence.[68]

Toynbee now undertook to identify the common essence of the higher religions, and in the process appeared to come close to abandoning his Christian philosophy of history in favour of what might be construed as a common-denominator syncretic religion. But if so, he pulled back. In the last two chapters of the book, nineteen and twenty, he offered a statement of 'the essential truths and essential counsels' of seven higher religions. In addition to the four religions he usually mentioned – Christianity, Islam, Mahayana Buddhism, and Hinduism – he now included Judaism, Hinayana Buddhism, and Zoroastrianism. He picked out a number of generalized points: the universe is not self-explanatory, there is a spiritual presence greater than humans, the goal of life is communion with this greatest spiritual presence, the enemy is human self-centredness, and knowledge of truth is properly a means to right action. These points, Toynbee suggested, could be disengaged from 'non-essentials,' things like holy places, ritual, taboos, social practices, myths, and theology. He was not unaware that even his stripped-down statement of the essentials had a Christian ring to it and that the essentials were inaccessible except through the particularity of what he wished to regard as the non-essentials of each religion.

In the last chapter of the book Toynbee offered an exposition of the essentials. Almost in spite of himself he explicitly promoted Christianity and Mahayana Buddhism as higher than the other higher religions, and he named Christianity as the highest version of all because of its message of love for others through suffering. Toynbee again recalled the saying attributed to Symmachus – 'The heart of so great a mystery can never be reached by following one road only' – which he believed summarized his own view (and which Hindus might echo today), and suggested that it should be understood as an anticipation of the message of Christian love. Speaking as a Christian Toynbee urged, 'We can take Symmachus' words to heart without being disloyal to Christianity.' He finished the book by appealing to the words of St Paul in 1 Corinthians 13: 'Charity never faileth.'[69]

In 1954 Toynbee became a member of the international affairs section of the World Council of Churches. In the fall of 1955 he served with the Episcopal bishop of Michigan, Richard Emrich, as one of two keynote speakers at a large Episcopal congress in Albany on the theme of the church and work.[70] He also lectured at Andover Newton Theological School, Episcopal Theological School, and Union Theological Seminary in New York. The president of Union, Henry P. Van Dusen, helped him with the revision of the crucial chapters nineteen and twenty of his Gifford lectures. Toynbee corrected the proofs of his American seminary lectures in Japan in 1956 while surrounded by non-Christian religions. They appeared in 1957 under the title *Christianity among the Religions of the World*.[71] In the book he felt compelled to confront the charge that he projected a dismissal of Christianity and the erection of a new syncretic religion in its place. He contended that even though he sought to embrace the other religions in his understanding he in no way desired to create a new syncretism of the higher religions. Indeed, he argued that according to his philosophy of history, as published as long ago as the volumes of 1939, syncretism would deprive each religion of its spiritual power and would be an important symptom of the disintegration of a civilization.[72]

Toynbee spoke as a Christian to Christians. He urged that 'we Christians' should practise Christian charity and not let doing so 'prevent us from holding fast to what we believe to be the essential truths and ideals in our own Christian faith.' What were those Christian essentials? They were expressed by St Paul in Philippians 2:5–8. Toynbee put the essence of Christianity succinctly in his own words: (1) 'God loves His creatures so greatly that he has sacrificed Himself for their salvation'; (2) 'human beings ought to follow the example God has set for them in His incarnation and crucifixion'; and (3) we ought 'not just to hold this conviction theoretically but to act on it as far as one is able.'[73] Genuine progress in history would be to overcome self-centredness by following the true Christian vision of self-sacrificing love for others. In mundane terms, such progress would effect an increasingly world-wide awakening to the Christian truth of the 'sacredness of human personality.' In supramundane terms, progress would mean attaining the true end of human life, which is, in words Toynbee borrowed from the Westminster Shorter Catechism, 'to glorify God and to enjoy Him forever.'[74]

Toynbee's other writings from 1956 and 1957 continued to give indications of his Christian emphasis. Notably in the book *Hellenism*, written in those years and published in 1959, he explained the triumph of Christianity in the Roman Empire as due primarily to the superiority of Christian spirituality in fulfilling the need of 'hungry Hellenic souls' in an era of spiritual decadence.[75] And in *East to West*, a book on his journey around the world in 1956 and 1957, he spoke of finding evidence of spiritual hunger in Japan that Christianity already may have begun to fill with 'the bread of life' at an unconscious level.[76] In works that appeared in the years immediately after 1957 we find Toynbee continuing to express many of the Christian views we have become accustomed to hearing from him. For example, in *The Present-Day Experiment in Western Civilization*, presented as lectures in Montreal in 1961, he still regarded the message of Christian charity to be a lasting gift of Christianity to the world.[77] And in his dialogue with his son Philip Toynbee, published in 1963, he still affirmed the picture of the Incarnation presented by St Paul in Philippians 2:5–8.[78] Yet we can detect a notable change in emphasis and orientation during these same years. It would appear that Toynbee, now in his seventies, moved away from centring his religious attentions upon Christ and Christianity. This he did in the same manner in which he had moved away from his Christian upbringing long ago as an Oxford undergraduate – undramatically, without deliberate plan, but decisively none the less.[79]

It is not easy to tell what Toynbee moved towards after 1957. What we note is that he no longer talked about Christ as the highest expression of God. He allowed his Christian framework and language to recede, and he relativized his concern for the future of Western civilization and of Christianity within it. In place of this concern he emphasized, at least for a while, his sympathy and solidarity with Hinduism and he preached the message of world unity. As he put it in his Montreal lectures in 1961, Christianity had two veins, the one of charity that yielded concern for social justice and liberal democracy, the other of intolerance that issued in exclusivism and hubris. This he had said in various ways many times before, but now he changed the emphasis. He now counted the trait of intolerance to be so prominent a feature of Christianity as to warrant his abandoning his previous attraction to Christianity as the highest expression of the divine. To his Montreal audience he acknowledged his appreciation of Hinduism as the religion that 'takes it for granted that there is more than one valid approach to truth and to salvation, and that these different approaches are not only compatible with each other but are complementary.'[80] In New Delhi in 1960 Toynbee commended India's spiritual experience, which he described as characterized by large-mindedness and broad-mindedness, and called it India's special contribution to world unity. He said he believed that Mahatma Gandhi exemplified the spiritual character necessary to lead the world to tolerance, and that Hinduism was the world's supreme candidate to serve as 'the religion of co-existence.' Gandhi or his avatar might be the 'modern saviour of society,' he suggested.[81] In the dialogue with Philip, he stressed that of all the religions of the world he now felt the strongest attachment to Hinduism. He continued to feel the second strongest attraction to Mahayana Buddhism, and he demoted Christianity on his list.[82] Whereas Toynbee had for many years used the quotation attributed to Symmachus about many roads to the divine as an important symbol and accepted it as an anticipation of Christian charity, he now spoke simply of Symmachus's words as an anticipation of Hinduism, and made them his supreme message and the key to his philosophy of history.

While Toynbee tended to favour Hinduism during the 1960s and early 1970s, what he seemed to have in mind was not a conversion to Hinduism or a synthesis or fusion of all the religions, but their coexistence within the same world, the same local society, even the same person.[83] For a moment in the early 1970s, when asked, Toynbee looked extremely favourably upon the possibility of an authentic renewal of Christianity, although he supposed that it would have to be a new Christianity unlike the orthodoxies of the past. He also continued to have sympathies towards Buddhism.[84] Aware in 1958 that he was in the process of changing his emphasis in religion he wrote Columba that he would now define himself as an unorthodox transrationalist.[85]

It is possible that before his death in 1975 Toynbee passed into another stage in his religious pilgrimage – a reversion to pantheism, nature religion, and the worship of Mother Earth. But that would be another question.[86]

CONCLUSION: TOYNBEE'S CHRISTIAN PERIOD

We have enough before us to conclude that the years from about 1937 to about 1957 were a distinct period in Toynbee's philosophy of history, a period when he came to give pre-eminence to Jesus Christ and Christianity and to work his attachment to Christ into the categories and theses of his philosophy of history. We may regard it as the Christian period of his philosophy of history. He entered the period quite gradually, long before the early 1950s, and left it just as gradually. While it is clear that he held to his Christian orientation undogmatically, he none the less explicitly accepted Christianity as his primary orientation within his philosophy of history for around twenty years. In particular, his Christian view underlay the inversion of his general theory of universal history that became apparent with the publication of the 1954 volumes of *Study*.

Understanding Toynbee in this fashion requires us to disagree with his self-interpretation of his religious history. We have already noted his assessment in his autobiography of 1969 that he had become an agnostic at Oxford and remained one ever since. In *Reconsiderations* (1961), volume twelve of the *Study*, he counted that he had experienced three stages so far in his religious journey – the ancestral Anglicanism of his youth, the agnostic rationalism of his Oxford and post-Oxford days, and his then current stage, which he called 'agnostic transrationalism.'[87] As a result of our analysis of his writings we know enough to suggest that he omitted a stage, the period discussed here when he adopted a Christian view of history into his philosophy of history. We may grant that he was quite right in considering himself during that period to be an agnostic towards the dogmas and authority of ecclesiastical Christianity, but, with respect to his philosophy of history, between the late 1930s and the late 1950s he was a Christian believer. Saying this about Toynbee means that we also disagree with those orthodox Christians, whether Protestant or Roman Catholic, including even Columba until at least 1944, who looked on him as not in the Church or not Christian. Even though Toynbee held back from conversion to the Roman Catholic church, and could appear as a syncretist to evangelical critics and others, we may observe that during the years of his Christian period he came to act broadly as an Anglican and to give himself and his historical analysis in service of the Church.

It is important to note that Toynbee's Christian period corresponded with the peak of his career – from about age forty-seven to sixty-seven – when he produced seven of the ten primary volumes of *A Study of History*, and established his world-wide reputation. Identifying this as his Christian period will require us to revise our interpretation and assessment of Toynbee's work as a whole. His adoption of a Christian view of history was not a surface addition to his theory.

Nor was it simply a matter of his private beliefs. His Christian orientation was intrinsic to the character and structure of his philosophy of history and will need to be treated as such. We will need to take it into account when we analyse and criticize the primary ingredients of Toynbee's theory of civilizations and religions as well as his general vision, insights, and proposals for the future. Toynbee's work in those years formed, without premeditation, part of a wider movement to renew Christian interpretations of history. Others, like Reinhold Niebuhr, Herbert Butterfield, William Temple, Christopher Dawson, Henri-Irenée Marrou, Georges Florovsky, Kenneth Scott Latourette – to mention a few – each in their own way shared a common Christian vision of history. How we assess Toynbee's philosophy of history during his peak years will depend to no small degree upon what we ourselves think of the possibility and merits of using Christian insights to illuminate history. That, in part, is what Toynbee sought to do during the Christian period of his philosophy of history.[88]

NOTES

1 Toynbee, *A Study of History*, 12 vols (London and New York: Oxford University Press 1934–61), 7: 420–5
2 Toynbee, *Experiences* (New York and London: Oxford University Press 1969), 127, 138; Arnold and Philip Toynbee, *Comparing Notes: A Dialogue across a Generation* (London: Weidenfeld and Nicolson 1963), 8–9; Toynbee, 'Toynbee on Toynbee,' *Fides et Historia* 6, no. 2 (spring 1974): 66–7
3 Pieter Geyl, 'Toynbee as Prophet,' and 'Study of Toynbee: A Personal View of History'; and A.J.P. Taylor, 'Much Learning,' in *Toynbee and History: Critical Essays and Reviews*, ed. M.F. Ashley Montague (Boston: Porter Sargent 1956), 360–77, 103–10, and 115–17; see Sherman B. Barnes, 'The Personal Religion of Arnold J. Toynbee,' *Fides et Historia* 6, no. 1 (fall 1973): 30–5.
4 Linus Walker, 'Toynbee and Religion: A Catholic View,' in *Toynbee and History*, 338–46; see Toynbee's response in *Study*, 12 (1961): 583–4; Martin Wight, 'The Crux for an Historian Brought up in the Christian Tradition,' annex in *Study*, 7 (1954): 737–48
5 William McNeill, 'Arnold Joseph Toynbee,' *British Academy Proceedings* 63 (1977); 456; Roland N. Stromberg, *Arnold J. Toynbee: Historian for an Age in Crisis* (Carbondale: Southern Illinois University Press 1972), 37, 88; Edward

Rochie Hardy, 'The Historical Validity of Toynbee's Approach to Universal Churches,' in *The Intent of Toynbee's History* (Chicago: Loyola University Press 1961), 154

6 It seems to be an occupational hazard of those who interpret a thinker as apparently systematic as Toynbee that they attempt to treat his thought as if it were one unchanging system. Virtually every interpreter who attempts to analyse Toynbee's philosophy minimizes the changes in his thought and cites references indiscriminately from different phases of his thought.

7 C.T. McIntire, 'History, Christian Views,' in *The Encyclopedia of Religion*, ed. Mircea Eliade (New York: The Free Press/Macmillan 1987), 6: 394–9; *God, History, and Historians: Modern Christian Views of History*, ed. C.T. McIntire (New York: Oxford University Press 1977), 177

8 *Study*, 1: 56–7

9 Ibid., 3: 248–376

10 Ibid., 1: 129–33, 271–2; and 3: 191–2

11 Ibid., 4: vii–ix

12 Ibid., 4: viii–ix

13 *Experiences*, 176

14 Toynbee to Columba Cary-Elwes, 5 Aug. 1938, in *An Historian's Conscience: The Correspondence of Arnold J. Toynbee and Columba Cary-Elwes, Monk of Ampleforth*, ed. Christian B. Peper (Boston: Beacon Press 1986), 19–21

15 *Historian's Conscience* contains much essential information about Toynbee's daily and personal life.

16 Toynbee to Columba, 19 March 1939, in *Historian's Conscience*, 32–3

17 *Study*, 7: ix; and Bridget R. Reddin to Columba, 3 July 1944, in *Historian's Conscience*, 165–6

18 Toynbee, 'Post-War Paganism versus Christianity,' *The Listener* 17 (1937): 123–4. His lecture was also published in the United States, as 'The Menace of the New Paganism,' in *Christian Century*, 10 March 1937, 315–17. See Columba to Toynbee, 27 Jan. 1937, and Toynbee to Columba, 31 Jan. 1937, in *Historian's Conscience*, 12–13.

19 Toynbee to Columba, 14 Feb. 1937, 27 July 1938, 5 Aug. 1938, 19 Oct. 1939, and 14 Jan. 1940, in *Historian's Conscience*, 14–15, 17, 19–21, 40–1, and 48–9

20 *Study*, 4: 5

21 Ibid., 1: 192–5, where he uses the metaphor of climbing the face of a mountain and reaching successive ledges.

22 Ibid., 4: 5–6

23 Ibid., 4: 260
24 Ibid., 4: 261–2, referring to Romans 1:25
25 Ibid., 1: 9; 4 (1939): 261–464, where idolatry became a major category for him; on pages 407–8 he mistakenly read his new emphasis on idolatry back into volume 1.
26 Ibid., 5: 35ff. and 376ff.
27 Ibid., 5: 376. Toynbee would have known of Archbishop William Temple's famous Gifford Lectures for 1933 and 1934 at Glasgow in which he suggested the metaphor of sacrament as apt for describing the universe as a whole – 'the sacramental universe.' See Temple, *Nature, Man, and God* (London: Macmillan 1934), chap. 19. See *Study*, 7 (1954): 429, 504, 559; and *Experiences* (1969), 138.
28 *Study*, 5: 394–9
29 Annex, 'Marxism, Socialism, and Christianity,' in *Study*, 5: 581–7
30 Ibid., 5: 428–9, 438–9
31 Ibid., 6: 300, 314
32 Ibid., 6: 149–68
33 Ibid., 6: 174–5, referring to John 3
34 Ibid., 6: 175–278 (esp. 278), and 376–539
35 Ibid., 6: 322–4
36 Ibid., 6: 325–6
37 Toynbee to Columba, 5 Feb. 1939, in *Historian's Conscience*, 29–30
38 Toynbee to Columba, esp. 19 Oct. 1939 and 23 June 1940, in *Historian's Conscience*, 40–1, 67
39 Toynbee to Columba, 19 Oct. 1939, 3 Feb. 1940, 5 Dec. 1940, and Columba to Toynbee, 18 July 1940, in *Historian's Conscience*, 40–1, 50–1, 80–1, and 73–4
40 Toynbee to Columba, 10 Oct. 1940, 8 Sept. 1944, and *passim* between 1940 and 1946, in *Historian's Conscience*, 77–8, and 171–5
41 Toynbee to Columba, esp. 29 March 1943, and Toynbee to Robert Darbyshire, 3 Oct. 1946, in *Historian's Conscience*, 134, 177–8
42 Toynbee to Columba, 16 Nov. 1943, in *Historian's Conscience*, 144–6
43 Columba to Toynbee, 14 July 1940, 10 Sept. 1941, 9 Feb. 1942, 12 Jan. 1944, and Toynbee to Columba, 14 July 1944, and note by Columba, in *Historian's Conscience*, 72–3, 99–100, 106–7, 152–5, 167–9, and 175. See McIntire, 'All History Is Spiritual,' *Christianity Today*, 2 Oct. 1987, 69. On Toynbee's Anglican tradition, see *Comparing Notes*, 8–9.
44 Toynbee, *Christianity and Civilisation* (London: Student Christian Movement

Press 1940). The lecture was reprinted with minor changes in Toynbee, *Civilization on Trial* (New York: Oxford University Press 1948), with a reference to the timing of the lecture in 'Acknowledgements,' vi.
45 *Christianity and Civilisation*, 8–19
46 *Christianity and Civilisation*, 19–24, 42–8
47 *Christianity and Civilisation*, 20, 24–30
48 Toynbee, 'Has Christianity a Future?' in *Beyond Victory*, ed. Ruth Nanda Anshen (New York: Harcourt, Brace 1943), 43–52
49 *Study*, 7: vii–x
50 Toynbee, 'The Meaning of History for the Soul,' in *Civilization on Trial*, vi, 260–3
51 *Civilization on Trial*, vi
52 Toynbee, 'Does History Repeat Itself?' in *Civilization on Trial*, 39–41
53 Toynbee, 'Churches and Civilizations,' *The Yale Review* 37, no. 1 (Sept. 1947): 1–8; and 'Civilisation on Trial,' and 'Western Tradition Still in the Making,' *The Listener* 40 (15 July and 30 Sept. 1948): 75–6 and 489–90
54 Toynbee to Columba, 24 Dec. 1946, and the quotation from Toynbee's Christmas card to Columba, n.d., in *Historian's Conscience*, 179–81. In volume six of *Study* (1939), Toynbee had used the episode surrounding the statue of Victory as an example of 'archaism' in religion, a sign of the disintegration of civilization. He had not mentioned Symmachus. In volume seven, however, written in 1947 and 1948, he used the Symmachus quotation as a symbol of the attitude he now wished to take towards the world's religions (*Study*, 6: 88–9, and 7: 428–9, 442). Actually, most of the remainder of the Toynbee-Columba correspondence after 1946 touches on the world religions.
55 Toynbee, *The Prospects of Western Civilization* (New York: Columbia University Press 1949). Only 400 copies of the book were published.
56 David P. Gaines, *The World Council of Churches: A Study of Its Background and History* (Peterborough, NH: Richard R. Smith 1966), 415, 559, 657; Toynbee, Amos N. Wilder, and C.S. Lewis, 'The Christian Hope – Its Meaning for Today,' *Religion in Life* 21, no. 1 (winter 1951–2), 3–32; *Christian Faith and Communist Faith: A Series of Articles by Members of the Anglican Communion*, ed. D.M. Mackinnon (London: Macmillan 1953), iii–vi, ix–xii; see Toynbee to Columba, 5 March 1950, in *Historian's Conscience*, 258–9.
57 Toynbee, 'The Christian Understanding of History,' in *Christian Faith and Communist Faith*, 198–9, 207–8; see McIntire, *God, History, and Historians*, 176–7.
58 Esp. *Study*, 7: 420–49 and 8: 88–97

59 Esp. ibid., 9: 618–28, a section entitled 'The Spiritual Odyssey of the Western World'
60 *Study*, 9: 636–7, 642–4, and 7: 428–9. Toynbee publicly took St Francis as his model of authentic Christianity in *The Prospects of Western Civilization*, 105.
61 *Study*, 7: vii–viii
62 Toynbee to Columba, 24 Aug., 14 Sept., and 17 Sept., 1948, in *Historian's Conscience*, 227–9, 232
63 *Study*, 7: 428–9, and the annex by Martin Wight in 7: 737–8. William Temple's statement comes from *Readings in Saint John's Gospel* (London: Macmillan 1939), 10.
64 *Study*, 7: 465–70
65 Ibid., 7: 388, 426–7, 441, 555–68
66 Ibid., 10: 140–4, and see 10:1
67 Toynbee, *An Historian's Approach to Religion* (London: Oxford University Press 1956), chap. 1–7. The triad of objects of worship recalled William Temple's famous book, *Nature, Man and God* (London: Macmillan 1935). He might have mentioned a fourth: Satan.
68 *Historian's Approach*, chap. 14, 16, 17, 19, 20
69 *Historian's Approach*, chap. 19 and 20 esp. 297–9
70 Toynbee, 'Man at Work in History,' in *Man at Work in God's World*, ed. Canon G.E. DeMille (New York: Longmans, Green 1956), 3–41
71 Gaines, *World Council of Churches*, 934–51; *Historian's Approach*, vi; Toynbee, *Christianity among the Religions of the World* (New York: Charles Scribner's 1957), v–viii
72 *Christianity among the Religions*, vii, 82, 85, 103–4; see *Study*, 5: 527–528.
73 *Christianity among the Religions*, 104–7
74 *Christianity among the Religions*, 89–90, 98–100
75 Toynbee, *Hellenism: The History of a Civilization* (London: Oxford University Press 1959), viii–ix, 213–24. In the preface he confessed that Gilbert Murray, later his father-in-law, commissioned the book for the Home University Library in 1914(!).
76 Toynbee, *East to West: A Journey around the World* (New York: Oxford University Press 1958), 74
77 Toynbee, *The Present-Day Experiment in Western Civilization* (London: Oxford University Press 1962), 43–50
78 *Comparing Notes*, 19–20
79 *Comparing Notes*, 8–9, and *Experiences*, 127–8
80 *Present-Day Experiment in Western Civilization*, 38–50

81 Toynbee, *One World and India* (New Delhi: Orient Longmans, for the Indian Council for Cultural Relations 1960), 3–4, 53–4; see *Present-Day Experiment in Western Civilization*, 49, 73.
82 *Comparing Notes*, 16–19
83 Toynbee, *Change and Habit: The Challenge of Our Time* (London: Oxford University Press 1966), 184–95; see also *One World and India*, 56–7.
84 Toynbee and G.R. Urban, *Toynbee on Toynbee: A Conversation between Arnold J. Toynbee and G.R. Urban* (New York: Oxford University Press 1974), 69–70; Toynbee and Daisaku Ikeda, *The Toynbee-Ikeda Dialogue: Man Himself Must Choose* (Tokyo: Kodansha 1976), *passim*
85 Toynbee to Columba, 12 Oct. 1958, in *Historian's Conscience*, 384–5
86 Toynbee, *Mankind and Mother Earth: A Narrative History of the World* (New York: Oxford University Press 1976); *The Toynbee-Ikeda Dialogue*, 300; Toynbee, *The Greeks and Their Heritages* (New York: Oxford University Press 1981), 313–14; see Thomas W. Africa, 'The Final Vision of Arnold Toynbee,' *Historical Reflections/Réflexions historiques* 10 (1983): 221–8.
87 *Experiences*, 127–8, 138; *Study*, 12: 97–102
88 McIntire, *God, History, and Historians*, 3–26; *History and Historical Understanding*, ed. McIntire and Ronald A. Wells (Grand Rapids, Mich.: Eerdmans (1984)

Toynbee and the Meaning of Athens and Jerusalem

Marvin Perry

Ever since Tertullian asked 'What indeed has Athens to do with Jerusalem?' Western thinkers have struggled with the relationship between the two traditions represented by these ancient cities. Leo Strauss reminds us that 'the broadest and deepest [qualities] of Western man's historical experience are indicated by the names of these two cities ... Western man became what he is, and is what he is, through the coming together of biblical faith and Greek thought. In order to understand ourselves and to illuminate our trackless way into the future, we must understand Jerusalem and Athens.'[1] Arnold Toynbee, who considered it the historian's duty to transcend analytical studies and to give the facts of history a larger meaning, was compelled to come to terms with the rationalism of Athens and the revelation of Jerusalem.

By regarding God as one, sovereign, transcendent, and good, the ancient Hebrews effected a religious revolution that constitutes one source of Western civilization. In confronting God, the Hebrews developed an awareness of self; the individual became conscious of his or her moral autonomy and personal worth. Central to the Hebrew outlook was the belief that God, who possessed total freedom himself, created men and women in his image, bestowing upon them moral freedom – the capacity to choose between good and evil. By making God the centre of life, the Hebrews envisioned themselves as free moral agents: no person, no human institution, no human tradition could claim their souls – an outlook that was inherited by Christianity. Also inherited by Christianity was the Hebrew view of history as a divine drama filled with sacred meaning and moral significance; it is a clash between human will and God's commands. From the Hebrew prophets Christianity acquired an overriding principle of human behaviour – that when people forget God and make themselves the centre of all things, they bring disaster to themselves and the community. In particular, the prophets railed against idol worship. The worship of false gods is the height of folly and arrogance, they said; it causes people to lust after power and wealth and to wage endless conflicts in pursuit of these idols. By holding out the hope that life on earth could be improved, that injustice need not be accepted as part of an unalterable cosmic order, the prophets also created a social conscience that has become an integral part of the Western tradition. This prophetic outlook, amplified by Christianity, pervades Toynbee's philosophy of history; for Toynbee, history is a spiritual encounter between the individual and God.

To ancient Greece we trace the origins of philosophic and scientific thought. The Greeks broke with the mythical view that physical nature is a 'thou' suffused with life, that natural objects are gods or the dwelling places of gods. Rather they saw nature as an 'it,' following general rules ascertainable by the mind. In self-consciously striving for rational rather than mythical explanations for natural occurrences and human events, the Greeks made possible a systematic investigation of nature and human culture. In addition to establishing the norms of reason, the Greeks conceived the principle of political freedom and upheld a humanist outlook that gave worth and significance to the individual; they called for the maximum cultivation of human talent, the full development of human personality, and the deliberate pursuit of excellence. Though man could not alter the universe, over which both humans and gods had no control, he could take control over his own life. 'Had Greek civilization never existed,' said W.H. Auden, 'we would never have become fully conscious, which is to say, that we would never have become fully human.'[2]

A classical scholar of eminence, Toynbee was intimately aware of the immense achievement of the Greeks, but what impressed him more were the limitations of classical civilization that Europeans have revered since the Renaissance. Toynbee viewed Greek humanism as the 'most whole-hearted and uncompromising practice of man-worship up to date,'[3] and it was precisely this idolization of man and his works

The Meaning of Athens and Jerusalem 95

that caused Hellenism's ruin. For Toynbee, the root cause of Hellenism's failure was the deification of a human institution – the city-state and the Roman Empire – and the deification of a human being – a Macedonian king and a Roman emperor. Toynbee drew several lessons from the history of Hellenism. Reason not guided by spiritual values cannot restrain the individual's basest impulses or unite the various social groups in a common purpose, and freedom derived from a nonspiritual source is fragile. Modern Western civilization, Toynbee concluded, has not learned the lesson of Hellenism: it too idolizes human creations and with the same disastrous results.

The rational-humanist tradition of Greece, including the Stoic conception of natural law that applies to all people, flowed into the Enlightenment. Dispensing with the scholastic premise that reason complements and serves faith, the *philosophes*, in the tradition of the Greeks, asserted that the intellect is autonomous: it depends upon no transcendent realm, upon no power beyond itself for comprehending nature and society. The *philosophes* also rejected the Christian doctrine that evil was intrinsic to human personality, a consequence of original sin. To them human wickedness was a product of a faulty environment that could be reformed.

Profoundly shaken by the First World War and the rise of totalitarianism, Toynbee lost confidence in the liberal-rational tradition of the Enlightenment. His Victorian optimism shattered, Toynbee was left with the distressing feeling that Western civilization was in deep crisis. 'I had continued to concur in Gibbon's judgment till, in the first days of August 1914, the disaster, unforeseen by me, into which my own world was now rushing, suddenly opened up my eyes to the truth. The illumination had caught me in a flash; my illusion that I was the privileged citizen of a stable world had been shattered by a thunderbolt. Since that moment I have seen the world with different eyes and have found that it is not the kind of world that until then, I had naively imagined it to be.'[4]

Like other thinkers between the wars – Paul Tillich, Reinhold Niehbur, Christopher Dawson, Nicholas Berdyaev – Toynbee challenged liberal and Marxist assumptions about history and the individual. The Great War, by calling into question core liberal beliefs – the essential goodness of human nature, the primacy of reason, the efficacy of science and technology, and the inevitability of progress – led some thinkers to find in Christianity an alternative view of human experience and a way of dealing with the crisis of the twentieth century.

Christian thinkers asserted the reality of evil in human nature and assailed liberals and Marxists for postulating a purely rational and secular philosophy of history and for anticipating an ideal society within the realm of historical time. In the Christian conception of life and history – the clash between human will and God's precepts – these thinkers found an intelligible explanation for the tragedies of human existence. They reminded Westerners of the central importance of religion in their historical development.[5] Thus in 1933 Christopher Dawson wrote: 'If our civilization is to recover its vitality, or even to survive, it must cease to neglect its spiritual roots and must realize that religion is not a matter of personal sentiment which has nothing to do with the objective realities of society, but is, on the contrary, the very heart of social life and the root of every living culture.'[6]

Toynbee's philosophy of history is part of this general trend. While an undergraduate at Oxford, Toynbee concluded that 'religion itself was an unimportant illusion.'[7] But the First World War and its aftermath led him to doubt basic liberal assumptions and to find meaning in the Christian philosophy of history. And yet, while Toynbee focused on the limitations of the Western liberal-rational tradition, it is misleading to regard him as an enemy of reason. Pervading Toynbee's world-view was the hope of a fruitful synthesis of reason and the spiritual values of religious prophets. Underlying his indictment of the Enlightenment was a profound desire to humanize reason, to wed it to values that liberate rather than distort human personality.

Toynbee viewed the emergence of a Christian society during the Middle Ages as a spiritual advance over Hellenism and our current post-Christian secular civilization as spiritual retrogression, 'at best ... a superfluous repetition of the pre-Christian Graeco-Roman one, and at worst a pernicious backsliding from the path of spiritual progress.'[8] He regarded the modern West as a depressing revival of Hellenic secularism and a repudiation of Christianity, for him the true essence of Western civilization. To Toynbee, the birth of the modern West out of the womb of *respublica Christiana* should not be thought of as progress, and should not command our admiration. 'If we can bring ourselves to think of it, instead, as one of the vain repetitions of the

Gentiles – an almost meaningless repetition of something that the Greeks and Romans did before us and did supremely well – then the greatest new event in the history of mankind will be seen to be a very different one. The greatest new event will then not be the monotonous rise of yet another secular civilization out of the bosom of the Christian Church in the course of these later centuries; it will still be the Crucifixion and its spiritual consequences.'[9]

A principal reason for Toynbee's dissatisfaction with the modern West was his hatred of nationalism, which he interpreted in religious terms – the worship of a false god. Since the Renaissance, maintained Toynbee, the West has revived the very practice that was the root cause of Hellenism's ruin – the deification of the state. Modern nationalism, he insisted, is the modern form of city-state worship; if it is not eradicated, the modern world will suffer the same fate as Hellenism. Toynbee defined nationalism as a 'spirit which makes the people feel and act and think about a part of any given society as though it were the whole of that society.'[10] It is a primitive form of religion that divides people, leads to the deification of parochial communities, and ignites tribal conflicts. Toynbee concluded that since the birth of civilization, nationalism has accounted for the 'death of no less than fourteen civilizations for certain, and perhaps of no less than sixteen, out of the twenty-one civilizations that had come into existence.'[11] He saw National Socialism, the most dangerous expression of modern nationalism, as a neo-pagan religion in conflict with Christian values. The decline of Christianity in the modern West, he said, created a spiritual vacuum and the loyalty once given to Christianity was transferred to secular ideologies of which nationalism was the most powerful and Nazism its most malignant expression. Toynbee viewed Nazism as 'the consummation ... of a politico-religious movement, the pagan deification and worship of parochial human communities which had been gradually gaining ground for more than four centuries in the Western world at large.'[12] The Nazi experience demonstrated the inherent deficiency of liberal-humanism, said Toynbee. As a result it was now impossible to retain a 'belief in the inevitable progress of a secularized Western Civilization and in the self-perfectibility of a graceless Human Nature.'[13]

While the Christian view of the individual and history pervades Toynbee's outlook, he came to believe that Christianity was not a unique and final revelation. All the higher religions have inestimable value; all are avenues to God. Toynbee believed that the higher religions – Christianity, Islam, Zoroastrianism, Buddhism, and Judaism – are humanity's finest achievement. The values taught by the world's great prophets – Isaiah, Jesus, Buddha – enable the individual to overcome an inherent self-centredness and the community a tribal-mindedness that ignites war. Higher religions liberate because they teach that God alone, not an individual or a human creation, is worthy of worship and that love is the greatest good. They provide a purpose to life, help the individual to deal with emotional distress, and foster social justice. By proclaiming that every soul is precious to God, prophetic values enable the community to overcome a narrow parochialism and to aspire to brotherly unity.

Toynbee valued prophetic teachings but did not adhere to dogma – the divinity of Jesus, the Virgin birth, the Resurrection – that seemed irreconcilable with what science teaches about the uniformity of nature, and criticized clergy who challenged science with theology. He also attacked Christian fanaticism and intolerance. The religious fanaticism of the wars of the Reformation, he said, became deeply rooted in the Western mentality; in the modern world, fanaticism became secularized and was channelled into wars of nationality. What Toynbee found most valuable in Christianity was its 'belief that self-sacrificing love is the most powerful of all spiritual impulses known to us.'[14]

Toynbee would not break with the modern spirit that pursues truth through the critical use of the intellect, but, with other thinkers, he also shared in the growing disillusionment with the Enlightenment tradition. The questioning and challenging of the Enlightenment outlook is a theme that is central to the intellectual life of the late nineteenth and early twentieth centuries; either explicitly or by implication this theme pervades Toynbee's world-view.

Most nineteenth-century thinkers carried forward the spirit of the Enlightenment, particularly its emphasis on science and its concern for individual liberty and social reform. But at the same time the Enlightenment tradition was being undermined. In the early nineteenth century romantics revolted against the Enlightenment's rational-scientific spirit. In the closing decades of the century, a number of thinkers, rejecting the Enlightenment's view of people as fundamentally rational, held that subconscious drives and impulses govern human behaviour more than reason does. Some theorists, like Nietzsche and Sorel, celebrated the irrational, which they saw as the true essence of the individual. Even theorists like Freud who valued reason and studied the individual and society in a scientific way pointed out that below a surface rationality lies a substratum of irrationality that constitutes a deeper reality. Toynbee shared this growing conviction that reason was a puny instrument that could not contain the volcanic strength of non-rational impulses, that these impulses pushed people towards destructive behaviour and made political life precarious, and that the non-rational did not bend very much to education.

Also like other early twentieth-century thinkers, Toynbee held that reason was a double-edged sword; it could demean as well as ennoble human personality. He too assailed modern technology and bureaucracy, creations of the rational mind, for denying people an opportunity for independent growth and a richer existence. Toynbee held that modern industrial society, in its drive for efficiency and uniformity, deprived people of their uniqueness and reduced flesh and blood human beings to cogs in a mechanical system.

In the decades shaped by world wars and totalitarianism, intellectuals raised questions that went to the heart of modern life. How can civilized life be safeguarded against human irrationality, particularly when it is channelled into political ideologies that idolize the state, the leader, the party, or the race? How can individual human personality be rescued from a relentless rationalism that reduces human nature and society to mechanical systems and seeks to regulate and organize the individual as it would any material object? Do the values associated with the Enlightenment provide a sound basis around which to integrate society? Can the individual find meaning in what many now regarded as a meaningless universe? Like other intellectuals, Toynbee struggled with these problems, which for him pointed to a larger issue: could Western civilization, indeed humanity itself, avoid self-destruction?

In a universe stripped of any overarching meaning, Toynbee found certainty in prophetic teachings. He believed that these values, humanity's finest achievement, provide the soundest basis upon which to reform Western society and to construct a world-state – a necessary condition if civilization is not to perish in a nuclear holocaust. In the tradition of the Hebrew prophets, Toynbee had a vision of the end of days – a world-state in which peoples of different nationalities dwell in peace, pursue social justice, and seek God. Towards this end, he would harness the tradition of Athens – the creative use of the intellect.

Like Aquinas, who sought to synthesize Greek philosophy and Christian belief, Toynbee tried to come to terms with the problems posed by the intellectual heritage of Athens and the spiritual message of Jerusalem. But unlike Thomas, Toynbee was a religious pluralist who held that all the higher religions are partial revelations of God's truth. Hence the synthesis that he sought was more encompassing – it would embrace the Western rational tradition, the Judaeo-Christian tradition, and all the world's higher religions. He sought a spiritual revival that would fit the requirements of a global age.

'To have stressed ... the fundamental oneness of mankind,' said Hans Kohn, 'will be a lasting merit of Mr. Toynbee's work and vision.'[15] In the twentieth century the world has entered into an age of globalism. Penetrating into every continent, Western civilization has transformed a fragmented world of differing cultural backgrounds into an emerging global city. Toynbee grasped this central fact of the contemporary world and sought to write a universal history that accorded with the needs of a global age. For the peoples of the world to live together, said Toynbee, they must know each other, for 'historical forces can be more explosive than atom bombs.'[16] Toynbee attempted to study world history free of Western ethnocentrism and distortions and to promote an ecumenical consciousness.

Toynbee held that only a world government, with national states as federated units, could deal effectively with the crucial problems of the contemporary world – national conflicts, nuclear weapons, a deteriorating environment, overpopulation, and poverty. In the tradition of the world's prophets, who taught the oneness of God and of humanity, he maintained that mankind is one family in the making; the world must become one family, he insisted, or it will destroy itself. If the world does become more knit together, Toynbee will be heralded as one of the prophets of world unity.

Toynbee's critics attacked his religious orientation as a repudiation of the Western rational-humanist tradition. Liberal humanists were particularly distressed by an approach, reminiscent of St Augustine, that self-consciously aspired to show the relationship between our world and a higher reality. Liberals are uncomfortable with and unforgiving of thinkers who hold that in studying history we should 'relegate economic and political history to a subordinate place and give religious history primacy.'[17] They regard as a regression to mythical thinking an attitude of mind that sees the vocation of the historian as 'a call from God to feel after him and find him.'[18] These critics were repelled by Toynbee's assertion that God's hand was at work in history, that history was a theodicy in which progress was measured by an awareness of God, and that communion with God was the ultimate goal of history. 'He is a man who believes in a strange mysticism about history ... His is not the talent of science but of belief,'[19] said Ortega y Gasset. To these scholars Toynbee was a modern-day St Augustine lashing out against the pagans, a prophet of doom preaching that dispensing with God is the root of humanity's undoing. Such an outlook befits a poet, a theologian, or a mystic, they said, but not a historian. H.R. Trevor-Roper, one of Toynbee's severest critics, held that Toynbee 'is fundamentally anti-rational' and detests Western civilization because it is basically liberal and rational.'[20] A.J.P. Taylor declared just as angrily: 'These monstrous volumes with their parade of learning are a repudiation of Rationalism.'[21]

It is misleading, however, to regard Toynbee as an enemy of the rational-humanist tradition associated with Athens and the Enlightenment. It is true that he considered philosophy an inadequate substitute for higher religions and philosophers lesser figures than saints, lamented the dissolution of Latin Christendom, and at times wrote like an inspired prophet rather than a sober-minded historian. Nevertheless, he rejected religious dogma that contradicted reason, criticized those who pitted dogma against the findings of science, affirmed religious toleration, and valued a humanist education that nurtured the intellect and refined aesthetic tastes.

Toynbee compels us to re-examine the efficacy and central meaning of the liberal-rational tradition associated with the Enlightenment. Liberalism, rationalism, and secularism, said Toynbee, are inadequate supports upon which to sustain Western civilization. The liberal-rational tradition, Toynbee believed, must be overarched by spiritual values, for reason, undirected by prophetic teachings (not dogma) that impel human beings to love one another and respect each other, produces a Frankenstein technology, ruthless social conflicts, and the totalitarian state. Toynbee rebelled against the reductionism inherent in the Enlightenment conception of reason. In its relentless drive to make everything intelligible, Toynbee said, reason degenerates into soulless mechanism, materialism, and technocracy. 'Man has now decisively overcome Nature by his technology; but the victor has been technology, not Man himself. Man has merely exchanged one master for another, and his new master is more overbearing than his former one. Man is still the slave of his environment, but this is now the environment that he has created for himself, not the environment which Nature originally endowed him. Nature used to chastize Man with whips; Man's own technology is now chastizing Man with scorpions.'[22]

Nor, for Toynbee, can reason compare with religion in awakening a human being's noblest sentiments – love and compassion. Enlightenment values, unbuttressed by Christianity, cannot restrain people's basest impulses. Rejecting as naïve the Enlightenment view of man's essential goodness, Toynbee believed in a spiritual division of the soul – the individual has an inherent capacity both for goodness and for wickedness. Without the guidance of prophetic values, people will be consumed by wickedness. Human nature contains an ineradicable spiritual element; if it is not directed towards prophetic values, it will be rerouted into lower religions, particularly the idolization of the parochial community, that bring out the worst in human beings. For Toynbee, civilization is only a thin veneer 'overlying a molten mass of wickedness that is always boiling up for an opportunity to burst out.'[23] The secular and rational tradition of the Enlightenment, he held, cannot contain this wickedness.

Toynbee also called into question the Enlightenment conception of individual freedom. Divorced from Christianity, he said, liberalism degenerates into selfish competitiveness that leads to the exploitation of the weak. Toynbee insisted that the idea of liberty originated in the Christian belief that each soul is sacred; separated from its Christian context, individual freedom proves to be an uninspiring doctrine that lacks the appeal of totalitarian ideologies.

In *The Philosophy of the Enlightenment*, written on the eve of Hitler's take-over, Ernst Cassirer lauded the Enlightenment because it 'discovered and passionately defended the autonomy of reason, and ... firmly established this concept in all fields of knowledge ... More than ever before ... the time is again ripe for applying ... self-criticism to the present age, for holding up to it that bright clear mirror fashioned by the Enlightenment ... The age which venerated reason and science as man's highest faculty cannot and must not be lost even for us.'[24]

Toynbee would agree that our age requires the application of a critical spirit, but he would add that through reason alone we cannot fully know ourselves, overcome a flawed human nature, cope successfully with social ills, or use science and technology for human advantage. Toynbee aspired to a creative synthesis of prophetic values and reason. Even if his commitment to reason and the Enlightenment was qualified, he did share in the Enlightenment's humanitarianism, tolerance, concern for human rights, cosmopolitanism, and distate for religious dogma. The anonymous reviewer for the *Times Literary Supplement* astutely concluded: 'For all that he professes to reject the Enlightenment, our new prophet is none the less its child and its disciple ... [*A Study of History* is] a deeply felt personal vision of the historical process, a vision which expresses the despair of a liberal who has seen the liberal dream turn to ashes as well as hope of a liberal who has turned again to God.'[25]

In an age that has seen reason soar and collapse, Toynbee raised essential issues. By questioning the ability of liberal humanism to guard against dangerous eruptions of the non-rational and to control an innate wickedness, Toynbee compels us to re-examine both the limitations and the potential of reason, both the promise and the failure of the Enlightenment tradition. In the same spirit, he reminds us that the religious impulse is not something that can be reasoned away, but constitutes a permanent part of human nature, and enjoins us to reflect on religion's immense historic significance and its meaning for a post-Christian age.

Even if, in the end, we reject Toynbee's mystical-religious worldview and are dismayed by his mythic-poetic approach to history, Toynbee remains a historian of stature for attempting a universal and synthetic history. And one aspect of Toynbee's synthesis that is of particular interest to students of culture is his effort to resolve the inherent tensions between Athens and Jerusalem.

NOTES

Some sections of this essay were published earlier in 'Arnold Toynbee Revisited,' *Continuity: A Journal of History*, Spring 1985.

1 Leo Strauss, 'Jerusalem and Athens,' *Commentary* (June 1967): 45
2 *The Portable Greek Reader*, ed. W.H. Auden (New York: Viking 1952), 38
3 Toynbee, *Hellenism: The History of a Civilization* (New York: Oxford University Press 1959), 10
4 Toynbee, *Experiences* (New York: Oxford University Press 1969), 167
5 See *God, History, and Historians*, ed. C.T. McIntire (New York: Oxford University Press 1977).
6 Cited in ibid., 9
7 *Experiences*, 127
8 Toynbee, *Civilization on Trial* (New York: Oxford University Press 1948); reprint ed. published with *The World and the West* (Cleveland: Meridian Books 1958), 207
9 *Civilization on Trial*, 208
10 Toynbee, *A Study of History*, 12 vols (New York: Oxford University Press 1934–61), 1: 9
11 *Study*, 9: 442
12 Toynbee, *Survey of International Affairs*, 1933 (London: Oxford University Press 1934), 111
13 *Study*, 8: 289
14 *Experiences*, 135
15 Hans Kohn, *Political Ideologies of the Twentieth Century* (New York: Harper Torchbooks 1966), 275
16 *Study*, 12: 139
17 *Civilization on Trial*, 89
18 *Study*, 10: 1
19 José Ortega y Gasset, *An Interpretation of Universal History*, trans. Mildred Adams (New York: W.W. Norton 1975), 251–2
20 H.R. Trevor-Roper, 'Arnold Toynbee's Millennium,' *Encounter* 8 (June 1957); reprinted in *Historical Essays* (New York: Harper Torchbooks 1957), 300, 322–3
21 A.J.P. Taylor, 'Much Learning,' in *Toynbee and History*, ed. M.F. Ashley Montagu (Boston: Porter Sargent 1956), 117
22 *Experiences*, 326
23 Toynbee, *Acquaintances* (New York: Oxford University Press 1967), 294
24 Ernst Cassirer, *The Philosophy of the Enlightenment* (Boston: Beacon Press 1950), xi
25 'Study of Toynbee: A Personal View of History,' in *Toynbee and History*, 109–10

Toynbee:
The Time Traveller
Thomas W. Africa

> Friends who set forth at our side
> Falter, are lost in the storm!
> We, we only, are left! ...
> On to the City of God.
>
> Matthew Arnold, 'Rugby Chapel'

In the shaken post-war era, history was briefly 'relevant,' and Arnold Toynbee had oracular status in many quarters.[1] Thanks to *Time*, television, and a string of best sellers, the public knew and revered him. Generally academics were less enthusiastic. Particularly shocking to many academics was Toynbee's frank antirationalism – he was 'soft on' religion, in favour of poetic inspiration, and prone to mystical states. Though few critics were as rabid as Trevor-Roper,[2] Toynbee's mysticism was as unwelcome in academe as Auden's homosexuality or Dylan Thomas's drinking – all these habits were tolerable only as long as they were performed in quiet. But, like his fellow celebrities, Toynbee flaunted his deviance – from scientism and secular orthodoxy.

As a poet of history, Toynbee had an elegant mentor, Plato the champion of myth and intuition, and later he discovered the arcana of Carl Jung.[3] Had he confined his poetic flights to the metaphors that are integral to grand historical systems, Toynbee might have fared better with the critics, but his poetizing tendency and the incorporation of biblical passages into his prose increased as *A Study of History* was completed in the post-war era. Similarly, his notion that civilizations exist to produce higher religions would have seemed unexceptional if Toynbee had remained an Anglican or converted to Catholicism, as he almost did in the thirties.[4] However, no quarter would be given – or asked – for the mystical experiences of which he boasts in the tenth volume of his major work. In most of these episodes, the historian travels through time to witness specific events, and the cumulative effect of these experiences is a preparation for the ultimate mystical revelation:

When the feeling for the poetry in the facts of History is thus transmuted into awe at the epiphany of God in History, the historian's inspiration is preparing him for ... 'the Beatific Vision' ... God is seen face to face ... To this process of progressive initiation, the first stage in a historian's spiritual pilgrimage is the experience of a communion on the mundane plane with persons and events from which ... he is sundered by a great gulf of Time and Space ... There are moments ... in which temporal and spatial barriers fall and psychic distance is annihilated; and in such moments of inspiration, the historian finds himself transformed in a flash from a remote spectator into an immediate participant.[5]

Toynbee carefully distinguished 'an historian's normal relation to the objects of his study' ('tenuous, long-distance ... intellectual') from the brief flash that can be triggered by a passage in a book or a glimpse of a site that is rich in associations.[6] That he did not view such episodes as acts of an over-excited imagination is evident in his fervent description of them and in the occurrence of other experiences when, in Wordsworth's words, 'the light of sense goes out, but with a flash that has revealed the invisible world.'[7]

In 1911, the invisible world first opened to Arnold Toynbee when, aged twenty-two, he was reading Livy at Oxford and 'was transported in a flash ... to Teanum in 80 B.C.' to witness the suicide of an Italian fugitive.[8] On 10 January 1912, touring Greece, he was stirred by the sounds of tinkling goat-bells and bleating sheep at Cynoscephalae to suddenly 'see' the defeat of Philip v by the Romans. Moved by the spectacle, the young scholar tossed off some Greek elegiac verses.[9] On 19 March 1912, at the ruins of a baroque villa in Crete, 'the spectator was suddenly carried in a "Time-pocket" ... to a day in the fifth decade of the seventeenth century' when the building was evacuated.[10] At a Laconian fort on 23 April 1912 'he fell again into the deep trough of Time' and 'was transported to the evening of the day' when the fortress was abandoned in 1715 or 1821.[11] On 23 May 1912 Toynbee sat musing at Mistra and gazed over Laconia when he had a sudden insight on the crucial role of geography in history and the consistent warfare between predatory highlanders and the farmers of the plain.[12] While not a 'Time-pocket,' the episode was a conscious imitation of Gibbon's 'illumination' on the Capitoline Hill on 15 October 1754.[13] Back at Oxford, a dream on 22 October 1913 warned Toynbee against the intellectually deadly fate of becoming a don.[14] As a disciple of Herodotus, he took the warning dream to heart. The next contact with the 'invisible world' defies description: 'Walking southward along the pavement skirting the west wall of Victoria Station, the writer ... one afternoon not long after the end of the first World War – he had failed to record the exact date – had found himself in communion, not just with this or that episode in History, but with all that had been, and was, and was to come. In that instant, he was directly aware of the passage of History gently flowing through him in a mighty current, and of his own life welling like a wave in the flow of this vast tide.'[15] Recalling the vision three decades later, Toynbee connected 'a sense of personal communion with all men and women at all times and places' with some sentimental verses by his first wife, Rosalind Murray.[16] In any case, 'that ineffable experience' outside Victoria Station fell short of the Beatific Vision of the Communion of Saints, permeated by the presence of God, that Toynbee visualized from a painting by Fra Angelico and suggested in the ecumenical litany that concludes *A Study of History*.[17]

The Great War had a decisive impact on Toynbee, who had contracted dysentery on his trip to Greece and was unfit for military service. He felt that fate had spared him from the slaughter in the trenches in order that he might explain the catastrophe that had destroyed the Victorian world order.[18] This self-imposed task was a debt of atonement for fallen friends. 'About half my contemporaries at school and at the university were killed in 1915–16,' he later mused. 'I have always felt it strange to be still alive myself.'[19] In 1974 he was still plagued by a survivor's guilt: 'I often think what could have been achieved by my contemporaries who were killed ... I feel the loss ...

more and more every year that's added to my life, because I feel the difference between their fate and mine, and how utterly unreasonable and irrational and barbarous it is that they should have perished.'[20] In their honour he wrote Greek and English elegies and he undertook *A Study in History*.[21] For a historical model, Toynbee turned first to Thucydides' comments on the wreck of Athens, which he now felt was a 'contemporary' disaster.[22] 'In the Summer of 1920, Professor Namier ... placed in my hands Oswald Spengler's *Untergang des Abendlandes*,'[23] but the German seer was not to Toynbee's tastes. On 11 February 1921 'the most vivid of the present writer's experiences of the local annihilation of Time ... had overtaken him at Ephesus ... The empty theater peopled itself with a tumultuous throng ... When the cries of "Great is Diana" are dying down ... the spectator is carried up again ... from an abyss, nineteen centuries deep.'[24]

On 17 September 1921 a dreamy train trip through Bulgaria and the sight of peasant garb 'must have released some psychic wellspring at a subconscious level,' for, before going to sleep that night, Toynbee sketched 'a list of topics, which ... was substantially identical with the plan of' *A Study of History*.[25] On 24 November 1929, 'Time stood still at Port Arthur,' and Toynbee saw the carnage that forced the Russians to capitulate to the Japanese in 1904.[26] A month later, attracted to the lovely Eileen Power, Toynbee 'was in a moral conflict between the better and the worse side of myself'; in his poems on this *agōn*, he symbolized the latter as 'the black primaeval bull.' When the beast seemed irresistible, 'a transcendent spiritual presence ... came to my rescue ... in the guise of Saint George ... A rationalist might suggest that ... I was externalizing ... a wholly internal psychic conflict, and ... I cannot disprove [it].' Nevertheless, Toynbee believed that the epiphany of Saint George was 'an immediate encounter with the godhead.'[27]

In the thirties, Toynbee laboured on *A Study of History* 'under enormous mental pressure.' The world lurched towards war again, and Toynbee's 'first marriage had collapsed, affecting me deeply.'[28] To the horror of her father, Gilbert Murray, Rosalind Toynbee had become a Roman Catholic in 1932, and her husband too was ripe for conversion.[29] Despite religious differences, Rosalind was close to her father and could communicate with him through 'extra-sensory' means. Toynbee was delighted by her 'psychic skills,'[30] but he balked at embracing formal Christianity, despite his mystical experiences and his recent contact with God. 'In the summer of A.D. 1936, in a time of physical sickness and spiritual travail, he dreamed, during a spell of sleep in a wakeful night, that he was clasping the foot of the crucifix hanging over the high altar of the Abbey of Ampleforth and was hearing a voice saying to him *Amplexus expecta* ("Cling and wait").'[31] Toynbee, who was a Symmachan by temper, continued to wait. In 1939, he was in need of spiritual support when his mother died and then his eldest son, Anthony, committed suicide. Shortly before he was to be married, the young man shot himself in the stomach and died on the Ides of March despite a blood transfusion from his father.[32] Overwhelmed by grief, Toynbee had a mystic experience, another divine epiphany. As in the crisis of 1929, the godhead seemed to intervene in a recognizable form, 'in the likeness of Michelangelo's vision of the Creator giving life to Adam ... God had revealed himself for an instant to give an unmistakable assurance of his mercy and forgiveness.'[33] During the war years, the Toynbee-Murray marriage finally disintegrated, and he found happiness in a second marriage in 1946. Meanwhile, the historian had turned to psychoanalysis for relief: 'Dr. Sylvia Payne helped me, in a time of great personal trouble, to find a way through the dark wood which I could not have found by myself.'[34] Though Toynbee favoured Jung, Dr Payne was a moderate Freudian and just what he needed: 'I was wonderfully relieved from pain. It untwisted me and released me from a sense of guilt.'[35]

The post-war decade was one of marital happiness, worldly fame, and the completion of *A Study of History*. Toynbee also had four more trips through time. On 21 April 1947 he visited the field at Gettysburg and 'was in momentary personal communion' with those who had fought there in 1863.[36] In 1949 the historian was reading accounts of the Fourth Crusade when he suddenly caught a glimpse of Constantinople in 1203. At another moment, he was present at the rescue of a Greek girl during the sack of the city in 1204.[37] In 1951 Toynbee was reading Bernal Diaz when he suddenly saw Tenochtitlan in 1519.[38] In 1952 the historian had a 'vivid recollection of six ... experiences in which he found himself participating in a historic past event through a momentary annihilation of the intervening time on the hypnotizing spot.'[39] These reinforced episodes had taken place in 1912 (three), 1921, 1929, and 1947 at Cynoscephalae, Crete, Laconia, Ephesus,

Port Arthur, and Gettysburg, respectively, where the sites triggered the vision. The four experiences prompted by reading presumably took place in libraries in 1911, 1949 (two), and 1951. The grand vision of past and future, outside Victoria Station not long after the First World War, occurred in prosaic surroundings. The dreams of 1913 and 1936 and the divine epiphanies of 1929 and 1939 do not qualify as time travel, though they reveal much about the Time Traveller. In *Reconsiderations* Toynbee commented that many critics were disconcerted by the candour and detail of his autobiographical passages.[40] He might have added that only Colin Wilson approved of his time travels.[41] As a profession, historians relish gossip and dote on autobiography, but they do not appreciate frank revelations by fellow scholars.[42] Perhaps they are put off by what J.H. Plumb calls 'the ache within.'[43] Since Toynbee was candid about his visions, let us try to understand them.

Breaking the barrier of time is a topic of absorbing interest to mystics and poets, and Toynbee fits both categories. Few would argue with T.S. Eliot's dictum that 'the historical sense, which we may call nearly indispensable to anyone who continues to be a poet beyond his twenty-fifth year, ... involves a perception, not only of the pastness of the past, but of its presence.'[44] Many writers have toyed with the notion of a visitable past, but the trip into time has not always been a happy one. The hero of Henry James's unfinished novel, *The Sense of the Past*, was a historian of sorts who wanted 'to recover the lost moment, to feel the stopped pulse, ... to be again consciously the creature that had been; ... he wanted the very tick of the old stopped clocks.'[45] In an eerie London mansion, he tumbled back into 1820, into a world of ghosts. In Kipling's 'The Finest Story in the World,' a simple lad recalls bits of prior lives as a galley slave or a Viking, until 'love of a woman kills remembrance!'[46] After reading Malory, Mark Twain dreamed of the discomforts of wearing armour. Chronic despair and financial frustration turned the dream into an apocalyptic parable, *A Connecticut Yankee in King Arthur's Court*, where the Machine Age and progressive thought wrought havoc in the past. Originally, Twain intended the Yankee to commit suicide.[47] As Max Beerbohm's Enoch Soames learned, visiting the future can be unpleasant too. The grimmest trip through time is the most famous. H.G. Wells's *The Time*

Machine deposited the traveller in the nightmare world of decadent Eloi and cannibal Morlocks, a morality play tuned to *fin-de-siècle* despair.[48]

Of course, contrived tales of time travel are not comparable to Toynbee's glimpses into the abyss. The closest approximation, albeit fictional, is the celebrated passage in *The Mayor of Casterbridge*, where Thomas Hardy concludes an account of the Roman amphitheatre at Dorchester: 'Some old people said that at certain moments in the summer time, in broad daylight, persons sitting with a book or dozing in the arena had, on lifting their eyes, beheld the slopes lined with a gazing legion of Hadrian's soldiery as if watching the gladiatorial combat, and had heard the roar of their excited voices; that the scene would remain but a moment, like a lightning flash, and then disappear.'[49] The shouts and mood of violence were echoes of a No-Popery demonstration, replete with burning effigies, which Hardy as a child had witnessed on that spot.[50] Like Toynbee, Hardy was stimulated by historic sites: on the Palatine Hill in 1887, 'each ranked ruin tended to beguile the outer sense,' and strains of music 'stirred me as I stood, in Caesar's House, ... and blended pulsing life with lives long done, till Time seemed fiction, Past and Present one.'[51] As a kindred spirit, Toynbee was fond of Hardy's works, especially *The Dynasts*,[52] and when he wanted examples of 'even the smallest city,' the historian cited three: 'Abraham's Ur or Goethe's Weimar or Thomas Hardy's "Casterbridge."'[53] The three towns held much significance for him.

Whether Toynbee's descents into the abyss of Time were concoctions of an overwrought imagination or, as he believed, the first rungs on Jacob's ladder, his claims of divine epiphanies and a glimpse of all Time mark the historian as a true mystic. Appropriately, Toynbee begins his account of time travel by evoking Ezekiel's vision of breathing life into skeletons in a valley of bones.[54] The company of distinguished mystics is a roster of renown. 'The trances of Socrates, Plotinus, Porphyry, Boehme, Bunyan, Fox, Pascal ... [and] Swedenborg will readily come to mind,' notes Emerson. 'But what as readily comes to mind,' he continues, 'is the accompaniment of disease.'[55] Many of these god-intoxicated men have been regarded as mad. Karl Jaspers considered both Swedenborg and Ezekiel 'schizophrenic'; George Rosen disagreed on Ezekiel.[56] William Blake, of course, frequently saw God and the prophets, interviewed heroes of the remote past, and conversed with the ghost of a flea.[57]

Toynbee, however, was not a contemporary of Swedenborg or Blake, and his visions should be compared with those of Victorian bourgeois intellectuals. For instance, the hero of Romain Rolland's *Jean-Christophe*, at a crucial moment of departure, 'suddenly had one of those moments of giddiness which open great distances in the plain of life. A chasm in Time ... Christophe had a feeling that it had already been, that what was now was not now, but in some other time.'[58] Though embodied in fiction, this episode was not a novelist's fancy, for Rolland had three major 'mystical disturbances.' In 1882 he was literally ravished by a view of the mountains at Lake Geneva: 'I was possessed by nature like a violated virgin. For a moment, my soul left me to melt into the luminous mass of the Breithorn.' In 1886, while reading Spinoza, Rolland was possessed by God: 'Out of my icy room ... I escape into the depth of substance, into the white sun of Being.' Not long after this vision, he had a *pan-en-henic* experience in a railway tunnel.[59] At Rome, in 1890, 'the revelation of the Janiculum ... drew creativity up out of the ground; it revealed to me ... all that I was later to do, all that I have done ... It took me twenty years to bring it to completion.'[60] Whatever transpired on the Janiculum Hill was not a conventional mystic moment, but it was on 'sacred soil' in the city sacred to Montaigne as well as Gibbon.[61]

On Mount Marcy in the Adirondacks, on 8 July 1898, William James 'got into a state of spiritual alertness ... The influences of Nature, [thoughts of family], the problems of the Edinburgh lectures, all fermented within me till it became a regular *Warpurgis Nacht* ... The streaming moonlight lit up things in a magical checkered play, and it seemed as if the Gods of all the nature-mythologies were holding an indescribable meeting in my breast with the moral Gods of the inner life ... I understand now what a poet is.'[62] His elation bore fruit at Edinburgh in the lectures that became *Varieties of Religious Experience*. William James fell into the arms of Dame Kind as a middle-aged man,[63] but John Addington Symonds had known a nightmarish mystic experience since childhood: 'That was a kind of trance ... Irresistibly, it took possession of my mind and will, lasted what seemed an eternity, and disappeared in ... [what] resembled the awakening from anaesthetic influence ... It consisted in a gradual but swiftly progressive obliteration of space, time, sensation, and the multitudinous factors of ... ourself ... At last, nothing remained but a pure, absolute abstract self. The universe became without form and void of content ... I had followed the last thread of being to the verge of the abyss and had arrived at ... eternal Maya.'[64] By the age of twenty-eight Symonds was spared the trances that threatened dissolution of the self.[65] 'In a recital like this,' mused William James, 'there is certainly something suggestive of pathology.'[66] Of course, James, like Rolland, was delighted with Dame Kind, but poor Symonds shrank back from a glimpse of Maya, the other face of Dame Kind.

Toynbee, too, saw the shining face of a deity who snatched him from sin and despair and showed him the vistas of Time. Yet, the brotherhood of mystics includes those who wander through the valley of terror. Anton Boisen spent years in madhouses: 'I have visited the same infernal regions and been branded with the same psychiatric label. I am very sure that George Fox also has visited the little-known country ... so also Swedenborg and Jeremiah and Ezekiel and Paul.'[67] Boisen quotes the confession of a less renowned mystic, a patient called James G.: 'I had a vision, and it seemed to me as if I could see way back to the beginning of all creation! I could see the evolution of man up to his present being ... When I was in the rage, there was something telling me that I was the true spirit of Christ.'[68] Boisen had similar delusions. But, did Arnold Toynbee?

The urge to escape into Time is no proof of lunacy. It is the chief subconscious motive of all historians, and many novelists and poets have felt the irresistible lure of the past. As Gibbon sighed, 'the abbreviation of time and the failure of hope will always tinge with a browner shade the evening of life.'[69] Nostalgia suffices for most people, but some would break the bonds of time. In 1846, Jacob Burckhardt lamented: 'I, who am so tired of the present, will be refreshed by the thrill of antiquity as by some wonderful and peaceful tomb. Yes, I want to get away from them all, from the radicals, the communists, the industrialists, the intellectuals ... the "ists" and "isms" of every kind ... [A few months later in 1847] I should say, let's go to America together! But I simply could not live there; I need an historical terrain, and what is more a beautiful one ... Doesn't it sometimes seem to you as though one fine day on a lonely path, you would meet a dwarf who would open a secret door in the moss and stones of the forest and lead you into a new world?'[70] In a Renaissance Italy of his own imagining, Burckhardt would find such a world.

Are such escapes limited to flights of imagination or mystic trances? The best documented claim of a break in time was made by two Victorian ladies, Misses Charlotte Anne Moberly and Eleanor Jourdain. While strolling near the Petit Trianon, on 10 August 1901, they encountered individuals in antique dress and beheld buildings and paths that had existed at Versailles in the days of Marie Antoinette but were no longer extant in 1901.[71] Miss Moberly wrote a most interesting account of their adventure, and her veracity is unimpeachable, for she was a bishop's daughter and principal of St Hugh's Hall, Oxford. To be sure, she had other contacts with ghosts and once spotted Constantine strolling down the grand staircase at the Louvre. At first, she thought he was Charlemagne, an understandable error since both men were tall.[72] Miss Moberly's truthfulness is not in doubt, but the significance of her experience is open to more than one interpretation. Cicely Wedgewood will have none of it: 'The historian need not (even in the gardens of Versailles) either fear or hope for one of those kinks or knots in time, dear to writers, that will project him suddenly into an earlier epoch.'[73] I assume that Dame Cicely had Miss Moberly in mind. Her strictures, of course, do not apply to Toynbee, who has the mystic's hallmark of familiarity with the ineffable.

Ironically, Toynbee was critical of a famed tale of time travel. In the sixth volume of *A Study of History*, he dealt with creative individuals in a disintegrating society who advocate archaist or futurist solutions. The historian calls such an individual a 'Saviour with a Time-Machine,' which is not a positive image in his vocabulary. The metaphor prompts him to digress on H.G. Wells's *The Time Machine*, which he misrepresents as a paean to *Homo mechanicus* roaming through time as well as space. Toynbee chides Wells for not recalling Lewis Carroll's parable of a time machine, the 'Outlandish Watch,' in *Sylvie and Bruno*. In Carroll's tale, an individual tries to prevent an accident by mechanically interfering with time and removing the cause of the mishap, only to wind up with the same result, an accident.[74] While worthless as a critique of Wells, the invocation of Carroll's peculiar novel reveals much about Toynbee, who was one of the few readers to think well of the book. *Sylvie and Bruno* and its sequel, *Sylvie and Bruno Concluded*, are long, mawkish fantasies about a virginal mother figure, Lady Muriel, and two saccharine fairy children, one of whom babbles baby-talk.[75] Throughout both novels the narrator slips from 'the ordinary state' to either (1) 'the "eerie" state in which, while conscious of actual surroundings, he is also conscious of the presence of fairies,' or (2) 'a form of trance, in which, while unconscious of actual surroundings and apparently asleep, he (i.e. his immaterial essence) migrates to other scenes in the actual world or in Fairyland.'[76] Carroll even provides a convenient chart of the 'historian's locality and state,'[77] all of which made an impression on Toynbee, who probably read the book as a child.

As every reader of *A Study of History* knows, Toynbee was a bookish man, who not only read omnivorously but had an almost rabbinical veneration of the written word. Indeed, one of his major methodological flaws as a historian stemmed from his reliance on obsolete notes; he boasted repeatedly of using 'notes that I had taken five, ten, or twenty years before the opportunity came for using them.'[78] These unchanging words were sacred to a man who built his life around books. 'When I travel,' he told Ved Mehta, 'I carry in my pocket a copy of the Bhagavad-Gita, a volume of Dante, an anthology of the metaphysical poets, and "Faust" – books I read over and over again. Some people live by Freud and "Hamlet." I live by Jung and "Faust."'[79] From *Faust*, Toynbee learned the dialectic of challenge-and-response and that Good can come from Evil,[80] but he was also sensitive to the ultimate revelation of the drama: 'Das Ewig-Weibliche zieht uns hinan.'[81] Most relevant to Toynbee's psychic life was Faust's assignment to revive Helen and Paris; he achieved the task by descending to the Mothers, the matrices of creation, who permit some of the once-living to return in nocturnal dreams and some as daytime visions.[82] These themes are suggestive of Toynbee's descents into the abyss of Time to glimpse the once-living as they were.

Carl Jung, of course, was alert to the sexual symbolism of the Mothers sequence in *Faust* with its phallic key and uterine themes.[83] Like the historian, Jung was fond of Goethe, subject to visions, and prone to imagery that Toynbee found attractive – withdrawal and return, mandalas, night journey of the hero, and submarine voyages through 'the Psyche's subconscious abyss.'[84] As a compulsive traveller and devout Jungian, Toynbee must have read the Swiss psychiatrist's observation on wanderers, a few lines before a long quotation from Goethe on the Mothers: 'Wandering is a symbol of longing, of the restless urge which never finds its object, of nostalgia for the lost mother.'[85] Jung also considered the sea a maternal symbol; 'the great primordial image of the mother, who was once our only world.'[86] In a long, ornate passage in the ninth volume of *A Study of History*, Toynbee rhapsodizes on the sea as 'the Great Mother of Life on Earth ... the fount of Poetry and Prophecy' and follows the stream of consciousness to ponder 'a stage of early infancy in which God's future place in the Soul's universe has been occupied by the infant child's Mother, ... who represents Authority as well as Love in her own indivisible person.'[87] In Toynbee's poetic view, the sea, his mother, and God are easily interchangeable images, different forms of the same entity that inspires, comforts, and sustains him.[88] In the words of one of Toynbee's favourite poets, Wordsworth, 'Heaven lies about us in our infancy ... Our Souls have sight of that immortal sea, which brought us hither, can in a moment travel thither, and see the Children sport upon the shore, and hear the mighty waters rolling evermore.'[89]

Like Augustine and Proust, Toynbee was extraordinarily devoted to his mother, and his autobiographical passages are filled with references to books read with her, places visited together, and personal belongings presented by Sarah Toynbee to her adoring son. Her husband, Harry, was a social worker whose mind collapsed in 1908 when their son was nineteen. The 'death-in-life' of his father, who spent the next third of a century in a mental institution, terrified Arnold Toynbee,[90] but Harry's tragedy intensified the already close bond between Sarah and her son. A minor writer of popular history, she was his muse and role-model:[91] 'I am a historian because my mother was one before me,' he boasted.[92] Toynbee fondly recalled 'the intimate companionship that his mother had given him,' her bedtime stories about British history, and her personal books, the volumes on the Ancient Near East that 'shook him out of the Yin-state of receptivity into a Yang-movement of curiosity ... The child flung himself upon the Ocean of History.'[93] Twenty years later, the historian merged with the Ocean of History in his vision outside Victoria Station, when he was 'in communion ... with all that had been, and was, and was to come. In that instant, he was directly aware of the passage of History gently flowing through him in a mighty current, and of his own life welling like a wave in the flow of this vast tide.'[94] Oddly, he gives no time reference other than 'not long after the end of the First World War' for the awesome moment 'when that ineffable experience travelled through him,'⁹⁵ though he usually provides precise dates for his visions. Perhaps Toynbee instinctively realized that time was inappropriate in a uterine environment.

On 5 December 1927 Romain Rolland wrote to Sigmund Freud about his own religious feeling, 'the sensation of the Eternal, which may very well not be eternal, but simply without perceptible limits, and in that way oceanic.' Rolland also compares this 'oceanic feeling' with 'an underground bed of water which I feel surfacing.'⁹⁶ In *Civilization and Its Discontents*, Freud alludes to the 'oceanic feeling' that Rolland felt was widely experienced, but the psychoanalyst identified it as 'the restoration of [the] limitless narcissism' of infancy.⁹⁷ On this matter, Freud's insight was correct, and Rolland, as we know, was prone to *pan-en-henic* visions – he was also fixated on his mother.⁹⁸ As for Toynbee, with the amniotic fluid of History flowing through his veins, he might well say with another of his favourite poets, 'In my beginning is my end.'⁹⁹

In retrospect, what do Toynbee's psychic adventures reveal about the man? The divine epiphanies in 1929 and 1939 were responses to emotional crises, and Toynbee admitted that he 'cannot disprove these demythologizations,'¹⁰⁰ but he is fond of quoting Pascal: 'La coeur a ses raisons que la raison ne connaît point.'¹⁰¹ Toynbee's 'ineffable experience' by Victoria Station puts him in company with Pascal, who on 23 November 1654, 'from about half past ten at night to about half past twelve,' saw 'Fire, God of Abraham, God of Isaac, God of Jacob, not of the philosophers and the learned,' and found 'certitude, feeling, joy, peace.'¹⁰² Toynbee, too, saw God in conventional forms, St George and the Sistine Deity, but by Victoria Station, he presumably saw only people, albeit *all* people, past, present, and future.

Were it not for these three extraordinary visions, Toynbee's on-site glimpses of the past would not be remarkable. Many people get moony visiting famous spots. In an expansive mood, Ernest Hemingway claimed that he could recall the feel of ancient armour and being at past battles: 'When I am a little crazy, I can remember the damndest things, and *Salammbo* always bored me because I remembered how it really was.'¹⁰³ Unfortunately, Hemingway was more apt to lie than he was to have visions, and he was probably only trying to impress Bernard Berenson.¹⁰⁴ Toynbee, by contrast, was not arguing for reincarnation, but for present-day descents into the abyss to recapture a bit of the past from the Mothers. Visiting a historic site or reading a vivid book might trigger the experience, just as the taste of a madeleine soaked in tea pierced the veil of time for Proust: 'I can hear the echo of great spaces traversed.'[105] For Toynbee, as for Proust, the 'true paradises are the paradises that we have lost,'[106] specifically the childhood monopoly on the affections of an adored and adoring mother.

Nineteen twelve was a year filled with time travel for Toynbee, as he toured Greece and reacted to hallowed sites with the enthusiasm of an imaginative visitor, trained as a classicist and by nature a poet. Yet, his first descent into the abyss of Time had taken place *the year before* at Oxford while he was reading a summary of Livy. Suddenly, the reader witnessed a scene evoked by only four lines of Latin: a proscribed Italian general sought refuge in his own home, but was rejected by his wife and killed himself on the spot.[107] Though only part of an account of numerous acts of violence under Sulla, this minor episode 'transported' Toynbee 'across the gulf of Time and Space.' Why? The key lies in what Toynbee calls 'the traitor-wife's infamy'; she rejected the fugitive husband and thus prompted his final despair. Surely, this was not the outward behaviour of Sarah Toynbee at her husband's recent collapse and incarceration: 'When my Father went out of his mind and my Mother became entirely absorbed in him ... I virtually lost my Mother (with whom I had a particularly close relation till then).'[108] What was Arnold's subconscious reaction to what he called the 'death-in-life' of his father, other than the horror to which he admits? After depicting the ancient scene in graphic detail, Toynbee adds, in a footnote, that the wife's 'infamy was the more heinous' because in comparable situations the wives of proscribed men had 'showed the greatest loyalty, ... their sons none.'[109] Although he translated the Livy passage in the text, Toynbee left the footnote quotation on the unfilial feelings of sons in the original Latin, but he did add some significant New Testament texts (for instance, 'I have come to set a man against his father'!).[110] In his readings in Roman history, the young scholar had encountered guilty sons, and the words 'filiorum nullam' rankled in his mind until he chanced upon the wife who spurned her doomed husband, as sons abandoned their fathers supposedly without exception. Whatever guilt he felt about his reaction to his father's 'death-in-life,' Toynbee deflected onto the infamous wife of Livy's account.[111] So important was this solution to Oedipal guilts that he conjured up the historic scene in vivid intensity. By seizing on the guilt of wives, even of his angel mother, Toynbee 'loosed the silver cord' that connected him with Sarah.

The following year, in Greece, Toynbee had more conventional travels in time and a Gibbonian inspiration on a hill in Laconia. Returning to England, he assumed adult roles, taught at Oxford, married the daughter of Gilbert Murray, and started a family of his own. The world war broke up his tidy universe and presented him with a historical dilemma to solve. His acute guilt as a survivor added a sense of obligation to carry out the task on behalf of his slaughtered comrades. For psychological support in this heroic endeavour, Toynbee turned again to his mother, as Achilles had turned to Thetis. Appropriately by *Victoria* Station, he avowed his vocation as a historian in the vision which took the explicit form of a uterine return and a restoration of his bond with his mother and muse, who was now History incarnate. He spent the rest of his life devoted to her service, and periodically he would refresh himself at the primordial fount with descents into the abyss of Time. As T.S. Eliot notes, 'history is a pattern of timeless moments ... But to apprehend the point of intercession of the timeless with time, is an occupation for the saint.'[112] Like any aspiring saint, Toynbee constructed his visions from expectations and memories gleaned from books and art. Like most late Victorians, he knew the King James Bible well, not to mention Wordsworth, Tennyson, Thomas Hardy, and Lewis Carroll; he was also indebted to continental sages – Pascal, Goethe, and Jung. Above all, he was imbued with Greek and Roman thought, and his first time trips focused on Mediterranean subjects. However, the chief wellspring of his visions came from deep within his psyche, where his mother reigned supreme.[113] 'Locke said, "God, when he makes the prophet, does not unmake the man,"' Emerson agreed, and added that 'Swedenborg's history points the remark.'[114] So do the visions of Arnold Toynbee.

NOTES

1 The most thorough biographical sketch of Toynbee is by William H. McNeill, 'Arnold J. Toynbee,' *Proceedings of British Academy* 63 (1977): 441–69. An

invaluable source of personal data is *An Historian's Conscience: The Correspondence of Arnold J. Toynbee and Columba Cary-Elwes, Monk of Ampleforth*, ed. Christian B. Peper (Boston: Beacon Press 1986). See also Richard Clogg, *Politics and the Academy: Arnold Toynbee and the Koraes Chair* (London: Frank Cass & Co. 1980).

2 Hugh Trevor-Roper, 'Arnold Toynbee's Millennium,' *Encounter* 8 (June 1957): 14–28. C.V. Wedgewood, *The Sense of the Past* (New York: Collier Books 1967), 73, notes: 'When a philosopher historian of the scope and vision of Professor Toynbee arises to suggest an overall pattern, the specialist scholars who are writhing like Laocoön in the toils of their more detailed research, wrench themselves free from their devouring doubts for just long enough to shoot him as full of arrows as Saint Sebastian.'

3 Toynbee, *A Study of History* (London and New York: Oxford University Press, 1934–61), 10: 228

4 Arnold and Philip Toynbee, *Comparing Notes: A Dialogue across a Generation* (London: Weidenfeld and Nicholson 1963), 11

5 *Study*, 10: 129–30; *Historian's Conscience*, 385

6 *Study*, 10: 130

7 William Wordsworth, 'The Prelude,' in *Selected Poems* (London: J.M. Dent & Sons 1975), 145

8 *Study*, 10: 130–1

9 Ibid., 134–5

10 Ibid., 136

11 Ibid., 136–7, esp. n. 1

12 Ibid., 107–11

13 Ibid., 103–4. Edward Gibbon, *Autobiographies*, ed. John Murray (2d ed., London: John Murray 1897), 270, 302, 405. The differing drafts prompted Ernst Badian to consider Gibbon's account 'demonstrably fictitious'; *Gibbon et Rome*, ed. P. Durcey (Lausanne: Université de Lausanne 1977), 103. *Non liquet*.

14 *Study*, 10: 21–2n. Toynbee expands on the topic in *Experiences* (London and New York: Oxford University Press 1969), 68. Eric R. Dodds dreamed that his tenure at Oxford would be a 25-year coma (*Missing Persons* [Oxford: Clarendon Press 1977], 128).

15 *Study*, 10: 139

16 Ibid., 140

17 Ibid., 140–4. As of 1951, 'the runner has not yet reached his goal.'

18 *Experiences*, 37–40

19 *Experiences*, 119
20 *Toynbee on Toynbee*, ed. G.R. Urban (New York: Oxford University Press 1974), 110; cf. Toynbee, 'Toynbee on Toynbee,' *Clio* 2 (1973): 171.
21 *Study*, 10: 236–7; *Experiences*, 386–7
22 Toynbee, *Civilization on Trial* (New York: Oxford University Press 1948), 7–8
23 Ibid., 9
24 *Study*, 10: 138–9; cf. Acts 19:23–40.
25 *Study*, 7: ix–x
26 Ibid., 10: 137–8
27 *Experiences*, 176–7, 389–91; *Historian's Conscience*, 21–2
28 Ved Mehta, *Fly and the Fly-Bottle* (Boston: Little Brown 1963), 147–8
29 Francis West, *Gilbert Murray: A Life* (London: Croom Helm 1984), 170–1
30 *Experiences*, 141
31 *Study*, 9: 634–5
32 *The Times*, London, 16 March 1939. The inquest and a brief appreciation appear in the 21 March issue, pp. 13 and 18. Toynbee's beloved mother also died in the spring of 1939 (*Study* 4: viii), but the 'private grief in March 1939' refers to Tony. In a poem of 1943, the still stricken father alludes to 'Tony's window ... and the lawn haunted by print of Tony's melancholy play'; *Experiences*, 393.
33 *Experiences*, 176–7; *Historian's Conscience*, 32–3
34 *Study*, 10: 237, which includes Dante, *Inferno*, 1.4–6. Toynbee had considered suicide; *Historian's Conscience*, 178, 473.
35 *Comparing Notes*, 106; *Historian's Conscience*, 160, 162, 164, 166, 170
36 *Study*, 10: 138
37 Ibid., 133–4
38 Ibid., 132–3
39 Ibid., 134
40 Ibid., 12: 574
41 Colin Wilson, *Religion and the Outsider* (Boston: Houghton Mifflin 1957), 109–25; *The Occult* (New York: Random House 1971), 61
42 William L. Langer, *In and Out of the Ivory Tower* (New York: N. Watson Academic Publications 1977), 170–2, describes his panic before audiences after February 1938. See Peter Loewenberg, *Decoding the Past* (New York: Alfred A. Knopf 1983), 81–95. William E. Leonard depicts a harrowing lifetime obsession in *The Locomotive God* (New York: The Century Company 1927). E.M. Forster's *Goldsworthy Lowes Dickinson* (New York: Harcourt,

Brace & Co. 1934) is not a candid portrait of the famed academic, whose frank autobiography was published by Dennis Proctor in 1973.
43 J.H. Plumb, *Studies in Social History* (London: Longmans, Green 1955), xiii: 'Men write history for many reasons; to try to understand the forces which impel mankind along its strange course; to justify a religion, a nation, or a class; to make money; to fulfill ambition; to assuage obsession; and a few, the true creators, to ease the ache within.'
44 T.S. Eliot, *Selected Essays* (New York: Harcourt Brace & Co. 1959), 4
45 Henry James, *The Sense of the Past* (New York: Charles Scribner's Sons 1922), 48–9
46 Rudyard Kipling, *A Selection of His Stories and Poems*, 2 vols (New York: Doubleday & Co. 1956), 2: 3–24
47 Justin Kaplan, *Mr. Clemens and Mark Twain* (New York: Simon & Schuster 1968), 344–54; see also Susan K. Harris, *Mark Twain's Escape from Time* (Columbia, Mo.: University of Missouri Press 1982).
48 Bernard Bergonzi, *The Early H.G. Wells: A Study of the Scientific Romances* (Toronto: University of Toronto Press, 1961), 33–61
49 Thomas Hardy, *The Mayor of Casterbridge* (London: Macmillan 1974), 98. See also the acoustic effects in his short story 'A Tryst at an Ancient Earthwork.'
50 'Maumbury Ring,' in *Thomas Hardy's Personal Writings*, ed. H. Orel (Lawrence: University of Kansas Press 1966), 225–32; Florence Hardy, *The Early Life of Thomas Hardy* (London: Macmillan Company 1926), 27
51 Thomas Hardy, *Complete Poems* (New York: Macmillan Co. 1976), 102–3
52 *Study*, 1: 451; 10: 124
53 *Experiences*, 360
54 *Study*, 10: 130; Ezek. 37:1–10
55 Ralph Waldo Emerson, *Essays and Lectures* (New York: Library of America 1983), 663
56 Karl Jaspers, *Strindberg and Van Gogh*, trans. O. Grunow (Tucson: University of Arizona Press 1977), 115–25; George Rosen, *Madness in Society* (New York: Harper Torchbooks 1969), 60
57 Mona Wilson, *The Life of William Blake*, rev. ed. (New York: Cooper Square Publishers 1969), 60–6, 256–61, 346. Alan Ginsberg, in turn, heard the voice of Blake in 1948; *Paris Review* 37, no. 10 (1966): 35–41.
58 Romain Rolland, *Jean-Christophe*, trans. G. Cannan, 3 vols (New York: Modern Library n.d.), 1: 596
59 Harold March, *Romain Rolland* (New York: Twayne Publishers 1971), 21–4

60 Ibid., 36
61 Michel de Montaigne, *Essays*, trans. D. Frame (Stanford: Stanford University Press 1958), 762–3. Gibbon, *Autobiographies*, 267: 'At the distance of twenty-five years, I can neither forget nor express the strong emotions which agitated my mind as I first approached and entered the *eternal* City. After a sleepless night, I trod with a lofty step the ruins of the Forum, each memorable spot.'
62 William James, *Selected Letters*, ed. E. Hardwick (Boston: David R. Godine Publishers 1980), 173–4
63 W.H. Auden, *Forewords and Afterwords* (New York: Vintage Books 1974), 58: 'The Vision of Dame Kind. The objects of the vision will be inorganic – mountains, rivers, seas – or organic – trees, flowers, beasts – but they are all non-human ... The basic experience is an overwhelming conviction that the objects confronting him have a numinous significance and importance, that the existence of everything that he is aware of is holy. And the emotion is one of innocent joy, though this joy can include, of course, a reverent dread.'
64 Horatio F. Brown, *John Addington Symonds*, 2 vols (New York: Charles Scribner's Sons 1905), 1: 29–32
65 Ibid., 168–9: His nightmare of 5 July 1861 indicates low self-esteem and guilt. For the 'crisis at Cannes' in 1868, see Phyllis Grosskurth, *The Woeful Victorian: A Biography of John Addington Symonds* (New York: Rinehart & Winston 1964), 124–5.
66 William James, *The Varieties of Religious Experience* (New York: Modern Library n.d.), 377
67 Anton T. Boisen, *The Exploration of the Inner World* (New York: Harper Torchbooks 1962), 114. On Swedenborg's visions, see Signe Toksvig, *Emanuel Swedenborg* (New Haven: Yale University Press 1948), 142–3, 151–3, and Inge Jonsson, *Emanuel Swedenborg* (New York: Twayne Publishers 1971), 120–8.
68 Boisen, *Exploration*, 168–9; cf. 116.
69 Gibbon, *Autobiographies*, 348
70 Jacob Burckhardt, *Letters*, trans. A. Dru (New York: Pantheon Books 1955), 96, 105; cf. his account of 'Julia's' tomb in *The Civilization of the Renaissance in Italy*, 2 vols (New York: Harper Torchbooks 1958), 1: 190–1.
71 Charlotte Anne Moberly and Eleanor Jourdain, *An Adventure*, ed. Joan Evans (New York: Coward-McCann 1955); Evans's edition is the most scholarly. Cognoscenti of time adventures may also enjoy John W. Dunne, *An Experi-*

ment with Time, 3d ed. (London: Faber & Faber 1934); Mr Dunne advocates 'serialism.'

72 Edith Olivier, *Four Victorian Ladies of Wiltshire* (London: Faber & Faber 1945), 24–44, esp. 41–2
73 Wedgewood, *Sense of the Past*, 40–1
74 *Study*, 6: 214–15. Lewis Carroll, *Complete Works* (New York: Modern Library n.d.), 456–8, 475–81. Toynbee is kinder to Wells in *Study*, 1: 4–5.
75 The saga of Sylvie and Bruno (Carroll, *Works*, 275–749) is lucidly examined by Phyllis Greenacre in *Swift and Carroll: A Psychoanalytic Study of Two Lives* (New York: International Universities Press 1955), 192–205.
76 Carroll, *Works*, 512. Cf. *Study*, 10: 235, where Toynbee, like Tennyson, 'used to tingle with the inaudible music of "the horns of elfland faintly blowing."'
77 Carroll, *Works*, 513
78 *Experiences*, 104. *Toynbee on Toynbee*, 52, mentions 'twenty or thirty years later.'
79 Mehta, *Fly*, 149. Despite their titles, Toynbee does not use Freudian concepts in such papers as 'Poetical Truth and Scientific Truth in the Light of History,' *International Journal of Psychoanalysis* 30 (1949): 143–53, and 'Aspects of Psycho-History,' *Main Currents in Modern Thought* 29 (1972): 44–6. For his dependence on Jung, see n. 84 below.
80 *Civilization on Trial*, 12
81 J.W. Goethe, *Faust*, 2.12110–11
82 *Faust*, 2.6427–38. 'Die Mütter! Mütter! 's klingt so wunderlich' (6217). Goethe told Eckermann that he found the Mothers in Plutarch, *Marcellus* 20; J.P. Eckermann, *Conversations with Goethe* (London: J.M. Dent & Sons 1930), 342.
83 Carl G. Jung, *Symbols of Transformation*, 2nd ed., trans. R. Hull (Princeton: Princeton University Press 1967), 124–6, 205–6
84 *Study*, 7: 716–20, 772; 10: 20, 225–6, 228; *Comparing Notes*, 108; see T.W. Africa, 'The City of God Revisited: Toynbee's Reconsiderations,' *Journal of the History of Ideas* 22 (1962): 282–92.
85 Jung, *Symbols*, 205. In its first avatar, this book was *Psychology of the Unconscious*, trans. B. Hinkle (New York: Dodd, Mead, & Co. 1916), and Toynbee could read this passage on p. 231.
86 Jung, *Symbols*, 251, 219
87 *Study*, 9: 399–401
88 As a child, Toynbee once crawled under a bed, exclaiming, 'Mother and

Nanny are good; Mother and Nanny are God; I am hiding from God'; *Study*, 10: 57 n. 1.
89. Wordsworth, 'Ode: Intimation of Immortality,' *Poems*, 107, 109
90. *Experiences*, 121. The phrase 'Death in Life' appears in Tennyson's *The Princess*, 4.40, not far from a phrase quoted by Toynbee (*Study*, 10: 235). The poem features the theme of madness, 1.5–20: 'None of all our blood should know the shadow from the substance, and ... one should come to fight with shadows and to fall ... Myself too had weird seizures ... I seem'd to move among a world of ghosts and feel myself the shadow of a dream.'
91. *Experiences*, 3, 89–90, 194; *Study*, 10: 18–19, 213, 217, 219, 223–5, 232
92. *Civilization on Trial*, 3, 5; *Study*, 4: viii
93. *Study*, 10: 19 incl. n. 2
94. Ibid., 139
95. Ibid., 140. In May 1919 Toynbee had a breakdown of some kind; Clogg, *Politics and the Academy*, 40.
96. David J. Fisher, 'Sigmund Freud and Romain Rolland,' *American Imago* 33 (1970): 1–59, quotes the complete letter (pp. 20–1) and Freud's response: 'Your letter ... about a feeling you describe as "oceanic" has left me no peace' (23).
97. Sigmund Freud, *Civilization and Its Discontents*, trans. James Strachey (Standard Edition, London: Hogarth Press 1961), 64–5, 72; see *The Letters of Sigmund Freud*, ed. Ernst Freud (New York: Basic Books 1961), 389.
98. March, *Romain Rolland*, 100–1. His obsession led Rolland to identify with women and at times fantasize himself as a woman. Like Toynbee, he was drawn to Fra Angelico 'to forget brutal reality in the mystic reality of this world of souls, to lose myself in the divine Love, alone capable of filling the void within me' (p. 20).
99. T.S. Eliot, 'East Coker,' *Four Quartets* (New York: Harcourt, Brace & Co. 1943), 11
100. *Experiences*, 177
101. *Study*, 9: 185; *Experiences*, 201
102. Blaise Pascal, *Pensées*, trans. H. Stewart (New York: Pantheon Books 1950), 383
103. Ernest Hemingway, *Selected Letters* (New York: Charles Scribner's Sons 1981), 785
104. Carlos Baker, *Ernest Hemingway* (New York: Charles Scribner's Sons 1969), 505–6

105 Marcel Proust, *Remembrance of Things Past*, 3 vols, trans. Moncrieff-Kilmartin (New York: Random House 1981), 1: 48–9; cf. 3: 958–9
106 Ibid., 3: 903. Toynbee was going on ten when he was 'thunder-struck' by the prospect of leaving home for boarding-school: 'Till that moment, I had felt completely secure. I have never since recaptured that Eden-like state of existence'; *Experiences*, 3.
107 *Study*, 10: 130–1; Livy, *Periochae*, 89
108 *Historian's Conscience*, 162; *Experiences*, 121
109 *Study*, 10: 131 n.4; Velleius Paterculus 2.67
110 *Study*, 10: 131 n.4; Matt. 10:35
111 Toynbee wrote an interesting digression on viragos, including Olympias: 'The Monstrous Regiment of Women,' *Study*, 8: 651–63.
112 Eliot, *Four Quartets*, 38, 27; cf. *Toynbee on Toynbee* (ed. Urban), 40.
113 In his last book, *The Greeks and Their Heritages* (New York: Oxford University Press 1981), Toynbee repudiated the 'Higher Religions' and monotheism in favour of a polytheism that was reverent of Nature, the Great Mother; see T.W. Africa, 'The Final Vision of Arnold Toynbee,' *Historical Reflections/ Réflexions historiques* 10, no. 2 (1983): 221–8.
114 Emerson, *Essays*, 684

Toynbee as a Prophet of World Civilization

W. Warren Wagar

Arnold J. Toynbee is best remembered nowadays as a prodigiously learned student of comparative civilizations who made an elaborate case for the cyclical theory of world history. So he was; and so he did. But he was also, and perhaps most passionately of all, an explorer of the human future. In curious and perhaps unexpected ways, his prophetic vision is still relevant in these closing decades of the twentieth century.

Toynbee lived a strangely bifurcated life. He devoted long years to writing and editing the annual surveys of current events for the Royal Institute of International Affairs. At the same time, he maintained his standing as a professional historian specializing in ancient Greece and comparative world history, and he published his most important work, the twelve volumes of *A Study of History*. Clifton Fadiman proclaimed that 'of all the books published so far in this century,' *A Study of History* was 'the one most assured of being read a hundred years from now.'[1] It is unlikely that more than a handful of enthusiasts actually turned more than a few pages of the *Study* even in its best-selling days. But some people did read it, and its salient insights and forecasts achieved a wide currency.

When I first encountered Toynbee in my graduate-school days in the mid-1950s, what caught my eye at once was the way in which all his thought, all the great baroque stage machinery of the *Study*, pointed by a kind of irresistible force to the future of the human race. The history had to be there, and preferably in the richest profusion possible, to make the futurism persuasive. But what mattered most was that in the end Toynbee touched the fabulous distant shore where all things human enjoyed their grand triumphant consummation. Most of the scholars of his time only splashed about in local puddles. But Toynbee sailed on the high seas of world history and – wonder of wonders! – he actually got somewhere. After a terrific voyage, he landed.

For some mid-century critics, Toynbee's concern for the future was so pervasive that it diminished the credibility of his scholarship. The English historian Hugh Trevor-Roper, for example, suggested with tongue in cheek that perhaps Toynbee had cast himself as the divinely inspired prophet of a new world religion. There was just enough truth in his gibes to make them sting. Philip Bagby described Toynbee as 'a prophet – a prophet disguised as a "modern Western student of history,"' and some years later Roland N. Stromberg brought his critical study of Toynbee to a close with the chilling observation that 'like Karl Marx's, Toynbee's system of history was one of the last febrile products of the romantic imagination, masquerading as science.'[2]

But for scholars in the 1950s searching for clues to the destiny of humankind in the pages of world history, Toynbee's vaticinations came as a welcome relief. Looking around us, we saw great numbers of historians, whole armies of academic moles tunnelling through archives; but only one prophet, among the living members of his profession, only one voice enlisting the vast resources of historical scholarship in the discovery of the future.

As time went by, I did find several other writers and scholars of Toynbee's generation who offered comparable visions of things to come, visions of an approaching world civilization with a syncretic universal culture, promised, if not by the laws of history, then by the light of some other lamp, whether sociology, philosophy, biology, or physics. They ranged from Karl Jaspers, F.S.C. Northrop, and Pitirim Sorokin to Lewis Mumford and Julian Huxley, and included even one man of the cloth, the French Jesuit Pierre Teilhard de Chardin.

The eventual result of my searching was an overheated little book entitled *The City of Man: Prophecies of a World Civilization in Twentieth-Century Thought*.[3] Stromberg, if he had reviewed it, might have characterized it as 'one of the last febrile products of the romantic imagination, masquerading as intellectual history.' In any event, Toynbee played the star role in the book, as a glance through its index soon bears out, and without him, I should not have had the courage to write it.

Later on, Toynbee was a prime exhibit in evidence in a book of mine on the recent history of the idea of progress, and he was one of the 'prophet-fathers of the coming world civilization' to whom I dedicated my experiment in utopography, *Building the City of Man*, published in 1971.[4]

In short, for about ten years I was an ardent Toynbeean, not only a historian influenced by Toynbee's scholarship, but a publicist for world order and world civilization borrowing a good part of his message from Arnold J. Toynbee, the Prophet.

Somewhere in the mid-1970s, Toynbee lost his grip on my imagination. I drifted belatedly into a New Left, meta-Marxist orientation. Frustrated by his sterile obsession with religion and his stunning ignorance of political economy, I stopped reading him or even thinking about him. Looking at his later works now, for the first time, I am embarrassed by their flatness and repetitiveness and strangely selfless self-importance. Even the earlier books, on re-examination, appear seriously flawed. Although clearly more sophisticated, they suffer from a windy religiosity and a pachydermal prose style that unites the worst qualities of Henry James with the dreary longueurs of an over-educated Anglo-Catholic pulpiteer.

All that remains after the settling of the dust is the recognition that Toynbee did struggle with the great issues of human destiny, and that he strove to anticipate a credible future keyed to an interpretation, however risky or far-fetched, of the dynamics of world history. But this effort is more than enough to justify his life and award him a place of high honour in the most secular of pantheons.

In assessing Toynbee's contribution to the discovery of the future, a point of special interest is his response to the modern Western faith in human progress. Over and over again, Toynbee excoriated modern civilization and escaped in his imagination back to earlier, simpler, sweeter days with the help of his considerable command of pre-modern texts and languages and myths. But he failed to shake himself loose from what is, after all, the most characteristic and inspiring dogma of our epoch, the conviction that the human race has made a better life for itself down through the millennia, and may do better still in times to come. Toynbee's ambiguous belief in progress went hand in hand with his 'knee-jerk liberalism'[5] on current public issues, and goes far to explain why his knee always did jerk.

It may be helpful to examine first the great pains Toynbee took to make clear that he was *not* an apostle of progress. The most obvious point is that *A Study of History*, all twelve volumes, describes the cyclical process by which civilizations germinate, flower, and decay. Toynbee saw progress of a sort in the earlier phases of the cycle, but in due course the progress was reversed. The creative minority changed into a dominant minority, as Dr Jekyll turned into Mr Hyde, and disintegration ensued. Like Oswald Spengler before him, Toynbee tended to idealize or romanticize the times of growth and denigrate the times of decay. *Saeva necessitas* left the men of the latter days with few options, and it would have been heartless to apply the term 'progress' to the choices fate constrained them to make.

Of course there could still be such a thing as cumulative progress, gains of one sort or another from one generation of civilizations to the next, but on several occasions Toynbee seemed to scotch that notion as well. In volume twelve (1981), for example, where he reconsidered his use of terms, he affirmed that no objective criteria for determining what constituted progress were possible, that progress occurred (when it did) only in discontinuous bursts, and that although one might discern progress along many separate lines, it was nonsense to speak of progress 'in the absolute.'[6] In his posthumously published dialogue with Daisaku Ikeda, he admitted that cumulative progress could be traced in science and technology, but denied that the power such progress had conferred on humanity made things one whit better for us. 'It merely increases,' he said, 'the material magnitude of the effect of good and evil actions,'[7] which is precisely what neo-orthodox Christian theologians had argued throughout Toynbee's lifetime.[8]

But elsewhere and even in the same texts, Toynbee contradicted himself on the question of progress. Or, let us say, he appeared to contradict himself. Having adopted a cyclical theory of the history of civilizations, he obviously could not afford to be suspected of simultaneously harbouring a theory of rectilinear progress: therefore, he had no choice but to reject what he called doctrines of progress 'in the absolute.' Nor, as a rebel against the materialism and secularism of modernity, could he very well associate himself even marginally with a reading of history that saw progress in science and technology and the powers of reason as an engine of social or spiritual progress. As he told Ikeda, *that* illusion began to crumble in 1914 and was finished off by the atomic bomb in 1945.[9]

Yet it remained possible for Toynbee to adhere to the essence of the progressivist tradition. Few of the upholders of that tradition since Turgot and Kant have preached a simple-minded doctrine of relentless rectilinear advance, and not all have made progress in science and technology the fundamental cause of human betterment. The heart of the faith in progress of modern Western culture has always been the belief that when everything is taken into full account, and assigned its full value (positive or negative, as the case may be), humankind experiences net gain in the spheres of life deemed most important by the believer. Such gain may be traced from the past into the future and enables the believer to stand back and say, of the human experience as a whole, that it has been good and may well get better. This is a distinctively modern and Western world-view, which one may discover not only in positivists and materialists but also in such other characteristic products of modernity as American Unitarian divines, German idealist philosophers, French and British vitalists, and prophets of the Italian Risorgimento.

To return to Toynbee, it is clear that in this broader sense, he did espouse a doctrine of progress. He was never, like many twentieth-century irrationalists and back-to-religionists, a cynic, a misanthrope, or a political reactionary. Although he told Ikeda there was 'no such thing as cumulative, social, spiritual progress,' by the end of the dialogue he was calling for a closure of the gap between the ethical and technological performances of humankind, which brings to mind the old 'culture lag' theory of William F. Ogburn.[10] If ethical progress were not possible, why bother to demand it?

In other works, Toynbee detected both social and spiritual progress in history. In volume twelve of the *Study*, he summed up his concepts of both;[11] and in *Surviving the Future*, a record of his conversations with another Japanese scholar, Kei Wakaizumi, published in 1971, he spoke of the two great 'waves' of human spiritual progress. The first had taken place in the earliest centuries of the history of civilization, leading to the first major religions and the building of complex urbanized societies. The second had occurred between the eighth century

BC and the seventh century AD, and had resulted in the rise of the so-called 'higher' religions and philosophies, such as Buddhism, Platonism, Christianity, and Islam. Now, said Toynbee, it was time for a third wave of spiritual progress, for a crash program (as it were) in religion and ethics, which citizens should make their governments subsidize, to shorten the growing 'morality gap' caused by the incredible progress of human power in modern times.[12]

But the best evidence for Toynbee as a believer in general human progress is the emphasis that he laid, in the last thirty years of his life, on the coming of a great, ecumenical, world-wide civilization higher than any known hitherto and made possible by that third wave of spiritual progress for which he appealed in *Surviving the Future*.

So long as he confined himself to the comparative history of those units of study he called civilizations, in the plural, he remained a cyclicist and a relativist, like Spengler before him. But Toynbee did not always confine himself to comparative history. From the 1940s onward, what most held his attention was the possibility that history as we know it can be transcended, and within – not just outside – time. As he argued in volume seven (1954), the rise of the higher religions was an event of unprecedented significance, of greater moment than the civilizations from which they sprang or to which they gave birth. The appearance of the higher religions prefigured, or so he devoutly hoped, the coming of a new planetary civilization in which the cycles of history would be abolished altogether.

Toynbee's most effective image for the course of history as a whole, embracing past and future alike, was his myth (in Plato's sense) of the climber's pitch, broached in volumes one and three (1934), and then developed more fully in the final chapter of volume twelve. In this age of plural civilizations, he contended, humanity 'has been making a number of attempts to scale the cliff-face that towers up from the ledge reached by Primitive Man. The next ledge above ... is invisible to climbers who are striving to reach it. All they know is that they feel compelled to risk their necks in the hope of gaining this next ledge and in the faith that the endeavour is worth while.'[13]

In other words, history was not properly seen as some kind of treadmill or Ferris wheel. It was a progress, both empirically and normatively, an advance from animality to the long lazy morning of savagery (the ledge below, in Toynbee's metaphor), then from savagery to civilization (which consisted of a series of desperate attempts to scale the cliff-face), and finally from civilization to what Toynbee hoped would be a long sunny afternoon of sainthood (the epoch of peace and unity on the ledge above, once we had finally scaled the cliffs of history).

On the next ledge, as all of Toynbee's later work reveals, great wars would be unknown, thanks to the establishment of a world state. The higher religions would 'school themselves to playing [their various parts] in harmony,' and there would be brotherhood and justice for all, ending the exploitation of man by man.[14]

Humanity might, Toynbee pointed out, choose to create such a world the easy way, by programs of social conditioning as foreseen by Aldous Huxley in *Brave New World*. But the alternative to this dismal empire of the ants was a kingdom of saints, the coming of a race of human beings who had raised themselves – like the saints of the past – 'above the average level of human goodness.' If, in the past, some men and women could achieve sainthood, he saw no reason why all men and women could not achieve it in the future, with the help of divine grace. Not that such saints would be perfect, any more than the saints of history were perfect. 'Even in a saintly society the victory over self-centredness, collective and individual, would never be complete ... This means that the next ledge will be the scene of a spiritual struggle ... not less intense than the struggle to climb, from ledge to ledge, up the face of the cliff.'[15]

Nevertheless, Toynbee left no doubts in the minds of his readers that the building of the City of Man would represent a triumph for all the human race, unique in history.

If mankind does respond to the challenge of its present self-imposed ordeal by saving itself from self-inflicted genocide, this will have been the reward of a common effort to transcend all the traditional divisions and to live as one family for the first time since mankind made its first appearance on this planet. This *union sacrée* in the face of imminent self-destruction will be, if it is achieved, Man's finest achievement and most thrilling experience up to date. From the new position of charity and hope which Man will thereby have won for himself, all the past histories of the previous divisions of the human race will be seen, in retrospect, to be so many parts of one common historic heritage. They will be seen as leading up to unity, and as opening out, for a united human race, future prospects of which no human being could have dreamed in the age of unfettered parochialism.[16]

Toynbee did not supply a utopian text comparable to Wells's *A Modern Utopia* or Shaw's *Back to Methuselah* depicting the coming *civitas sanctorum* of his prophetic imagination.[17] It is unlikely that he could have done so; in any case he kept shifting his ground through the long course of his scholarly career.

All that seems clear is Toynbee's intuition of the coming world society as an organism, much like the various full-blown civilizations of the past. Even today the foundations were being laid 'for a single world-wide society and for a uniform world-wide culture that will take its first shape within a Western framework.' But, Toynbee added, 'it will become less specifically Western in complexion as all the cultural heritages of all the extant societies come to be the common possession of the whole of mankind.'[18] In due course the human race would constitute a single family, culturally and socially unified.

At its heart, enabling it to live in peace and harmony, the human family would enjoy communion with all being through the ministry of the 'higher religions,' which Toynbee identified and defined in volume seven of the *Study*. Given the importance of religion in his world-view, one might expect that he would have called for the invention of a new ecumenical faith to undergird cosmopolis, but in most of his pronouncements on the subject, he inclined rather to a tolerant pluralism. In volume seven he observed that each of the higher religions – limited in that text to Christianity, Mahayana Buddhism, Hinduism, and Islam – met different psychological needs, and all would have their parts to play in the coming world civilization. Although they would recognize one another's validity and collaborate in the common task, each would go on flourishing as a separate entity. Enlarging the list to include Hinayana Buddhism, Zoroastrianism, and Judaism, he continued to assume in volume twelve that they would coexist peacefully in the ecumenical future. In *Change and Habit*, he devoted a whole chapter to the premise that 'fusion' of the higher religions, far from being desirable, would impoverish the culture of cosmopolis.[19]

But he was not consistent. His 1955 Hewitt Lectures, published as

Christianity among the Religions of the World, anticipated that one of the higher religions would eventually prevail, just as in a sporting event.

> In a peaceful competition, the best of the competing religions will eventually win the allegiance of the whole human race. If we believe that God is love, we shall also believe that the whole human race will eventually turn to whichever vision of God is the fullest vision and gives the greatest means of grace. We can also forecast that the winning religion, whichever it may be, will not eliminate the other religions that it replaces. Even if it does replace them, it will achieve this by absorbing into itself what is best in them.[20]

In his conversations with Ikeda, Toynbee went a step further. He anticipated the 'worldwide spread of some kind of common religion,' but insisted that because all the current religions had proved 'unsatisfactory,' humanity needed either a revolutionary new faith or 'a new version of one of the old religions ... transformed so radically that it would be almost unrecognizable.'[21]

His correspondence with Father Columba Cary-Elwes, monk and teacher at Ampleforth Abbey in Yorkshire, reveals a similar pattern. As early as 1947, Toynbee mused to Father Columba that some day the higher religions might coalesce. Or perhaps 'one will absorb the others and will be influenced by what it has absorbed: as Christianity already has digested Judaism, Zoroastrianism, Isis and Osiris, Ishtar and Tammuz, the Magna Mater and Attis, and most of Greek philosophy.' At other times he was content to observe that the higher religions all pursued the same ultimate goal, and needed to work together in peace and fraternity. 'I think we have to coexist,' he wrote to Father Columba in 1966, 'loving each other and working together for good against evil, while recognising that the claims that we each make for our own religions are not convincing to our neighbors.'[22]

The same waverings marked his thoughts on the political shape of things to come. At first he had joined the chorus of voices immediately after the Second World War that pressed the case for a world federation. In *Civilization on Trial* (1948), he urged the establishment of 'a constitutional co-operative system of world government,' assigning it a higher priority in the short term than even the recovery of religious faith.[23] Taking up the question of the prospects of Western civilization in volume nine of the *Study* (1954), he maintained that the elimination of distance and the multiplication of power made the arrival of a universal state inevitable, through conquest or through federation. His preference was a federal polity, which would bring the pattern of the first 6000 years of world history to a glorious finale.[24] Similar views found their way into volume twelve, where he added the notion that world-wide diasporas of kindred spirits would supplement and perhaps supplant the traditional national communities as components of a future world order.[25]

But his intimate familiarity with the universal states of the past and a growing impatience with the course of events in his own time led Toynbee more than once to suggest other outcomes. In *Change and Habit*, he repeated the assertion that a future world state would have to be a consensual federal polity, but later in the same chapter canvassed the possibility that the United States and the Soviet Union might use their virtual monopoly of nuclear weapons 'to put the World in order and keep it in order.'[26] The idea of a consortium of superpowers came back, two years later, in the form of a proposal for a 'Russo-American joint dictatorship,' admittedly undemocratic and yet preferable to atomic war.[27] George Orwell had foreseen exactly such a 'solution' to the nuclear dilemma in *Nineteen Eighty-Four*, the vision of a future world order made possible by the tacit collaboration of the superpowers, but Orwell, unlike Toynbee, viewed it as a fate worse than death.[28]

In his last years Toynbee became still more inclined to consider undemocratic alternatives, although he continued to find them disagreeable. 'As I look back on the social history of past ages,' he said in 1971, 'I do fear that, in the present state of the world, the establishment of a dictatorial world state in the style of the Akkadian, Persian, Roman, and Chinese Empires is the most probable development.' Such a dictatorship would arrive not through warfare but would be 'imposed on the majority by a ruthless, efficient, and fanatical minority, inspired by some ideology or religion.' Humankind would 'acquiesce in a harsh Leninian kind of dictatorship as a lesser evil than self-extermination.'[29]

The vision of a global Leninism reappeared in the Toynbee-Ikeda dialogue, with the further thought (foreshadowed by a passage in *Change and Habit*) that the initiative would be seized not by Soviet

Russia or the United States but by a resurgent China.[30] It all sounds like Toynbee's sometime muse, Oswald Spengler, writing of the coming Caesars in *The Decline of the West*. But Toynbee remained enough of an optimist to expect that in time this baleful regime would pass and yield to a truly democratic polity kindled by revolutions of the heart and spirit.[31]

His final reflections on world dictatorship remind one not only of Spengler but also of Marx and his anticipation of a future in two phases in the *Critique of the Gotha Program*: the necessarily harsh, necessarily flawed first age of communism, ushered in by a dictatorship of the proletariat; and the second, higher age, characterized by the dissolution of public power and the arrival of a kingdom of freedom and justice unlike anything known in history heretofore.

Indeed, as Roland Stromberg has hinted, in its broadest contours Toynbee's vision of history and the future parallels the vision set forth by Marx and Engels.[32] Both visions, in turn, derive at least some of their structure from biblical apocalyptic.[33] In Marx and Engels the stage of primitive communism corresponds to the ledge below in Toynbee. The cyclical agonies of Toynbee's twenty-odd civilizations correspond to the rise and fall first of slavery, then of feudalism, and ultimately of capitalism in Marx. And the city of saints occupying the next ledge in Toynbee corresponds to the stateless and classless future under communism. In both instances what we call history is a time of tribulations, a time of transition from innocence to beatitude. In both theodicies, as in the biblical version, history functions as a necessary evil – testing, trying, proving, and perfecting the finite, fallible creature of flesh, so that he may be ready, in the end, for true freedom and true life.

Both Marx and Toynbee would object strenuously to any comparison of their systems with biblical apocalyptic, because both imagined themselves wearing the spattered white smock of the laboratory scientist, and because both argued that the achievement of the next stage in world history would only inaugurate a whole new adventure for humanity, fraught with its own as yet unseen travails and challenges. But the parallels exist and should be noted for whatever they are worth. Perhaps there are just a limited number of ways in which it is psychologically satisfying for *Homo sapiens* to express its hopes and fears.

In any event, the way chosen by Toynbee is not really out of step with the march of modern thought. He was a thoroughly modern man, even and perhaps especially when he was most vigorous in his denunciations of modernity. On some points, at least, he also had more than an inkling of the shape of things to come. His Orwellian forecast of a global consortium of the superpowers or their managerial élites to keep the world's peace may yet prove accurate. So, in the longer run, may his vision of a democratic world state and the transcendence of the cyclical pattern of the past. If not, if Toynbee was wrong, if the present nation-state system is impervious to the winds of change, we are unlikely to have any future at all.

NOTES

Portions of this essay are reprinted, with permission, from *Futures Research Quarterly* 2, no. 3 (Fall 1986), published by the World Future Society, 4916 St Elmo Ave., Bethesda, Maryland 20814.

1 Quoted on the box of the Dell Laurel edition of D.C. Somervell's abridgments; Toynbee, *A Study of History*, 2 vols (New York 1965).
2 See Hugh R. Trevor-Roper, 'Arnold Toynbee's Millennium,' in *Men and Events: Historical Essays* (New York: Harper 1957), 299–324; Philip Bagby, *Culture and History: Prolegomena to the Comparative Study of Civilizations* (London: Longmans Green 1958), 181; and Roland N. Stromberg, *Arnold J. Toynbee: Historian for an Age in Crisis* (Carbondale: Southern Illinois University Press 1972), 113
3 W. Warren Wagar, *The City of Man: Prophecies of a World Civilization in Twentieth-Century Thought* (Boston: Houghton Mifflin 1963; revised, Baltimore: Penguin Books 1967)
4 Wagar, *Good Tidings: The Belief in Progress from Darwin to Marcuse* (Bloomington: Indiana University Press 1972), esp. 199–201 and 291–4; and *Building the City of Man: Outlines of a World Civilization* (New York: Grossman 1971; San Francisco: W.H. Freeman 1972)
5 Attributed to W.L. White in Stromberg, 82
6 Toynbee, *A Study of History*, 12 vols (London and New York: Oxford University Press 1934–61), 12: 266–7
7 Toynbee and Daisaku Ikeda, *The Toynbee-Ikeda Dialogue: Man Himself Must Choose* (Tokyo: Kodansha 1976), 325
8 See, for example, Reinhold Niebuhr, *Faith and History: A Comparison of Christian and Modern Views of History* (New York: Charles Scribner's 1949)

9 *Toynbee-Ikeda Dialogue*, 324
10 Ibid., 325 and 342
11 *Study*, 12: 267
12 Toynbee, *Surviving the Future* (London and New York: Oxford University Press 1971), 38–41
13 *Study*, 12: 562
14 Ibid., 7: 374
15 Ibid., 12: 568–70
16 Ibid., 12: 143
17 The general architecture of Toynbee's future world civilization, pieced together from widely scattered references, is discussed in Wagar, *The City of Man*, esp. 85–92, 146–7, 162–5, and 229–31. At the time *The City of Man* was published, however, Toynbee still had twelve productive years of life before him, and his views changed on various points during that period.
18 *Study*, 12: 309
19 Toynbee, *Change and Habit: The Challenge of Our Time* (London and New York: Oxford University Press 1966), chap. 10, 'Is a Fusion of the Higher Religions Desirable?'
20 Toynbee, *Christianity among the Religions of the World* (New York: Charles Scribner's 1957), 110
21 *Toynbee-Ikeda Dialogue*, 245 and 295
22 Toynbee to Columba Cary-Elwes, 31 Aug. 1947, in *An Historian's Conscience: The Correspondence of Arnold J. Toynbee and Columba Cary-Elwes, Monk of Ampleforth*, ed. Christian Peper (Boston: Beacon Press 1986), 199; and Toynbee to Cary-Elwes, 26 Nov. 1966, 471; see also ibid., 292–3 (where Toynbee admits his own preference for Christianity), 390, 478, and 544.
23 Toynbee, *Civilization on Trial* (New York: Oxford University Press 1948), 39–40 and cf. p. 27
24 See esp. *Study*, 9: 555
25 Ibid., 12: 215–17. The 1972 abridgment of the *Study* prepared by Toynbee in collaboration with Jane Caplan saw the world state beginning as 'a voluntary political association in which all the cultural elements of a number of living civilizations will continue to assert themselves'; Toynbee and Caplan, *A Study of History* (New York: Oxford University Press 1972), 318.
26 *Change and Habit*, 140 and 157
27 Toynbee, 'Peace, Empire, and World Government,' *Saturday Review*, 29 April 1967, 21
28 George Orwell, *Nineteen Eighty-Four* [1949] (New York: New American

Library 1961), esp. 152–64. This passage contains the third chapter, entitled 'War Is Peace,' of the alleged underground book by Emmanuel Goldstein from which Orwell's hero Winston learns how the international system of his day really works.
29 *Surviving the Future*, 113–14; and cf. p. 66.
30 *Toynbee-Ikeda Dialogue*, 217 and 233; see also *Change and Habit*, 157–8.
31 *Surviving the Future*, 66 and 117–18
32 *Arnold J. Toynbee*, 83, 91, 93, and 113
33 See Frederik L. Polak, *The Image of the Future*, 2 vols (Leyden and New York: Oceana Publications 1961), 1: 268–90 (on Marx) and 1: 391–401 (on Toynbee).

A Study of History and a World at War:

Toynbee's Two Great Enterprises

Roland N. Stromberg

Let us remind ourselves that the series entitled *Survey of International Affairs* constituted Arnold Toynbee's other lifetime project, taking probably more of his time (and certainly more pages) than *A Study of History*. He published the first three volumes of the *Study* ten years after he began his connection with the Royal (at first, the British) Institute of International Relations at Chatham House in 1924. During thirty-three years of active association with the RIIA, Toynbee wrote the annual *Survey*, a volume or volumes covering the world of international affairs for a given year, usually published within months of the year's conclusion, and offering both an authoritative factual record and a masterful analysis. This yearly publication is an achievement as remarkable in its way as the *Study* – certainly if considered sheerly as a physical *tour de force*. Toynbee was hired, evidently, because he was the only known person who could do this job at a time when the budget allowed for hardly any staff; and after he left, the volumes ceased within a couple of years, no one being able to replace him. No such enterprise has ever existed since. The long row of fat volumes of the *Survey of International Affairs*, each largely written by Toynbee and bearing his unmistakable stamp, represents as unrepeatable an accomplishment as the twelve volumes of *A Study of History*. Toynbee did both of them simultaneously! Beginning in 1927 he was able to complete the *Survey* by June, leaving his assistant (and future wife) Veronica Boulter to see the volume through the press, and then work on the *Study* from about July to November of each year.

I think the *Survey* is worth looking at as closely as the more celebrated *Study* because it is remarkably good, containing splendid writing and insights. In his modest way Toynbee later disparaged it,[1] but we should not let him mislead us. Indeed later research inevitably overtook this work to some degree, but it none the less contains many things that endure and that students of world affairs in this dramatic era should use. To the student of Toynbee, it reveals his vision and personality as much as does the other great opus. The *Surveys* are often insightful, and contain all manner of subtle perceptions, along with data carefully gathered from all that was known at the time, much of which remains relevant; elegantly expressed, reflecting the mood of the times, but valuable beyond that 'historic' significance.

To those who would urge that the two works represent entirely different levels of achievement, the reply might be that the level of thought, the organization of empirical data, and the style of the *Survey* compare favourably with the admittedly more pretentious *Study*. What is contained in this score of volumes on international relations is a vast history of one of the most important of all historical subjects, the world crisis of 1919–39.[2] Though some of the parts were always farmed out to a few experts (for instance, on economic matters), and Veronica Boulter was clearly an invaluable assistant, the *Survey* was as much Toynbee's personal achievement as the other work. It contains much of his most distinctive thought. Herein he gave expression to one of his two sides (Janus-like, as he often said). The mixture in Toynbee of shrewd practical realism and lofty moralizing has often been noted. If I might intrude a personal experience, the only time I ever met and had the opportunity to talk at some length with Toynbee (at College Park, Maryland, during his lecture tour of 1961), I recall being surprised that he wanted to talk not about some weighty theory or spiritual profundity, which in my innocence I expected, but about the immediate details of world affairs – with great zest and incisiveness. He was more like Walter Lippmann or Henry Kissinger than the Henri Bergson or Carl Jung I had anticipated. Or perhaps that evening Janus chose to reveal that side of himself.

Toynbee claimed that the two enterprises were intimately related. 'I do not believe I could have produced either the *Survey* or the *Study* if I had not been at work on both of them simultaneously.' 'In writing the *Study* I was providing myself with [the] indispensable historical background for the *Survey*, and providing it on the *Survey*'s own global scale.' 'Conversely, the *Survey* benefited the *Study*.'[3] His reasons may be somewhat questionable. Every historian, he said, must have a foot in the contemporary world, among real people, in order to understand the dead people that he as historian is writing about. This reasoning seems unhistorical: we cannot, it says, understand the people of former times except as analogues of living ones. If he means only that we must have met some real people, this comment is trivial and does not compel us to *write* contemporary history. And to argue that the *Study* was only background for the *Survey* is clearly wrong: the *Study* is crammed with exotic personages and periods having not the remotest connection to the crises of the 1930s, and was designed to serve the wholly different purpose of supporting laws about the cycles of growth and decline in different human societies.

Moreover, the *Study* is probably weakest on modern Europe, the focus of the *Survey*. Toynbee knew Greek and Roman history best, he became a considerable Islamic scholar, he struggled manfully with China, South America, and many an ancient and exceptional culture; but, oddly, on nineteenth- and twentieth-century Europe there is relatively little in the *Study* and what little there is is strangely focused. Our Western society, born in the early Middle Ages, experienced the first of its three death-rattles in the sixteenth and seventeenth centuries and evidently spent the nineteenth convulsed by the last deadly cycle of 'Wars of Nationality,' 'war followed war in an ascending order of intensity.'[4] This is about all we hear of the whole of the teeming, dynamic, revolutionary nineteenth century in the *Study*. In any case the essential nature of the *Study* is not to supply background for a sequential history, but to create a comparative schema for the necessary stages of all civilizations. It would hardly help you much to understand Hitler's 1936 foreign policy to know that every cycle of war is followed by a *pax oecumenica*, followed by the secession of internal and external proletariats, and so on.

Toynbee was clearly off base concerning the logical reasons he gave for the two projects supporting each other. That they did so psychologically has frequently been suggested: Toynbee fled from one extreme to another, finding relief from the meticulous fact-finding of the *Surveys* in the expansive speculations of the *Study*. But this view overlooks the fact that the latter is usually crammed with specifics, while the former not infrequently indulges in typically Toynbeean flights of moralizing and generalizing. The two projects are not really that different in form and style. It is more plausible to say that they jointly supported his Promethean ambition to 'drink the ocean.' 'Together they gave me the widest horizon that I was capable of attaining.'[5] Both projects demanded those qualities that Toynbee so superbly possessed. Both were things he could do and had perfected a technique for doing – things that suited his genius and his sense of mission.

Toynbee's obsession, frequently confessed, was this desire to drink the ocean. At other places in this volume we have heard about his mystic experience in 1919 of the wholeness of history flowing through him, and of his other mystic experiences akin to those in which the self is absorbed into Nature or God. Toynbee's method of work, as he described it, was the holistic one of first 'seeing your subject or your problem as a whole.'[6] His talent consisted in a combination of an extraordinary capacity for detailed empirical research with an equally remarkable ability to generalize and synthesize, and then to bestow upon the results an aesthetic effect of great charm – a fatal charm to devotees of AJT, but lost upon that considerable number who have always disparaged him. His capacity for work, his driving energy, and severe work ethic he variously attributed to his religious heritage, his examination-taking childhood, or his guilt feelings of having been spared death in the Great War that claimed so many of his schoolmates.

A key component in his synthesizing ability was a prodigious memory. 'I have a memory that makes it possible for me to pick out what I need,' he said, fact or quotation, from an enormous filing system that he was able to keep in his head, instantly available.[7] About the style, we ought only to note that it was the most important element of all. Toynbee was perhaps the last great historian, maybe even the only one apart from a rare few predecessors like Gibbon and Carlyle (in English), who is so distinctively recognizable that one need read only a few lines to know who is writing. I refer here to the great writings of the 1930s, the first six volumes of the *Study* and the *Survey*, especially for 1931–7. It seems that Toynbee greatly degenerated in his later writings, for reasons it would be interesting to explore. If he was at the height of his power in the tragic thirties, we should not make the mistake of leaving the *Survey* out of consideration. The writing of the *Survey* compares to the *Study* in the richness of metaphor, the meditative and allusive style, and the wide-ranging historical comparisons. It is quite as compelling as the *Study* and contains much of his finest writing.

We ought to be equally clear that these were the superb qualities of which Toynbee had the defects. He was not much of a thinker. Ortega y Gasset remarked that 'Mr. Toynbee is, in philosophical matters, a man of enchanting and paradisical innocence.'[8] This very (and very British) innocence of metaphysical depths actually facilitated Toynbee's generalizing, for he could ignore the subtleties and qualifications that were capable of inhibiting the generalizations of others. The urge to generalize also encouraged a tendency to be gullible about factual matters, which numerous critics of Toynbee have alleged.[9] This was the same gullibility Robert Conquest once noted in Bertrand Russell: so avid was his analytical faculty that he seized uncritically on the data that were grist for his mill, not bothering to question their validity as facts.

Both the *Study* and the *Survey* demanded the absorption of an immense amount of data and its reduction to an order. Each was global. And each perhaps dealt with human affairs at a level of abstractness that enabled them to be fitted into a pattern. It is one of the criticisms of Toynbee that he seldom engages with human actions in a really human way, but sees these as symbols or as ideas.[10] There is a mythic quality about the *Surveys*, just as there is about the *Study*. They helped create the myth of Collective Security.[11] Toynbee's is a marvellous make-believe world, yet we should note that it is also richly furnished with specific facts. Amid the general dismissal by historians of Toynbee's 'system' as too rigid, and doing violence to the full range of data, there is not enough recognition of the richness of his empirical data. Part of the wonder of Toynbee is that his hunger for facts was voracious, insatiable – an aspect of his drinking-the-ocean complex. The same is true of another systematizing philosopher-historian accused of ignoring mere facts: J.H. Randall, Jr, says of Hegel that 'he loved facts, hard facts and cold facts, and the harder and colder they were the better he loved them.'[12] (*Pace*, as Toynbee would put it, the conventional opinion.) The same may be said of Toynbee. His compulsion to travel, seeking to devour as much of the historic world as he could with his eyes, is a related trait.

Any reader of the *Study* – not the unfortunately abridged editions, so often the basis of popular views of Toynbee – knows that it is among other things a kaleidoscope of exotic facts, meant to be bathed in, read for sheer enjoyment. Fitting them into his great pattern is the least of the rewards, for many, in reading Toynbee. The whole, of course, communicates a certain vision – the most valuable part of any thinker – rather than his 'system.' But the *Surveys* abound in minor delights. 'He combined political insight with political unsophistication,' Martin Wight observed of Toynbee in a judgment all will echo.[13] In what follows we may be able to cite some examples of both the perceptiveness and the naïveté.

A co-reading of the two great texts, the *Study* and the *Survey*, reveals elements of one appearing in the other. The *Survey* volumes of the 1930s are filled with passages relevant to the *Study*, and vice versa. To begin with, it seems likely that the whole theme of Western civilization's decline and disintegration, developed so brilliantly in volumes four to six of *A Study of History*, germinated in the 1931 *Survey of International Relations*. True, Toynbee dated the inception of the *Study* from 1919–20, just after the Great War, as an idea 'swimming in his mind.' He made an outline in 1921, but, occupied first with his abortive career as Koraes Professor at the University of London and then with launching the *Survey*, he did not really get into the *Study* until 1930. Travels in 1929 interrupted the schedule for that year. Obviously he made rapid progress on the first three volumes, published in 1934. It seems likely that these were older ideas mulled over in his mind for a decade. Volumes four to six, written in the 1930s, are, it seems to me, work of a higher level than the first three; they contain his greatest writing and they rightly made his reputation. It was not until after their publication in 1939 that Toynbee took the world by storm. Coinciding with the coming of the Second World War, read during and just after it, their atmosphere of high tragic drama deeply impressed a generation.

But it was in 1931 that thinking people first felt impending doom. As Toynbee write in the 1931 *Survey*: 'The year 1931 was distinguished from previous years ... by one outstanding feature. In 1931 men and women all over the world were seriously contemplating and finally discussing the possibility that the western system of Society might break down and cease to work.'[14] And this, he thinks, for the first time in all its long history. We may well think of many other prophecies of doom from far back, and especially of many during and just after the terrible 1914–18 war. But Toynbee, who in the 1928 *Survey* had quoted Prime Minister Stanley Baldwin – 'Who in Europe does not know that one more war in the West and the civilization of the ages will fall with as great a shock as that of Rome?' – clearly meant to distinguish between a vague fleeting fear and a lively sense of certain doom. For him as for others, especially in Britain, the latter feeling suddenly came in 1931.[15] A year that saw the beginnings of conflict in the Far East, the upsurge of Nazism in Germany, Stalin's war on the peasants, the split and fall of the British Labour government, and above all the onset of the Great Depression was indeed, as Toynbee named it in the mordant essay that begins the 1931 *Survey*, *annus terribilis*. 'We are betrayed by what is false within' – those lines from Meredith that constitute the *leitmotif* of Toynbee's great world-symphony on the theme of nemesis appear here first.[16] It is plausible to suggest that Toynbee's drive to write *A Study of History* arose from the stimulus given to his mind by chronicling in the *Survey* the decline of the West in its relentless drift towards chaos and war from 1931 on. It was at this time that the *Study* was written, after having lain more or less dormant before, even if Toynbee did sketch an outline earlier.

Such a hypothesis receives support from a careful comparison of the two texts, the six volumes of the *Study* (1934–9) and the 1931–7 volumes of the *Survey*. There are numerous passages linking the two great enterprises. I would like to select for discussion a couple of instances in which Janus-Toynbee finds his two roles ambivalent or contradictory.

The 1933 volume of the *Survey* of course observed that the event of the year was Hitler's accession to power in Germany. Toynbee examines and analyses National Socialism with the aid of a concept drawn from *A Study of History*, viewing it as 'the consummation – or *reductio ad absurdum*' of the religion of nationalism, 'the deification and worship of parochial human communities,' heir of the medieval city-state and the Italian Renaissance state. National Socialism's most notable intellectual source was Machiavelli. The Nazi movement was also, Toynbee says, related in some secondary way to the more immediate context of recovery from the defeat of the First World War; but its basic and primary characteristic he situates in this deeply rooted and Europe-wide movement of nationalism. He also diverges to compare the Germany of 1918–33 with the France of 1815–30, as parallel cases of recovery, indulging in his familiar passion for such comparisons, and his tendency to find rather occult analogies – exactly fifteen years in both cases. Western nationalism is a 'ghost of the Graeco-Roman past' resurrected in the age of Machiavelli, masked at first by dynasticism, that is, the worship of a person rather than of the community directly, and retarded by a weakening Christianity, which Toynbee sees as ecumenical and anti-national, opposing the idolatry that, in Augustinian fashion, he thought is at bottom the love of self rather than God. Beginning in 1775 nationalism became a direct idolatry. Hitler's tribalism stands in the lineage of the Investiture controversy, the Medicis, and George Washington; it is nothing but the last stages of a steadily worsening attack of idolatrous self-worship that the pagan Greeks began and the modern masses have finished.[17]

Whatever we may think of this theory of Nazism, it does not seem to fit the immediate situation Toynbee must analyse as a commentator on international relations in 1933. He sees that Hitler is radically different and much more dangerous that other nationalists, uniquely brutal and aggressive, raising immediately the question of European stability. Toynbee offers no explanation of this violence, which in terms of the above analysis hardly follows. Why should the German Nazis be so drastically different from other modern forms of nationalism, since in Toynbee's view they must all be equally degraded and sinister? He uses the term 'totalitarian' without explaining it. He notes the instinctive British disgust at Nazi methods – again without offering an explanation. These pages of the 1933 *Survey* devoted to Hitler's new regime are perceptive indeed in identifying immediately the absolutely threatening, aggressive nature of the Nazi government – a new dimension, not just another regime. Few others can have seen this reality so early, so clearly. These pages show the genius of Toynbee the political analyst. But they do not at all fit the theory of Toynbee the theorist of history, which he imports into this context as an explanatory device.

One of the minor triumphs of this passage, worth mentioning as just an example of Toynbee's shrewdness in small details, is his explanation of why the French seemed so strangely calm and even pleased by Hitler's victory in Germany. It was because they were happy to see their dire predictions fulfilled, which the world had so long disbelieved – the satisfaction of being able to say, 'I told you so!'

Perceptive in these small touches and in identifying the nature of Hitler immediately, Toynbee fails to account for the specific Nazi qualities by simply appealing to his general theory that he develops in the *Study of History*. There are other philosophical reflections on nationalism and war dispersed through the *Survey*. The section in the 1928 volume on the background of the Kellogg-Briand Peace Pact, which greatly caught Toynbee's imagination, is one example. His enthusiasm for this product of the idealistic popular peace movement, the ban-the-bomb equivalent of its day, is characteristic of Toynbee, or one of the Toynbees; at other times in the *Survey* he is far from naïve, showing a keen appreciation of the realities of power politics and of human frailties.

His mastery of style may be illustrated by a passage from the 1934 *Survey*:

In Europe, the 'postwar period' after the General War of 1914–18 passed away in the course of the years 1933 and 1934. The first audible stroke of its death-knell was struck on the 30th of January 1933, when Herr Hitler came into power in Berlin; and, amid the gathering tumult of the next incoming age a sensitive ear might still catch, on the 15th October 1934, the last faint reverberation of a tolling bell in the announcement of the death of M. Raymond Poincaré, the presiding genius of the outgoing period,[1] who had been tragically preserved alive long after his eye had grown dim and his natural force had abated,[2] as though a Poetic Justice were unwilling to let him depart from this world until the Dead Sea Fruit of his statesmanship had unmistakably ripened into its predestined barrenness.

Footnote 1, a rather long one, finds Metternich an earlier counterpart of Poincaré, but not really, for the comparison suggests the dreadful deterioration of European statesmanship over the century. Footnote 2 cites Deuteronomy 29:7, adding that of course Poincaré was no Moses, though he might have been.[18]

The forceful bias evident in this delightful bit of Toynbee-ese, replete with biblical footnote, was somewhat characteristic. Like most Western liberals Toynbee long harboured a sense of the injustice of that peace settlement of 1919, in which he himself had been a restive participant; and his sympathy for a mistreated Germany manifested itself as late as his account in the 1935 *Survey* of the post-Hitler Saar plebiscite. His report of the 1934 *mésalliance* between France and the Soviet Union contains this thrust: 'In these French and Russian voices that were speaking the same pagan language naked and unashamed, we seem to hear Antichrist calling to Antichrist across the breadth of Europe.' And he paused to relish the irony of Herriot praising the Red Army while the French Communist party suddenly switched from denouncing to approving the military budget.[19] But this Toynbee who was pacifist, denounced all nationalisms equally, and bridled at any *realpolitik* was by no means the only Toynbee.

In fact, the Toynbee who revealed himself in the *Survey* from 1935 on was to be much more warlike and anti-'appeasement' than the great majority of his fellow intellectuals. Most of them were badly torn between their sworn pacifism, product of the reaction against 1914–18, and their growing desire after 1935 to oppose Hitler's Nazism. Most of them shrank from the realization that only armed force could restrain the German dictator and prevent him from dominating Europe and perhaps the world. They were driven to argue that their own government was quite as bad as Hitler, just another form of 'Fascism,' so that to fight against Germany under the British (or French or American) flag would serve no moral purpose. Some argued that it was vain to oppose Fascism by armed force, since one would be corrupted by the process into the same thing. Or they claimed that Hitler after all was a paper tiger who would soon fall of his own weight. With unusual clarity, or characteristic perversity, Bertrand Russell argued in 1936 that the alternatives were indeed either war or submission to Nazism, but the latter was preferable, an argument he abandoned only in 1940.[20] Orwell said that if England had listened to the intellectuals the Nazi boot would now be on her neck, forgetting that he himself until 1940 had been one of those offering that advice to disarm and refuse the challenge of the Nazis. The intellectuals overwhelmingly approved the Munich appeasement – 'a thousand times right,' as one of them said.[21]

Toynbee, while occasionally speaking of the horrors of war and the spiritual depravity of all nationalism, was in fact a resister almost from

Toynbee's Two Great Enterprises 151

the start. He accused the British government of 'a lack of courage and sincerity' in 1935–6 over Ethiopia. He cited Tom Brown as the wisest counsellor in such matters: try to keep out of fights but don't be a coward and if you do have to fight, see it through. Jeremiah provided the epigraph for the 1935 *Survey*: 'A wonderful and horrible thing is committed in the land ... and what will ye do in the end thereof?' He asked the 'deeply disturbing question' whether Great Britain was not abdicating her responsibilities as arbiter of Europe.[22] 'I am an abolitionist of war who is not a pacifist,' he later declared, adding that he would have gone to war with Japan over Manchuria in 1931, with Italy over Ethiopia in 1935, and with Germany over Czechoslovakia in 1938.[23]

It is true that like some others Toynbee took the dubious refuge of the League of Nations, arguing that it provided a 'nobler' way of checking aggression and defending the weak than 'military brute force,' as if somehow mere moral pressure might deter the dictators without the need of armed force.[24] But on the whole he did not shrink from responsibility to stand up to the dictator-aggressors, and, admiring the England that had defended Belgium in 1914, he eloquently indicted the whole 'British electorate of this generation' for lacking convictions and 'the courage to act upon them when the consequences of such action were likely to be unpleasant.'

The children of the Enlightenment fell under the yoke of the Goddess Tyche or Fortune, who, under many different names, had repeatedly established her paralyzing dominion over the souls of men and women who had been called upon to live in periods of social decadence ... They made their momentous choice neither on the absolute criterion of morality nor on the relative criterion of expediency, but on that trivial distinction between this moment and the next which keeps the sluggard cowering between the blankets when the house is burning over his head.[25]

After Munich, in a Chatham House address, Toynbee reiterated the dualism: one might choose to be a saint, or 'a man of power constructively in the world.' But, he continued, 'a man or a country that gives up the one ideal without embracing the other is irretrievably lost.'[26]

An intriguing, perhaps a dubious, duality: Toynbee was more the saint (or artist man of thought) in the *Study*, more the 'man of power' in the *Survey*. But he constantly wavered and waffled, hoping to be a 'constructive' man of power who might manage to avoid 'military brute force.' He moralized a great deal in the *Survey* even as he issued a call to stand up and fight, while in the solemn peroration to the sixth and (for the moment) final volume of the *Study* (written in the autumn of 1937, as he tells us in a footnote) he remarks that the 'catastrophe' of which people live in daily dread is 'hypnotizing us into a spiritual paralysis.'[27] This great concluding passage, which ends with a call to return with a contrite heart to the bosom of religion, warns against 'self-annihilation' through war and repeats the denunciation of all nationalism. At the same time it not only inveighs against spiritual paralysis but calls for the *pax oecumenica* that presumably can come only after a war which will, it is hoped, end the strife of parochial units within a society.

In the 1937 *Survey* Toynbee writes that while war is a sign of decadence, so is weakness and failure of nerve, and he again chastises the irresponsibility of the ostrich policy.[28] A part of the message of salvation in the *Study* is that we can, if we but will it firmly, break the chain of necessity and save ourselves. That 'schism in the soul' that afflicts disintegrating societies entails the lack of such a will, the psychology of chance and aimlessness, loss of control, 'the sense of drift.'[29] The 'what is false within' that betrays us in the declining days of a civilization seems at times to be materialism, power-lust, technology; but at other times it is weakness of will, the inability to respond to the challenge of adversity by resolute action. This portion of the *Study*, notably in volumes five and six, written simultaneously with the 1935–8 *Surveys*, clearly derives from Toynbee's reaction to the European crises of those years.

'Thus, in seeking to abolish the ancient institution of war, one finds oneself entangled in inconsistencies and frustrations,' Toynbee observed.[30] His ambivalence about war goes far back, for during the First World War, which he served so enthusiastically that he tarnished his scholarly reputation, Lady Ottoline Morrell classified him as a member of her anti-war circle. While he later regretted his propaganda work during the war, he continued to think that the war was a justified one for Britain. Later, though he had approved the 'stand against communist aggression' in Korea, he was almost hysterically anti-American in the Vietnam War of the 1960s.[31] Toynbee's equivocations about war may be seen as one instance of his larger ambivalence about the state, politics, and power. At times he denounced these with religious fervour as wicked, oppressive, lawless, immoral, yet at other times he sees them as necessary and even benevolent. The World State, the *pax oecumenica* that he believes we need so desperately, is a monster extruded by a civilization in decay, led by a dominant rather than a creative minority – a replacement that was itself the cause of war. (It is one of the more questionable inferences of Toynbee's system that in their creative, youthful stages societies knew no violent conflict.) Yet from this world state good things come forth, not the least a higher religion. No one can overlook the radical ambivalence of Toynbee, who once categorized himself as a Manichean dualist and who was always torn between his deeply unworldly, religious impulses and his desire to participate in the affairs of the world, reflected in his choice of research with the Royal Institute of International Affairs as a career.

It is obvious that Toynbee occasionally draws on the grand events of his own time in framing the generalizations of *A Study of History*. The metaphor in volume six of the Saviours with a Time-Machine (adopted from Lewis Carroll and H.G. Wells), the Archaists and Futurists who would turn the clock violently either backward or forward, both neurotic products of a civilization in crisis, was surely suggested by Fascism and Communism.[32] In volume two under 'The Stimulus of Pressures' (challenge-and-response subtheme) he contrasts the response of the Turks to their defeat in the First World War – a subject Toynbee knew well from his earlier book on the 1922–3 Graeco-Turkish War (which brought about his dismissal from the London chair by irate Greek sponsors) – with that of Austria-Hungary.[33] These and other examples[34] show the interaction between the two enterprises; yet of course the great majority of Toynbee's illustrations of his historical laws or processes in the *Study* are not drawn from contemporary history, or from modern European history. If there is one basic model tending to mould his theories, that would be the ancient world and especially the 'Hellenic Society' of classical Greece and

Rome. The interesting level of comparison between *A Study of History* and the *Survey of International Relations* is on the more philosophical level: the view of the state, power, war, and nationalism.

And also on the plane of style. It is possible that in the end we will come to value this aspect the highest in Toynbee. The re-evaluation of him, of which this volume is a sign, comes at a moment when we are prepared to take up his case again, broadly speaking for the third time. In the beginning, Toynbee tended to bowl over all criticism by what seemed the awesome weight of his wide-ranging erudition, combined with the great flair for generalization; 'a range of knowledge and subtlety of insight which leaves the reader breathless.'[35] The second phase, represented by such landmarks as the collection of critical articles edited in 1956 by M.F. Ashley Montagu (*Toynbee and History*), was a strong swing in the opposite direction, attacking Toynbee for concealing under his pretentious jargon a poverty of thought – a barrage of criticism in things both large and small that forced AJT to spend 675 pages answering his critics in the twelfth and last volume of the *Study* (*Reconsiderations*, 1961). From this onslaught, which surely gained strength from the level of Toynbee's popular writings in the 1950s, his reputation has scarcely yet recovered. True that the sheer energy of the man, who went on publishing book after book down to the end of his long life (and even beyond), forced admiration; but the quality of most of these numerous ventures, hopping on board every fashionable cause, did little to redeem him from the tag of superficiality. (And indeed a kind of awful platitudinousness permeates much of Toynbee's later writings.)[36]

But now, as we take a fresh look at him after an interlude of relative neglect, it seems to me that once again we are deeply impressed – not so much by the learning, certainly not by the 'system,' but by the sheer quality of his writing. At least, I have had this experience. I read him long ago when young and was 'bowled over,' indeed converted to a historian. Some years later I wrote a book about him that he was kind enough, in a review, to praise, but that in fact reflected a good deal of that disenchantment we had felt after professional historians had combed him over. Rereading him after a period of letting those green volumes gather dust, I find much of the old spell again asserting itself. The delight seems to come much more this time from the magic of his prose. I am referring to the work of the 1930s, both in volumes one to six of the *Study* and in the *Survey* down to 1938.

Toynbee's Two Great Enterprises 155

The latter books rise in importance if we come to value the macro-theorist less than the master of details. This tendency to elevate pure rhetoric over system-making had become a trend in recent criticism, so that in reacting this way we may feel ourselves quite in the current of our times. 'Not always the big bills, gentlemen, the small coins,' Edmund Husserl advised; and joining phenomenology in this relish for the concreteness of experience for its own sake are other groups of hermeneuticists, deconstructors, and Wittgensteinian language philosophers. We know that all systems are self-refuting, that only the surface is real, that all truth is in the particulars, and that thinkers are valuable for their intellectual personality not their theorizing as such. This is even true today in our appraisal of the great system-makers – of Hegel, Marx, Freud. The dogmas extracted from them by their disciples lie in ruins – but the masters themselves are still revered, having never really been dogmatists ('Thank God I am not a Marxist!' said Karl) and continuing to exert their appeal because of some elusive mastery of rhetoric, and of many particular insights.

I would argue, then, that the *Surveys of International Relations* are much worth rereading for their style and for insights into the interwar years; second, that to compare these volumes with the *Study of History*, especially the 1930s *Surveys* with volumes four to six of the *Study*, is rewarding for insight into Toynbee at his zenith; third, that such an exercise illuminates the gaps and contradictions between the two Toynbees, the person of omnivorous detail and the macro-theorist – a dualism that overlaps that between Toynbee the practical man of power and Toynbee the saintly, perfectionist denouncer of the ways of power; and, finally, that the *Surveys* rise in value as we learn to prefer the brilliant and gifted writer about politics to the maker of a system. There is of course much more to all these topics than this brief summary can reveal; let us hope we are in for a renewal of interest in this strange, great man, and that scholar-critics will soon give us the careful analysis and appreciation that we need.[37]

NOTES

1 *Toynbee on Toynbee: A Conversation between Arnold J. Toynbee and G.R. Urban* (London and New York: Oxford University Press 1974), 23–4. To the question 'How did your Survey of International Relations of the 1920s and 1930s stand up to scrutiny when the official documents became available?'

Toynbee replied, 'We gave alternative possible explanations of the facts as we knew them and of the purposes we suspected behind them. When we got the published German documents ... we found that none of our alternatives were entirely correct, but I don't think we were ever completely wrong.' This reply is vague and sounds like a non-answer to a hopelessly complex question. What seems important to stress is that Toynbee's account is uniquely valuable for its insight into the way the facts were perceived, by officials and the public. Factually, the *Surveys* are careful, scrupulously accurate summaries based on all available sources such as parliamentary debates, white papers, news stories, and government documents. My own admittedly non-specialist opinion is that the inside material later revealed does not add a whole lot. Of course it adds something; often at crucial points. As a test case, compare Toynbee's account of the presumed secret understanding between Laval and Mussolini giving Italy a green light on Ethiopia (1935 *Survey of International Affairs*, 1: 91–118) with later accounts.

2 After catching up by writing two massive volumes covering the world since 1920, Toynbee produced annual volumes of the *Survey* for the years from 1925 through 1937, the volume or volumes appearing in the year following; production of the 1938 volume was interrupted by the outbreak of the Second World War and it did not appear until late 1940. *The Eve of the War, 1939*, which contains significant portions by Toynbee, was published in 1958, and he supervised a ten-volume RIIA set on the Second World War, but wrote little of this himself except in *The Initial Triumph of the Axis* (1938); he left Chatham House at this time. The later volumes tend to fall between the stools of definitive research in the light of full documentation and an immediate, vivid, and incisive commentary such as the 1925–37 volumes provide. I have used the latter for this paper. Toynbee wrote the bulk of these volumes himself though sections were farmed out to others. They sometimes ran up to six to seven hundred pages and in two cases, 1935 and 1937, there were two volumes. For example, of 1937, vol. 1, Toynbee wrote all but eighty-three of the four hundred pages.

3 Toynbee, *Experiences* (London: Oxford University Press 1969), 112. It might be noted that the publisher and the format for the *Study* and the *Surveys* were the same; the *Study of History*, published by Humphrey Milford for the Oxford University Press, was 'Issued under the auspices of the Royal Institute of International Affairs.' Only the colour differed: the *Surveys* were bound in red and the *Study* volumes in green.

4 *Study*, 6 (1939): 315
5 *Experiences*, 112. Peter Calvocoressi, who replaced Toynbee as director of the Royal Institute, wrote that 'for him the *Study* and the *Surveys* were part of one another in the sense that both were part of his singularly large but singularly unified view of what is history'; Memorial Lecture on Toynbee, *International Affairs*, January 1976, 1.
6 *Experiences*, 87, 112
7 *Toynbee on Toynbee*, 52–3
8 José Ortega y Gasset, *An Interpretation of Universal History* (New York: W.W. Norton 1973), 279
9 Elie Kedourie charged Toynbee with 'a dismissive and insouciant attitude to historical evidence': *Encounter*, May 1974, 57. Martin Wight (whose criticisms Toynbee so often politely included as footnotes in *A Study of History* without ever changing his own view) notes his imperviousness to criticism in *International Affairs*, January 1976, 12. Against this stands the whole enterprise of *Reconsiderations*, an unexampled case of an author looking at most criticism made of him, and sometimes yielding to them. But this was the work of the later Toynbee.
10 Cf. Shirley Robin Letwin: 'What men have suffered and done ... does not seem to interest Toynbee in itself ... He is the prophet of a humanitarianism without human beings'; *Spectator*, 4 September 1974, 339–40. Toynbee himself said, 'I love the facts of history not for their own sake. I love them as clues to something beyond them'; *Experiences*, 90.
11 See article on Collective Security by Roland Stromberg in *Encyclopedia of American Foreign Policy*, ed. Alexander DeConde (New York: Scribner's 1978), vol. 1. Toynbee of course thought that resistance to aggression would diminish war by discouraging the aggressors; 1937 *SIA*, 1: 55.
12 John Herman Randall, Jr, *The Career of Philosophy*, 2 vols (New York and London: Columbia University Press 1965), 2: 277
13 *International Affairs*, January 1976, 12
14 1931 *SIA*, 1–2
15 For example, Eileen O. Blair remarked in 1940, 'I have known since about 1931 (Spender says he has known since 1929) that the future must be catastrophic'; Bernard Crick, *George Orwell: A Life* (Boston: Little, Brown & Co. 1980), 265. This of course was the moment of the apotheosis of Auden, Day Lewis, John Strachey, and the other young Communists (for the moment) responding to 'a world that has had its day' with visions of Marxist apocalypse.

16 1931 *SIA*, 5; cf. the memorable introduction to *Study*, vol. 4.
17 1933 *SIA*, 115–34; on nationalism see also, among other places, the opening pages of 1937 *SIA*, vol. 1.
18 1934 *SIA*, 322
19 Ibid., 385
20 Russell, *Which Way to Peace?* (London: M. Joseph 1936)
21 Simone Weil, *Ecrits historiques et politiques* (Paris: Gallimard 1960), 357. The left-liberal *New Statesman & Nation* was pro-appeasement until after Munich. 'Chamberlain's choice between evils was the best one,' Aldous Huxley explained. 'Most people ... would prefer to be alive under a tyranny to being dead under a democracy in process of being transformed into a tyranny by war or revolution,' (Letter of October, 1938 in Naomi Mitchison, 'Aldous Huxley on War and Intellectual Survival,' *Times Literary Supplement*, 11 June 1982, 635). This representative voice of 'civilization' seems to bear out Toynbee's point. One of Huxley's reasons for approving the price paid for peace was 'because even in the lives of people who are no more active than Mr. Micawber things do sometimes just "turn up" and the potentialities of accident, even of happy accident, are enormous.'
22 1935 *SIA*, 2: vii, 296, 481
23 *Experiences*, 84
24 This argument may be found in the 1936 *Survey*, re the German reoccupation of the Rhineland, as well as in the impassioned 1935 plea for the defence of Ethiopia (Abyssinia).
25 1935 *SIA* 2: 449–50; cf. *Study*, 5: 414–15, on 'the omnipotence of Tyche' as a factor in leading Western civilization to 'the pass in which it found itself in the autumn of 1938.'
26 'After Munich: The World Outlook,' *International Affairs*, January 1939, 18–19
27 *Study*, 6: 314
28 1937 *SIA*, 1: 52–5
29 *Study*, 5: 412ff.
30 *Experiences*, 84
31 'Toynbee on Korea,' interview with R.M. Bartlett, *Christian Century* 67 (1950): 946–7. A.V. Fowler usefully brought together Toynbee's words on war in the *Study* in *War and Civilization* (Oxford: Oxford University Press 1950). See also Marvin Perry, 'Arnold Toynbee: Nationalism as a "False God,"' *Interpretation* 4, no. 1 (winter 1974), and 'The Evolution of Modern European Nationalism,' *Journal of East and West Studies* 13, no. 2 (fall-winter 1984).

32 *Study*, 6: 213–42. Toynbee's only brief mention of 'the Anti-Semitic enormities of a Third Reich which has taken the French archaist's [Gobineau] fantasy in deadly earnest' (p. 217) and 'the extraordinary genius who succeeded in establishing a 'Dictatorship of the Proletariat' on the ruins of the empire of Ivan the Terrible and Peter the Great' (p. 240) masks this origin of the concept, as he discusses at much greater length examples from the later Roman Empire; but a careful reading makes one feel that this is a calculated downplaying of what his readers would certainly recognize as the crowning examples of Futurism and Archaism in politics.

33 *Study*, 2: 184–7

34 As an example only, here are some pages in vol. 5 of the *Study* that allude to incidents, events, or processes that come from international relations since the First World War: 76, 88, 316–18, 448, 479–80, 508, 525–7. The nature of these cross-references may be illustrated by the one on pp. 479–80: the reference is to Abyssinia's conquest by Italy, very much on Toynbee's *SIA* mind, as we know; but this case is used to illustrate the theme of conquerors being barbarized by the conquered. In vol. 2: 258n, Toynbee refers to the 1925 *SIA* re the Druse as a 'fossil' society in the Middle East. Toynbee's extraordinary knowledge of the Middle East derived from his work during the Paris Peace Conference and subsequently from his 1920–3 professorship of Byzantine and Greek history. His awareness of the many fastnesses in the Middle East where remnants of deviant religions survived suggested to him that notion of the 'fossil' society that he applied to the Jews with unfortunate repercussions.

35 R.H. Tawney, in *International Affairs*, November 1939, 433

36 For example, *The Toynbee-Ikeda Dialogue*, ed. Richard Gage (Tokyo: Kodansha 1976), which must contain a higher concentration of pretentious commonplaces than any volume this side of Msgr Sheen. One might speculate that termination of his role as analyst of day-to-day practical politics released the reins on Toynbee's idealistic, unworldly political visions, to some disadvantage.

37 Such additional research might include an exploration of the influence of the *Surveys*. We know that no less a person than Hitler thought them important enough to justify his seeking an interview with their author in 1936, which Toynbee has described in his book *Acquaintances* (London: Oxford University Press 1967). They obviously did much to mould Anglo-American perceptions of pre-Second World War international politics.

Toynbee's Interpretation of Russian History

Bernice Glatzer Rosenthal

Arnold Toynbee's interpretation of Russian history exemplifies the strengths and weaknesses of his overall approach. He fits Russia into his general scheme of history, which indeed explains important aspects of Russia's development, but ignores those aspects that do not fit into his scheme, and these omissions result in major distortions. Toynbee's discussion of Russian history, Marxism, and Bolshevism is scattered over the corpus of his works. This paper will set forth Toynbee's views before discussing them.

Russia and the West, Toynbee maintains, are two distinct civilizations set apart by religion. However, he does not consider Russia one of the world's twenty-one distinct civilizations; rather it is an offshoot of Byzantine Orthodox civilization that developed independently, owing to its isolation from the parent stem. Russia, Toynbee states, 'had always been a satellite, yet always one of an unusual kind.' Not only did Russia more than hold its own 'against the foreign body that had drawn her into its field of attraction,' but reversing the usual order, the satellite had threatened to usurp the sun's place and reduced the original sun to the status of a satellite.[1] Nevertheless, the original underlay of Russian civilization remains Byzantine to the present day.

The ebb and flow of pressures on Russia's frontiers explains Russia's development. The first set of pressures was from the steppe nomads of the East; the second set, from the West – an aggressive Western Christianity, then Western technology and liberalism. Now, however, the West is on the defensive, for the spiritual initiative has passed to

Russia. Marxism, a Christian heresy according to Toynbee, has displaced Orthodoxy as the new Russian religion, is attacking the West on its own soil, and is competing with the West for the allegiance of the world.

The first challenge, from the steppe nomads of the East, led to the formation of the Kievan state, 'an exotic plant of Orthodox Christian culture' kept alive artificially in a hothouse.[2] But the Kievan state was not strong enough to resist a renewed onslaught of nomadic invasions. Disintegration ensued and Russian society lapsed into anarchy and coarseness. A 'time of troubles' followed between the first and second phases of the Russian universal state. (The first phase was merely the cessation of feuding among the princes of Kiev; the second was the creative period – the arrest of disintegration and the full-blown emergence of a Russian universal church.) The 'time of troubles' began in 1157, when the capital was transferred from Kiev to Vladimir in the north, and ended in 1478, the date of the union of Novgorod and Muscovy.[3] Note that what Toynbee calls the Russian 'time of troubles' is not the same as what Russians themselves call their 'time of troubles' – c. 1598–1613. Toynbee considers the Mongol yoke a symptom rather than a cause of disintegration, for disintegration was well advanced in 1238 when Batu arrived to take advantage of it. ' "The beginning of the evils" was the work, not of Mongol but of Russian hands.'[4]

The origins of the Russian universal church are in the Kievan period (Russia converted to Eastern Orthodoxy in 988). The Church retained its vitality during the 'time of troubles' and, by passive resistance against the Mongols, paved the way for Orthodox Christendom to pass over to the offensive; Christendom became an ever more important factor in the Russian national identity, a true universal church. Several factors made this association of Orthodoxy and nationality possible. The fall of Constantinople (the Second Rome) was widely regarded in Moscow as Byzantium's punishment for accepting union with papal Rome at the Council of Florence (1439). 'The dramatic contrast between the final downfall of Orthodox Constantinople and the definitive triumph of Orthodox Moscow made a profound impact on the Russian imagination.'[5] It inspired the monk Filofei's prophecy (c. 1515) that Moscow was destined to be the Third Rome, the effect of which in turn 'seems to have been to precipitate, focus, and express a Russian sense of the uniqueness of Russia's own destiny as the sole surviving repository and citadel of an impeccably Orthodox Christianity.'[6] The marriage of Zoe Paleologue, niece of the last Orthodox emperor of Constantinople, in 1472, reinforced the idea of successor status. The concept of the Third Rome, says Toynbee, led to a threefold legacy that survives to the present day: a conviction that Russia is always right, messianism, and totalitarianism, the latter deriving from Byzantine Caesaro-papism. 'As heirs, *malgré lui*, of the Orthodox Christian heritage, they [the Russians] could not find the principle of totalitarianism either unfamiliar or shocking.'[7]

The Russian universal state that emerged full-blown in 1478 lasted until 1881, with the assassination of Tsar Alexander II. It constituted, Toynbee holds, a remarkably original, creative, and successful response to the challenge of unusual severity posed by the steppe nomads. The universal state entailed 'nothing less than the evolution of a new way of life and a new social organization which enabled a sedentary society, for the first time in the history of civilizations, not merely to hold its own' or to make punitive raids, 'but actually to make an enduring conquest of Nomad ground and to change the face of the landscape by transforming the Nomad's cattle ranges into peasants' fields and replacing their mobile camps by permanent villages.'[8] The Cossacks were crucial in this process. Toynbee considers them the 'frontiersmen of Russian Orthodox Christendom,'[9] the 'disciplined hunting dogs of the Russian Empire ... wild wolves snapping at the flanks of the Golden Horde.'[10] Incidentally, Toynbee regards the Cossack rebels Stenka Razin and Emilian Pugachev as exemplars of archaism, 'saviors with the time machine,' because of their reputed Old Believer faith.

The Russian universal state experienced one notable 'relapse' and one 'rally.' The relapse was what Russians themselves call their 'time of troubles' (1598–1613), the period of chaos and anarchy that followed the death of Tsar Fedor, sole surviving heir of Tsar Ivan IV (the Terrible). The resulting power vacuum triggered a struggle for the throne that in turn set off peasant revolts and foreign intervention, but Russians rallied to the defence of their nation, drove out the foreigners (Poles and Swedes), and established the new Romanov dynasty in 1613.

The challenge from the East was hardly mastered, Toynbee continues, when a new challenge threatened from the West, first in the form of aggressive Western Christianity and then Western technology and liberalism. Indeed, Moscow was hardly aware of its western frontier until Ivan IV 'rashly provoked his Western neighbours'[11] into the Livonian War, resulting in huge losses of Russian territory to Poland and Sweden; Russia already lagged behind them technologically. From this point on, according to Toynbee, Russian history was 'one plot, recurring with successive performances.' The initial event was a sensational Western military success at Russia's expense accounted for by her backwardness. Russia then tries to save her independence by mastering the new technology. There is a fresh ordeal by battle, which Russia wins, then a new technological advance in the West that begins the cycle again.[12]

In this case, the tide was turned in 1610–13; Moscow began to liberate territory conquered by Poland-Lithuania, regaining Kiev in 1667, which became a channel of Western cultural radiation into Russia in the seventeenth century. By the eighteenth century, Poland was no longer a threat. The abatement of danger on Russia's western frontier made possible the founding and flourishing of St Petersburg in the eighteenth century, but in the nineteenth and twentieth centuries successive Western invasions restored awareness of the strategic importance of Moscow.

Toynbee considers Russia the victim and the West the 'arch-aggressor of modern times,'[13] citing Western invasions in 1610 (Poland and Sweden), 1709 (Sweden), 1812 (Napoleon), 1853 (the Crimean War), 1915 (Germany), and 1941 (Germany). Sometimes he adds foreign intervention in the Civil War (1918) to his list. In short, Russia was the first civilization to confront and respond to the technological challenge of the West. Its response oscillated between archaism and futurism on the one hand, and zealotry and herodianism on the other. As Toynbee defines these terms, archaism and futurism are both utopian, for archaism involves a forcible stopping or change, a return to primitivism, while futurism involves a forcible accomplishment of change, a desire to create a new world.[14] Zealotry, a fanatic attachment to the past, denotes a passion surging (usually) from below, while herodianism tends to be a policy imposed from above, as rulers attempt to come to terms with 'an alien civilization of decidedly superior potency.'[15] Peter the Great was a Herodian, a 'Homo Occidentalis' along with Edison, Ford, Rhodes, Northcliff, Mark Twain's *Connecticut Yankee* in *King Arthur's Court*, or Shaw's Straker in *Man and Superman*. 'Both for good and for evil, he displayed an American vitality, an American impatience with pomp, an American delight in skill, and also an American ruthlessness.'[16] Peter's most American trait, according to Toynbee, was the 'combination of manual ability with the lynx eye of the prospector and the entrepreneur.'[17]

Peter's view of the West, Toynbee emphasizes, was narrowly utilitarian and military; even his educational reforms had military intent. But the westernization movement broadened after Peter's death, thereby demonstrating, according to Toynbee, the operation of a cultural law, 'that in any encounter between contemporaries, a single element of a radioactive alien culture when once admitted into a receptive society's body social tends to draw in after it other elements of the same alien culture-pattern.'[18]

Peter's Herodian policy was to convert the Russian Empire from a Russian Orthodox Christian universal state into one of the parochial states of the modern Western world, to make Russia 'like all the nations' after all. But this policy implied the renunciation of Moscow's pretensions to the unique destiny of being the citadel of Orthodoxy, the one society in the world that was pregnant with the future hopes of mankind.[19] Undermining the very basis of the Russian universal church, Peter was never totally accepted by the Russian people. His acts precipitated the zealot reaction of the Old Believers, who considered him Antichrist. Continued Westernization led to another, more muted form of zealotry, that of the Slavophiles of the nineteenth century, who maintained that Russian civilization was fundamentally different than Western, and that Russian problems required distinctively Russian solutions illuminated by Russian Orthodoxy and by the Russian cultural heritage.

The Herodian policy initiated by Peter lasted more than two hundred years, but ultimately failed. The long-suppressed insistence on the uniqueness of Russia's destiny reasserted itself in a Communist reaction to the modern West that found its opportunity in the Petrine regime's failure.[20] The ultimate failure to catch up with the West doomed the universal state and led to the Bolshevik Revolution.

A Tsardom that had the wisdom to take the sting out of the Russian people's suffering, defeat, and humiliation in the Crimean War by conceding the reform of the 1860s [the abolition of serfdom] paid with its life for its stiffneckness in refusing to forestall trouble once again by paying a corresponding ransom for the subsequent military reverses [of the Russo-Japanese war] ... and the far worse tribulations of the General War of AD 1914 proved to be the limit to Russian endurance and provoked the double revolution of 1917.[21]

Toynbee considers Bolshevism a response to the West that was both economic and religious. He views Marxism as a positive utopian response to the industrialization process that romantics hoped to undo. A powerful ideological weapon against the West, Bolshevism also 'served Russia's need to hold her own against the West economically, in forced marches.'[22] But Bolshevism is not just economic materialism; if it were, Toynbee believes, it would not be all that different from western liberalism, which has dropped the religious element and is equally materialistic. Bolshevism contains a powerful spiritual element, drawn from the fact (according to Toynbee) that Marxism is a Christian heresy. Thus it has become the new Russian religion and is now fighting the West with its own weapons on its own soil and is competing with the western faith of liberalism for the spiritual allegiance of mankind. 'The substitution of a Marxist ideology derived from the West, for an Orthodox Christianity derived from Byzantium, as the true faith of which Russia was the hollowed repository, was a paradox that was at the same time an inevitable corollary of militant reaction toward Western pressures for which Russian communism stood.'[23] Elsewhere, Toynbee considers Bolshevism a zealot attempt to break away from Westernization and claims that it satisfies two Russian desires – to escape from the West and to return to it in order to recast it according to a Russian pattern.[24]

Lenin, according to Toynbee, was at once a zealot and a Herodian, the direct heir of Peter, but also of Avvakum, the Old Believers, and the Slavophiles, a second Russian Antichrist.[25] The founder of the new Russian religion, Lenin put the West on the defensive as it had not been since the Turkish siege of Vienna. The Bolsheviks typefy the founding of a new universal church by a dissatisfied internal proletariat that had withdrawn to play the role of a creative minority.

Toynbee views Stalin's reign as an episode in Russia's never-ending race to catch up with the West. As the heir of Peter and Lenin, Stalin appropriated the international flag of Marxism to serve as the new banner of Russian nationalism, 'a paradox as illogical as it was statesmanlike.'[26] The first Five Year Plan he views as 'so radical a Westernization that it put Peter's work in the shade'; its goal was a new society 'with American equipment and a Russian soul.'[27] Combined the 'ideals of Lenin and the methods of Ford,' Stalin led the Russian people in a forced march from 1928 to 1941, but his 'tyrannical course of technological westernization was eventually justified, like Peter's, through ordeal by battle, the successful repulsion of invasion by the West in 1941.'[28] Note that Toynbee considers the Nazis the West.

But the same scenario recurred. Again the West made an advance in technology that revolutionized the art of war.

In AD 1945, the duration of the Soviet government's rest cure in a fool's paradise was limited, by a rocketborn *zeitgeist*, to a period of 90 days [from Germany's surrender to the dropping of the first Atomic bomb on Japan] ... In the never ending technological war between Russia and her Western sister, the West had again forged ahead of Russia so far as to leave her militarily at the mercy of her Western contemporaries unless and until she could catch up again with the formidable competitors for the third time, as she had succeeded in catching up with them twice before.[29]

Toynbee is sympathetic to Russia's attempts to deal with the problem of what he calls an 'oecumenical peasantry' shaken out of long-established political and economic inertia by the impact of Western democracy and technology. Russians, he says, could rightly argue that they were the only ones to grapple with the problem on a scale worthy of the challenge, for not even Peter or Alexander II (liberator of the serfs) tried to solve the problem of the peasantry or to cure the technological malady. Indeed Peter's heavy exactions of toil and taxes made the lot of the peasant worse.

It could hardly be denied that the Russian peasantry had been first deceived and then coerced by their demonic latter day rulers, but it would have been more difficult to refute the Soviet government's contention that the Russian peasantry, and with them Russia herself had been dragooned into economic salvation by this high-handed and unscrupulous act of state. If it is possible for human beings to be saved in spite of themselves, and if physical survival were not too dearly bought at the price of forfeiting both liberty and happiness, the Soviet government might claim to have been the Russian peasantry's saviour from economic disaster; and since the establishment of their ascendency over the peasant countries of Eastern Europe after the General War of 1939–45, they had seen to it that the same medicine should be administered to the agrarian economics of these satellite states.[30]

In the *Survey of International Relations*, Toynbee repeatedly described Communism as a religion. In 1924 he referred to Communism as a 'missionary religion' and to the Bolsheviks as 'zealots of the communist faith' who regard the sufferings of the Russian people as secondary. Nevertheless, he predicted, since Russia is their base of operations, the Bolsheviks would not allow the economic situation to deteriorate too far.[31] In 1927, he alluded to the 'church militant' and compared the struggle for power that followed Lenin's death with the 'struggle among the companions of the prophet for the heritage of the mantle.'[32] He maintained that capitalist society was out of danger and predicted a future of increasing economic stability. In 1934 he alluded to the eclipse of the apocalyptic vision and the transformation of the Marxian church in Russia, comparing this process to the 'daily round and common tasks, of "serving tables" in the temporary dwelling place in which the church has found herself in an unregenerate world.'[33] In 1936 he argued that a new nationalism was developing in Russia; it was not based on linguistic or racial bonds, but on a Stalin-Lenin-Marxian ideology that had transformed Russia into a totalitarian state. For Toynbee, nationalism inevitably degenerates into totalitarianism.[34] He also discussed the social and political counter-revolution of 1936 (changed divorce law and elimination of most legal abortions), alluded to the purges then going on, and referred to a Procrustean bed devised by Stalin for the Russian people, but said nothing about collectivization.

The competition between the US and the USSR for the allegiance of the world is discussed in several of Toynbee's books and articles written after the Second World War, including *A Study of History*. Russians, he argued, have an advantage in the competition, because they are not perceived as white and Russification is perceived as a short-cut to catching up with the West. By contrast, he notes, Russia's lack of cultural prestige is a disadvantage and will prove to be a formidable obstacle to her attempt to become a universal state, even on her own borders. Russia was never a middle kingdom for her neighbours as was China or even eighteenth-century France. Indeed, Russia's western neighbours resisted Russification, and still do, because they consider themselves more culturally advanced than Russia. Her best prospects, Toynbee concludes, lay in the backward areas of the world and on her eastern and southern borders – Central Asia, the Caucasus, and Siberia. He also predicted that because of China's feeling of her own superiority, the Soviet-Chinese alliance would not last.[35]

The overriding significance of Russian history, for Toynbee, is the challenge it now poses to the West, especially to Christianity. He compares the role of Communism to that of Goethe's Mephistopheles 'who wills evil but forever works the good.'[36] This 'new menacing presence' is actually a familiar presence that has merely assumed new dress, for 'in the world of the Judaic religions [Judaism, Christianity, Islam] has not Soviet communism been playing the traditional role of the Devil, alias Satan or Iblis? The devil's traditional service to human beings has been to scare them into doing things that they ought to do rather more quickly than they might have been willing to move if they had not observed that the devil is on their tracks.'[37] In line with his earlier views, Toynbee states that 'the abortive Russian challenge' (note his assumption) 'might turn out to have rebounded to the benefit of the vast depressed proletarian majority of mankind.'[38]

Toynbee attributes the success of Marxism to the failure of the Christian churches of both the East and the West to fulfil their social responsibility in the nineteenth and twentieth centuries.[39] For Toynbee, the spiritual and material fruits of civilization have been branded with the mark of Cain; they have been the monopoly of a privileged minority who had in effect repudiated 'the human social creature's inalienable obligation to be his brother's keeper.'[40] Marxism, however, proclaims Christ's commandment in a 'challengingly un-Christian voice.' It fights for 'one grievously neglected Christian truth,' but denies the necessity of placing this truth in a Christian context.[41] Nevertheless, Marxism challenges Christians to examine their consciences and to throw themselves once more into an essential Christian activity that has been neglected or even abandoned in modern times,[42] especially since the industrial revolution gave humanity the means to raise the standard of living and to lower the 'level of provocative inequality.'[43] In short, Marxism has reopened for Christianity a prospect of reconverting Christian Western souls to the Christian Gospel in its integrity, including its social implications.[44] Moreover, Toynbee maintains, suffering humanity will opt for whichever of the two superpowers that is carrying out the social gospel of Christianity de facto. Therefore, the self-interest of the West requires,

to achieve its purpose, a calculated policy of philanthropy ... caught up and carried away by a spontaneous outburst of love, and if the grace of God were to bring about this miracle in ex-Christian Western hearts, genuinely smitten with contrition and not merely with a self-interested alarm, by the hammer stroke of a communist challenge, then the encounter between the Western world and Russia, which had already changed the course of Russian history by prolonging the life-span of a time expired Russian universal state might also change the course of Western history by rejuvenating the body social in which the familiar symptoms of disintegration had already made their appearance. If this encounter were to have this outcome, this might prove to be the opening of a wholly new chapter in the history of mankind.[45]

Russia's destiny, then, is to engender a revival of Christian social teaching, namely Christian socialism. Proclaiming that Christian socialism is 'the brotherhood of man in consequences of the fatherhood of God in a *civitas dei*,' Toynbee believes that Marxism is an experiment which is doomed to failure, because it lacks the spiritual power that alone will enable it to succeed. 'The Christian critic will have no quarrel with Marxian socialism for going as far as it does; he will criticize it for not going far enough. Its fatal flaw in his eyes will be a sin of omission and not a sin of commission.' Thus, from the Christian point of view, the Marxist experiment may be tragic, but it is not the last word.[46] Again and again Toynbee repeats the same conclusion: 'The verdict of history may turn out to be that a reawakening of the Christian social conscience has been one of the great positive achievements of Karl Marx ... awakening from its inopportune slumber and speeding upon its abandoned paths that primitive Christian charity which does know the secret of making socialism work as one of the terrestrial institutions of a supramundane *Civitas Dei*.'[47]

Toynbee's treatment of Russian history has been criticized by historians of Russia who point to major omissions and the forcing of data to fit his own grand theory. Jesse Clarkson considers Toynbee's view a 'fantastic caricature' that ignores political, intellectual, and economic developments and omits Russia's rapid industrialization after 1860, especially the industrial spurt of the 1890s. Critical of Toynbee's insistence that Marxism is a religion, Clarkson points out that Filofei's prophecy of the Third Rome (c. 1515) was hardly known by his contemporaries, that Toynbee vastly exaggerated its importance and impact, and that these and other distortions demonstrate the danger of reading history backwards.[48] Dmitri Obolensky maintains that Toynbee is wrong on Byzantium, misunderstands Caesaro-papism, and absolutizes the differences between the West and Russia. Soviet totalitarianism, Obolensky argues, derives not from Byzantine Caesaro-papism, which was a symphonia of church and state, but from Peter the Great who subordinated the church to the state, following the Lutheran model. Moreover, Byzantine intolerance was never actively aggressive; Kiev was not isolated from the West, but an integral part of its trade patterns, and saw itself as part of one Christendom. Byzantium was a gateway to Europe for Russia, not a barrier. Zoe Paleologue's marriage was arranged by the pope – she was accompanied by a papal legate – for the pope wanted to unite Christendom against the Turks. Finally, Obolensky maintains that Byzantium ceases to be an 'intelligible field' for understanding Russian history in a larger context after the eighteenth century, that its influence was already receding in the fifteenth to sixteenth centuries, for by then Russia was drifting away from the Byzantine orbit into the eastern European one, and that by the eighteenth century eastern Europe definitely becomes the 'intelligible field.'[49]

Responding to Obolensky, Toynbee conceded several points, but still insisted on the importance of the fall of Byzantium to the Russian national identity. The idea of the Third Rome 'may or may not have been taken seriously, but still, remaining the sole surviving independent champion of Orthodoxy gave them a sense of being a country with an unusual destiny.'⁵⁰ Russia became the 'heart and citadel of Orthodox Christendom instead of remaining the outlying province that she had originally been.'⁵⁰ In his chapter treating Russia's Byzantine heritage, Toynbee insisted that the Byzantine underlay remains in the Russian soul and that the political climate was shaped by it. Russia, he claims, was attacked on two fronts by Tartars and by Poland-Lithuania, and in the long struggle that ensued sought salvation in a totalitarian state on the Byzantine model, working out a Russian version of it in the Grand Duchy of Muscovy.⁵² Moreover, he implies that since the Eastern Orthodox church remains powerful in the Soviet Union fifty years after the Revolution, its survival indicates that the Byzantine outlook survived along with it.⁵³

Other criticisms abound. Heinrich Stammler, a student of Russian literature and philosophy, confesses sympathy with Toynbee's transcendental view of history, but then reproaches Toynbee for claiming to be an empiricist when he is not. Stammler regards as major omissions Toynbee's neglect of Hesychast asceticism and of the part played by the Byzantine church in the formation of a national pattern of piety and in Russians' attitudes to the state and society.⁵⁴ Hans Kohn holds that Prussia, not Russia, was the first country to respond to the West, after being defeated by Napoleon at the battle of Jena. The response was the Prussian reform movement and the beginning of a debate – very similar to the Slavophile-Westernizer debate in Russia – of Germany's relation to the West. Kohn objects to Toynbee's equation of the West with technology and of liberalism with capitalism. He claims that Toynbee distorts the essence of Western civilization, which is an ethos of liberalism in the broadest sense of the word, tolerance, and respect for the individual. He abhors Toynbee's regarding the Nazis as Western when in reality they were the culmination of the anti-Western, anti-liberal trend in German thought.⁵⁵ Geoffrey Barraclough objects to Toynbee's transcendental Olympian view of history, and accuses Toynbee of 'breathtaking oblivion to the enormous genocide involved' in the breakdown of a civilization. Shocked by Toynbee's view that 'Hitler performed the same service for some future architect of a Pax Oecumenica' as Julius Caesar for Augustus, Barraclough points to Toynbee's statement 'the breakdown of a civilization is not a catastrophe if it is an overture to a church's birth' as evidence that

Toynbee has lost interest in civilization as such. 'All that matters to him is man's mysterious spiritual ascent on the wings of material catastrophe.'[56]

There are other omissions and distortions in Toynbee's treatment of Russian history. He ignores the centralizing impact of the Mongols on Russian governmental institutions, as well as their policy of religious toleration, which actually strengthened the Russian church *vis-à-vis* other institutions, and made it into a key component of the national identity. His use of the term 'time of troubles' for a time period (1157–1478) other than the Russian 'time of troubles (c. 1598–1613) is not only confusing but distorting, for it omits the reign of Ivan the Terrible as a major turning-point in Russian history and as the seedbed for the real 'time of troubles.' Ivan's capricious and cruel policies, culminating in the *oprichnina*, a kind of private kingdom to be managed entirely at the tsar's discretion, created social chaos, depopulated the central core of Muscovy, alienated key groups from the state, and weakened Russia *vis-à-vis* Poland-Lithuania. Ivan's policies, and not just the death of Fedor, brought on the 'time of troubles,' which was the result of primarily internal factors and cannot be explained away as the product of Western aggression.

Apropos of the latter, in the centuries-long struggle for territories once part of the disintegrated Kievan state, especially Galicia and Volyhnia, it is difficult to determine whether Muscovy (or its predecessor Vladimir) or Poland-Lithuania was the aggressor or the victim, and while militant Catholicism was indeed a factor in forging the Polish-Lithuanian identity and its sense of hostility to Orthodox Russia, it was by no means the only factor. Toynbee's treatment of the Cossacks ignores the socio-economic factors in their formation, especially their flight from serfdom. Over-emphasizing their links with the Old Believers, he makes religion appear as a much more important factor than it actually was, even though he does recognize the savagery of the Cossacks.

Toynbee's tendency in *A Study of History* and subsequent works to gaze on civilizations from Olympian heights leads him to ignore human suffering. True, it was his horror at the unprecedented suffering of the First World War that motivated his decision to become a historian, but by the time he wrote *A Study of History* he had become reconciled, it seems, to suffering, provided that it serves a higher purpose. A corollary of this orientation is Toynbee's tendency to treat events that fit into his scheme as almost predestined and therefore desirable, or at least not blameworthy. For example, reading Toynbee on the union of Novgorod, one would have no way of knowing that its involuntary incorporation into Muscovy was accomplished by massacres and terror. The tendency to ignore human suffering is even more glaring in his treatment of the Soviet Union. He hails Stalin's agricultural policy, considers the horrors of collectivization merely 'harsh,' and does not mention at all the planned famine in the Ukraine that resulted in anywhere from three to seven million deaths by starvation. To him collectivization is medicine – foul-tasting, but necessary – even though it is now recognized that agriculture is the weakest sector of the Soviet economy and that collectivization was abandoned in the satellites because it did not work, and in China for the same reason. Finally, justifying Stalin's policy by the defeat of the Nazis, Toynbee does not consider the issue of whether the purges in the army actually weakened the Soviet Union's ability to defend the nation in the first months of the war, nor does he consider the possibility that the purges were counter-productive, resulting in massive passing of the buck in order to avoid accusations of wrecking, counter-revolution, and sabotage, in the event of non-fulfilment of the Plan. Also ignored is the irrational component of Stalin's rule – the lust for power. In Toynbee's eyes everything is explained and justified by Russia's attempt to catch up to the West. But while there was indeed a 'forced march' for industrialization, Stalin wasted millions on monuments to himself and on schemes such as the one to change the climate of Asia.

Toynbee's Olympian abstract view also results in a blurring of essential differences and the loss of any sense of degree. For example, he compares the methods of Stalin with the methods of Ford, as if Henry Ford ever ran a *gulag*. Peter the Great he considers an example of American ruthlessness, but does not give an American equivalent to Peter's abuse of state power. For Toynbee, British liberalism is for all practical purposes equivalent to Russian Bolshevism merely because, as he sees them, both isms are materialistic, lack a sense of the transcendental, and focus on economic factors.

Gratuitous Jew-baiting also mars his treatment of Russian history.

To give a few examples, he considers the Cossack rebels Stenka Razin and Emilian Pugachev replications of 'Jewry's uncompromising Pharisees,' but fails to mention the savage Cossack pogroms against the Jews that were a perennial feature of their revolts.[57] Incidentally, perpetuating a common error among Christian historians, Toynbee does not seem to realize that the Pharisees were the liberals of the Second Commonwealth; their opponents, the Sadduccees, were the uncompromising conservatives. In the 1934 volume of the *Survey of International Relations*, Toynbee alludes to the 'rabbinical problem of reconciling expediency with the law,'[58] but why 'rabbinical'? Why not scholastic, or Jesuitical, or Machiavellian, or simply pragmatic? According to Toynbee, uncongenial aspects of the Russian outlook stem from the Judaic spirit.

> The Russian spirit and outlook would continue to be Judaic, since this Judaic ethos was common to the Byzantine and the Western tradition. Communism was as patently Judaic in its ideology as Eastern Orthodoxy was; and though the modern version of the Western culture, dating from the seventeenth century spiritual revolution, represented a resolute attempt to *purge the western tradition of its ancestral Judaic fanaticism and intolerance* [italics mine] we have seen that this vein in the Western tradition was not after all driven off the field, but was merely driven underground to erupt, in our day, in such ideologies as communism, fascism, and national socialism.[57]

Though this is not the place to discuss in detail Toynbee's minimizing of the horror of the Holocaust by comparing the well-provisioned Arab refugee camps to the crematoria of Auschwitz, it is perhaps significant that Toynbee, using Old Testament models for his operative concepts, considers the zealots, who were simply trying to maintain Jewish national identity, fanatics, and Herod, a despotic tyrant who massacred entire villages, but attempted accommodation with Rome, an exemplar of creative adaptation. He could not forgive the Jews for not assimilating.

Toynbee's views on Russia are remarkably similar to those of the Slavophiles of the nineteenth century and their neo-Slavophile successors of the early twentieth century. The Slavophiles maintained that

Russia was a distinctly different civilization, resisted Westernization (Toynbee considered them zealots in muted form), and believed that Russia would solve the social question through application of a key Orthodox doctrine, *sobornost'* (unity in which individuality is retained). A Russian version of organic society theory, *sobornost'*, they argued, would enable Russia to avoid the social conflicts of the nineteenth-century West. Their direct heirs were the neo-Slavophiles of the Russian religious renaissance – Nicholas Berdyaev, Sergei Bulgakov, Vyacheslav Ivanov, and others. Berdyaev and Bulgakov were expelled from the Soviet Union in the early 1920s and settled in Paris; Ivanov left voluntarily and settled in Rome. Toynbee might have been influenced by them, especially by Berdyaev and Bulgakov, for several of their works were translated into English; Berdyaev, especially, was very influential on the Catholic left in France after the Second World War, and he participated in a symposium at Oxford University on the state, religion, and society. Another channel of possible influence was the Russian *émigré* Nicholas Zernov, author of *The Russians and Their Church* and *The Russian Religious Renaissance* (which describes the neo-Slavophiles' views), and professor at Oxford.[60] In short, what I am suggesting is that Toynbee's views of Christian socialism in general, and of Russia's destiny in particular, stem not just from the many versions of Christian history that were 'in the air' in the 1930s and after, but have a specifically Russian source, for there are three specific parallels between Toynbee's views and those of the neo-Slavophiles.

The first parallel is Toynbee's view of socialism as religion. A commonplace by the 1920s and 1930s, this view was first enunciated by Berdyaev in 1906, in an essay 'Socialism as Religion,'[61] and then repeated in various books including *The Origins of Russian Communism* and *The Russian Idea*, both available in English translation, as was another work, *The Meaning of History*, which we know that Toynbee read. Bulgakov's key theme was the problem of the demonic, the 'man-God,' which he developed in works such as 'Karl Marx as a Religious Type,' 'The Religion of the Man-god and L. Feuerbach,' and 'The Spiritual Drama of Herzen.'[62] Though these were not available in English, Toynbee may have learned about them from Zernov. Moreover, Toynbee was definitely aware of Herzen's aristocratic distaste for the bourgeois West and his prediction of a collision of cultures, for he argues that, although Herzen is generally considered a Westernizer, his views on the distinctiveness and messianic role of Russia are somewhat Slavophile in tone. Toynbee's source is the English translation of Herzen's *My Past and Thoughts*.[63]

The second parallel is the tendency to equate Western liberalism and communism as similar doctrines because of their economic materialism and atheism. That communism is bourgeois, because of its emphasis on economic factors, was almost a cliché for thinkers of the Russian religious renaissance. Like Toynbee, who considered the Reformation a misfortune for mankind,[64] Berdyaev and Bulgakov were hostile to it and to what they considered atomistic individualism. Unlike Toynbee, however, they credited the Reformation for quenching the pyres of the Inquisition. To them, the Protestant Reformation was a reaction to the Catholic emphasis on power and obedience; thus, once the Catholic church returns to true Christianity, all the churches will be reunited.

The third, and perhaps most striking parallel, is Christian socialism. The neo-Slavophiles often referred to 'the truth of socialism' and maintained that the good things in it, and also in liberalism, stemmed from Christianity, rather than from Enlightenment rationalism. Like Toynbee, they too predicted the failure of Marxism, and for the same reason, claiming that Marxist materialism and 'class egoism' will never unite people as only Christianity can, on the basis of love and common faith. Like Toynbee, they criticized capitalism on religious grounds and objected to American mass affluence. Were they alive today, they would almost certainly endorse Toynbee's predictions, for they dovetail with their own on Christian socialism and on Russia's messianic destiny.

In conclusion, Toynbee's challenge and response does fit Russia, to a point, for reaction to the West was indeed a shaping force in her history. But it was not the only shaping force. Choices as to how to respond to the West were made and these were affected, even determined, by internal pressures and domestic conflicts. The multiplicity and variety of Russian history cannot be reduced to one all-enveloping factor.

Toynbee's Interpretation of Russian History 177

NOTES

1 Arnold Toynbee, *A Study of History*, 12 vols (London and New York: Oxford University Press 1934–61), 12: 539
2 Ibid., 6: 398
3 Ibid., 4: 91; 6: 308–30; 7a: 32; 7b: 690
4 Ibid., 4: 96
5 Ibid., 7a: 33
6 Ibid., 7a: 37
7 Ibid., 8: 140; see also the chapter 'Russia's Byzantine Heritage' in *Civilization on Trial and The World and the West* (Cleveland: Meridian Books 1958), 160–3
8 *Study*, 2: 155
9 Ibid.
10 *Study*, 6: 313
11 Ibid., 8: 137
12 Ibid., 8: 136
13 'Russia and the West' in *The World and the West*, 236
14 *Study*, 5: 382–4
15 Ibid., 8: 610–21
16 Ibid., 3: 277
17 Ibid., 3: 280
18 Ibid., 8: 675
19 Ibid., 8: 133
20 Ibid.
21 *Study*, 9: 516
22 Ibid., 8: 135
23 Ibid., 8: 134
24 Ibid., 3: 365
25 Ibid., 3: 201
26 Ibid., 8: 134
27 Ibid., 3: 202
28 Ibid., 8: 134
29 Ibid., 8: 141
30 Ibid., 8: 688
31 1924 *Survey of International Affairs*, 163, 170
32 1927 *SIA*, 248
33 1934 *SIA*, 357
34 1936 *SIA*, 371

35 Toynbee, 'Looking Back Fifty Years,' Introduction to *The Impact of the Russian Revolution* (New York: Oxford University Press 1967), 12–14, 16–18
36 *Study*, 8: 147
37 'Looking Back Fifty Years,' 30–1
38 *Study*, 8: 147
39 Ibid., 5: 586
40 Ibid., 8: 148
41 Ibid., 8: 148–9
42 Ibid., 5: 586
43 Ibid., 8: 147
44 Ibid., 8: 149
45 Ibid.
46 *Study*, 5: 585–6
47 Ibid., 587
48 Jessie D. Clarkson, 'Toynbee on Russian and Slavic History,' *Russian Review* 15, no. 3 (July 1956): 165–72
49 D. Obolensky, 'Russia's Byzantine Heritage,' *Oxford Slavonic Papers* 1 (1950): 37–63
50 *Study*, 12: 540
51 Ibid., 541
52 Toynbee, 'Russia's Byzantine Heritage,' 160–3
53 Ibid., 163
54 Heinrich Stammler, 'Russia between Byzantine and Utopia,' *Russian Review* 17, no. 2 (April 1958): 94–103
55 Hans Kohn, 'Toynbee and Russia,' in *The Intent of Toynbee's History*, ed. E. Gargan (Chicago: Loyola University Press 1961), 111–31
56 Geoffrey Barraclough, 'The Prospects of the Western World,' in *Toynbee and History*, ed. M.F. Ashley Montague (Boston: Porter Sargent 1956), 118–21, esp. 119
57 *Study*, 8: 606
58 1934 *SIA*, 377
59 *Study*, 12: 541–2
60 Nicholas Zernov, *The Russians and Their Church* (London: SPCK 1958); *The Russian Religious Renaissance* (New York: Harper & Row 1963). Though published after *A Study of History*, Toynbee and Zernov may well have discussed key aspects of these works.
61 N. Berdyaev, 'Sotsializm kak religiia' (1906); English translation in *A Revolution of the Spirit*, ed. B.G. Rosenthal and M.B. Chomiak (Newtonville, Mass.:

Oriental Research Partners 1982). See also N. Berdyaev, *The Russian Idea* (New York: Macmillan 1948); *The Origins of Russian Communism* (Ann Arbor, Mich.: University of Michigan Press 1960); *The Russian Revolution* (London: Sheed & Ward 1931; reprinted Ann Arbor, Mich.: University of Michigan Press 1961).

62 S. Bulgakov, 'Karl Marks kak religioznyi tip [Karl Marx as a Religious Type],' in *Dva grada* 1 (Moscow, 1911), 69–105; excerpt in *A Bulgakov Anthology*, ed. N. Zernov and J. Pain (Philadelphia 1976), 57–62. Also relevant is 'Two Cities,' *A Bulgakov Anthology*, 61–2; 'Religiia chelovekobozhiia u L. Feuerbakh [The Religion of the Man-god and Ludwig Feuerbach],' in *Voprosy zhizni*, no. 10–11 (1905); and 'Dushevnaia drama Gertsena' [The Spiritual Drama of Herzen],' in *Ot Markizma k idealizmu* (St Petersburg 1903), 161–94

63 *Study* 8: 701–3, 'The Weltanschauung of Alexander Herzen'

64 Matthew A. Fitzsimmons, 'Toynbee's Approach to the History and Character of the United States,' in *Intent of Toynbee's History*, 137

Toynbee on the United States

Edward Pessen

Arnold Toynbee's observations on the United States and its relatively brief history are no less fascinating, if more sparse, than are his appraisals of the many older civilizations he evaluated. While, as he himself was aware, his knowledge of America did not approximate his knowledge of the older worlds whose histories he had absorbed, it was nevertheless sufficient, consisting as it did in part in firsthand observations, to enable Toynbee to offer judgments of interest to both scholars and general readers. Toynbee had read responsibly, if neither widely nor sophisticatedly, in the historical literature on the United States.[1] But to a mind as quick and imaginative and far-ranging as Toynbee's, the slimness of his American bibliography no more inhibited him from offering large generalizations about American life and values than a somewhat similar innocence concerning the extant literature had earlier inhibited Alexis de Tocqueville.[2] This is not to say that Toynbee's interest in American traits and character was as great as his brilliant French predecessor's or his insights as profound. For all the flaws that have been detected in Tocqueville's *Democracy in America*, it is hard to disagree with the conventional scholarly wisdom that no book yet written about the United States matches it in profundity. Yet one can fall short of Tocqueville's achievement and still be admirably insightful and provocative as, in my judgment, was Toynbee. Certainly I disagree with a recent summary judgment that Toynbee's treatment of the United States is 'inaccurate and distorted, insufficient and indefinite.'[3] Some of Toynbee's observations may be guilty as charged. But the insightfulness of other of his judgments undermines so harsh a verdict.

No doubt because it is so youthful a nation, the United States does not figure heavily in *A Study of History*.[4] The allusions to it, however, are rarely lacking in interest. For Toynbee discerns in American history, no less than he does in the history of other states and empires, what seem to him clear illustrations of the great impersonal processes that govern the human past. Examples drawn from Toynbee's writings illustrate this point most vividly.

Writing in 1934, he contrasts Massachusetts with neighbouring Maine. The former state, he observes, 'is still one of the principal seats of North American industrial and intellectual activity, while Maine survives as a kind of "museum-piece" – a relic of seventeenth-century New England and of woods and lakes, which is still inhabited by woodmen and watermen and hunters.' 'How,' he asks, 'is this contrast between Maine and Massachusetts to be explained? It would appear that the harshness of the New England environment, which stands at its optimum in Massachusetts, is accentuated in Maine to a degree at which it brings in diminishing returns of human response to its challenge.' He continues with a fairly precise estimate of the latitudinal limits for successful responses. Thus, the 'North Atlantic seaboard has a northern limit at the northern boundary of Massachusetts which corresponds to its southern limit at the more celebrated Mason and Dixon line.' 'If it is a fact,' he continues, – and nothing indicates that Toynbee doubts that it is a fact – 'that, beyond the southern boundary of Pennsylvania, the challenge of the physical environment becomes deficient in severity and therefore positively relaxing in its effect upon human energies, it is also a fact that, beyond the northern boundary of Massachusetts, the challenge becomes excessive in severity and therefore repressive. And, in terms of the human response, the effects of repression and of relaxation are identical.'[5] In a few deft phrases, Toynbee is here explaining antebellum differences between the North and South by reference to the dissimilar climates of the two regions.

Since American historians are not trained to explain social and cultural differences between states or regions monocausally, whether the cause be climatic and geographical or any other, it is not surprising that many of them have reacted hostilely to Toynbee's argument. The ebb and flow in Massachusetts's own fortunes since 1800, despite essentially constant climatic conditions, is only one of the grounds for the scepticism that many of us feel about an interpretation lacking the requisite complexity. As to North/South differences, even Ulrich B. Phillips, who attributed them largely to the weather, does not go nearly as far as Toynbee in stressing the role of climate, precisely because Phillips was so much more knowledgeable than Toynbee about the matter. Nor were the differences between the North and South quite as great as Toynbee assumed. In fairness to Toynbee, it should be reported that two historians of the South before the Civil War have recently argued, as did he, that southerners did not work nearly as hard as northerners, ostensibly because they did not have to and above all because they were Celts, inheritors of a culture that frowned on work. In fairness to the critics of the latter interpretation, they have punched many holes in it.[6] Yet I suspect that I am not alone in being charmed by Toynbee's intellectual intrepidity and in finding interest in his admittedly excessively geographical-determinist explanation as a possible *partial* explanation of the dissimilar fates of regions, sections, and nations of dissimilar location.

Another bravura example of Toynbeean analysis is his explanation of why Virginia and South Carolina fell from their formerly lofty estate after the American Civil War, while lowly North Carolina ascended. 'Here again,' he advises, 'the explanation is not to be found in any inborn merits of the community which has achieved an eventual eminence, but rather in its freedom from the incubus that has weighed its fallen neighbours down. The former exaltation of Virginia and South Carolina is the verifiable cause of their abasement now [1939]. They have failed to rise again from their prostration in the Civil War because they have never succeeded in forgetting the height from which that fearful catastrophe once hurtled them, whereas North Carolina, who lost so much less because she had so little to lose, has found it relatively easy to recover from a slighter shock.' Toynbee then cites Luke, as though in proof of the rightness of his appraisal: 'For whosoever exalteth himself shall be abased, and he that humbleth himself shall be exalted.'[7] Actually, the biblical citation is not quite apposite. And more disturbing to American historians is an analysis of historical change that is so unconcerned with the myriad particulars that historians, above all, should know are most responsible for it. That general readers would find Toynbee's interpretation both provocative and strikingly clear does not negate its intellectual or scholarly deficiencies.

I am intrigued if not persuaded by the intellectual playfulness of a historian who finds a kind of spiritual similarity in the American poet's ode to the 'embattled farmers' who 'fired the shot heard round the world' and in Wordsworth's paean to the French Revolution, (when 'Bliss was it in that dawn to be alive, But to be young was very heaven.') To Toynbee, these are 'rejoicings' both, 'at a dawn [in which] historians should have had to let the poets be their spokesmen; for the joy awakened by the dawn of a new era of history is the soul's response to an epiphany that is something more than a merely temporal event. The demands that awaken such joy as this are irruptions into Time out of Eternity.'[8]

In *A Study of History*, Toynbee in effect glances swiftly at aspects of the American past for further illustrations of the operations of the great motifs, such as challenge and response, rise and fall, that he discerns and imposes on the past. He gazes more searchingly at the United States as a civilization or thing in itself in the book he wrote after his visit to the United States and Puerto Rico in 1961 and 1962.[9] *America and the World Revolution* is not a great historical work. Certainly it is not substantially researched. Consisting largely of three lectures that Toynbee gave at the University of Pennsylvania, it is essentially a series of opinions on America's recent role in international affairs, both before and after the onset of the Cold War, concise explanations of the historical origins of that role, and critical appraisals of that role. Neither in their substance nor their tone do Toynbee's observations have the weight or character of serious historical analysis. Yet, informed as his remarks are by his high intelligence, unique perspective, and matchless capacity to relate American behaviour to the earlier behaviour of the Roman and other empires – not to mention his intellectual integrity – Toynbee's evaluations are always interesting and in some cases piercingly insightful. Intellectual honesty such as Toynbee's is no slight matter. For during the hottest days of the Cold War, rare was the Western scholar who, like Toynbee or Hans Morganthau, seemed capable of appraising East-West conflicts without wearing as it were the uniform of the Free World.[10]

This is not to say that Toynbee was unsympathetic to the United States or its cause. A year earlier he had suggested that 'if either

Germany or Japan had emerged from the Second World War victorious, with the atomic weapon in her hands and with a monopoly of it, one may guess that she would have taken advantage of this unique military opportunity [to create] a universal state' under her domination. 'The people and administration of the United States did not do this and were not tempted to do it.'[11] Forget for the moment that post-Second World War policies of the United States with regard to atomic weapons were not quite as selfless as artful American propaganda convinced much of the world they were.[12] What is germane in this context is Toynbee's readiness to applaud what he regarded as yet another example of America's historical unselfishness.

Not that Toynbee's discussion of the modern United States was confined to its recent foreign policy. As a historian whose own evaluation of the pre-Civil War United States has called attention to the resemblance of ante-bellum American values, politics, and social developments to the values, politics, and social-mobility patterns of ancient Rome,[13] I am delighted by the resemblance that Toynbee found between the post-Second World War United States and Rome of the late Republic and Empire. Toynbee does not mince words. America, he reports, 'is today [1961] the leader of a world-wide anti-revolutionary movement in defence of vested interests. She now stands for what Rome stood for. Rome consistently supported the rich against the poor in all foreign communities that fell under her sway; and, since the poor, so far, have always and everywhere been far more numerous than the rich, Rome's policy made for inequality, for injustice, and for the least happiness of the greatest number. [And] America's decision to adopt Rome's role has been deliberate.'[14]

Toynbee is of course quite aware that this so-called American empire is not a thing of vast overseas possessions. But it is an empire none the less. History tells us that 'conquest and annexation are not the only means, or indeed the most frequent and most effective means, by which empires have been built up in the past.' Noting that 'the principal method by which Rome established her political supremacy in the world was by taking her weaker neighbours under her wing and protecting them against her and their stronger neighbours,' and that 'the most that Rome asked of them in terms of territory was the cession, here and there, of a patch of ground for the common security of Rome's allies and Rome herself,' Toynbee finds a striking parallel to Rome's behaviour in America's acquisition of ever more military and air bases in all parts of the world.[15]

Toynbee does not find the ancient Roman and the modern American empires similar in all respects. 'The new American Empire,' he explains, 'has at least two obvious and acknowledged merits which the older Empire lacks. Its first merit is that it has come into existence against America's own will – in contrast to the usual eagerness of empire-builders to dominate their neighbours. The American Empire's second merit is [that] America has been the first imperial power to give instead of taking,' as in its administration of the Marshall Plan after 1948.[16] Toynbee suggests elsewhere, however, that American 'giving' is motivated less by altruism than by a realistic desire to ensure long-run American gain and profits.

As historian, Toynbee understands empire and he displays a detached critical stance in explaining, even in accepting, it. He thus gives Augustus high grades for his shrewdness and good sense in imposing a salutary order on the ancient world, finding that his comforting pragmatism more than compensated for his selfishness and diverse cruelties. Yet Toynbee has no love for empire, deploring its harmful consequences not only for the foreigners it exploits but for the native population it appears to enrich. For, as I shall try to show shortly, Toynbee appears to think that, in accumulating pelf and power, nations simultaneously diminish, if they do not lose entirely, their souls.

Toynbee treats the American Revolution (1775–83) as indeed the shot heard round the world, praising it not only as the great pioneering effort by which a people successfully threw off the shackles of empire, but as the great clarion call to all the subsequent revolutions that shook the modern world. The French, Bolivarian, and Greek revolutions, the revolutions of 1848, the Paris Commune, the revolutions in Russia (1905), Persia (1906), Turkey (1908 and again between 1914 and 1928), China (1911), and Mexico (1910), the Russian October revolution, the independence movement in India, and the recent revolutions in China and Cuba are, all of them, in Toynbee's phrase, 'true daughters of the American Revolution.'[17] (I wonder: was Toynbee here playing with words in order to ridicule our friends the DAR?) The sad irony, according to Toynbee, was that precisely at the same moment when the American Revolution was 'circling the planet' and 'had come within sight of inspiring the whole human race,

America herself had disowned paternity, at least for the younger and less decorous batches of her offspring.'[18]

Toynbee glorifies the American Revolution as he does, the better to underscore his thesis that American foreign policy underwent a sea change after 1917. The great champion of, as well as inspiration to, revolutions before that date, the United States subsequently assumed the mantle and spoke the language of Metternich in its hostility to drastic overturns of an inequitable status quo. According to Toynbee, the United States has since 1917 become 'the arch-conservative power instead of the arch-revolutionary one' because of the fears created in American minds by the Bolshevik Revolution.[19]

Toynbee's explanation of America's reaction to the Russian Revolution is starkly clear and amazingly simplistic, coming as it does from a renowned historian. (If historians in the West are taught reverence for any intellectual canon, it is the one counselling the complexity of human affairs, the diversity of human motives.) Toynbee's answer to the question 'Why did the Russian Revolution inspire the dread it did in Americans?' puts one in mind of the answer given by Warren Beatty, playing John Reed in the film *Reds*, to the question 'What were the causes of the First World War?' 'Profits,' answered Reed. In Toynbee's view, the American reaction to Lenin's victory in Russia was the same as the reaction of rich people in all countries. Only, in the United States, it was a nation-wide reaction because in the United States 'the well-to-do section of the population had become [by 1917] a large majority, not the small minority that the rich have been and still are in most other parts of the world. 'Rich people,' in America and elsewhere, have 'taken Communism in a very personal way [because they see] in Communism a threat to their pocket books.'[20]

In Toynbee's fascinating version, the wealth that had ostensibly been accumulated by most Americans also triggered among them a wave of xenophobia, to accompany their red phobia. Why did the United States enact restrictive immigration laws in 1921 and 1924? Toynbee's answer is clear as crystal. Fearing that a 'flood of penniless Europeans' in unprecedented numbers 'might pour into the United States' in the wake of the Great War, the rich Americans who were ostensibly the numerically predominant element in the population, felt that a foreign influx would 'be a menace to the economic interests of the existing inhabitants of the United States.' America thus opposed European immigration 'for the same reason that made America react so strongly against Communism.' (Note: he uses the word 'reason' in the singular.) 'America's reactions were those of a rich man who is concerned to defend his private property against the importun[ing] of a mass of poorer people who are urging all round him and are loudly demanding a share in the rich man's wealth.'[21] In the years that followed, America's mastery of 'the techniques of industrial productivity' made her 'rich beyond all precedent.' The United States has opposed the revolutions of the mid-twentieth century because America supposedly 'felt herself impelled to defend the wealth that she had now gained against the mounting revolutionary forces that she herself had first called into existence.'[22]

This is economic interpretation of political behaviour with a vengeance. Given the brief time available to him to state his case, Toynbee's strategy was no doubt to cut through what he understood was a more complex motivation in order to jolt an American audience that was accustomed to perceiving its own imperial behaviour in unrealistically lofty terms. Toynbee appears to have been seeking to hold a mirror up to Americans in order to reveal to them that what they were really up to was protecting filthy lucre, for all their brave talk of defending the 'free world.' Very far indeed from being sympathetic to Marxism, let alone an outright Marxist himself, Toynbee reminded us anew that concern about the sordid effects that a preoccupation with accumulating gold (and protecting the gold accumulated) has on human thinking and conduct is as old as antiquity and has been characteristic of acute thinkers from classical times to the present – Plato, Thomas More, Shakespeare, Dickens, Ibsen, Dürenmatt, and Brecht, among them.

Since Toynbee's American lectures were shortly put to print, he could, had he wished, have edited them, explaining America's opposition to revolution in more nuanced terms. He chose not to. The moralist – and certainly Toynbee was a moralist – would not water down his harsh appraisal of what he believed to be America's sordid behaviour. Whatever may have been Toynbee's own motives in interpreting American motives as he did, his interpretation remains one-sided, marred, among other things, by its dubious factual premises.

Toynbee is very much like Tocqueville, at least in one particular, in believing, on the basis of thin impressionistic evidence, that the great mass of people in the United States were affluent and in possession of most of its wealth.[23] Evidence from the *Historical Statistics of the United States* and other primary sources indicates that in fact the great majority of American families, combined, held only a small portion of the nation's wealth and were far from affluent, however the latter term might be defined.[24] The point is not that Toynbee sinned grievously in being oblivious to the actual distribution of wealth in the United States. Eminent specialists in modern American history have been guilty of the same error and with much less excuse for it. The point rather is that, in attributing America's anti-revolutionary zeal to the allegedly bulging pocket-books of most Americans, Toynbee was grounding an important interpretation on a mere inference, and one that was in fact inaccurate. An even more glaring weakness than factual error in Toynbee's discussion of this matter is his omission of the part played by such other-than-economic factors as the rhetoric of political leaders, the media, the church, and government propaganda and coercion in engineering the consent of the American people, of whatever economic circumstances, to the anti-Communist and anti-revolutionary crusade launched by the Truman administration and pursued by later administrations.

Toynbee's simplistic and erroneous interpretation, attributing excessive influence to the popular element in wealth-holding and therefore in policy-making, is related to what I regard as his similarly unpersuasive discussion of democracy and the part the common people play in it. Toynbee's appraisal of democracy is unsentimental, even hard-boiled. Democracy, to him, is an inefficient, even a wasteful, form of government. Far from being the great source of Western power that Toynbee says non-Western peoples think it is, 'the truth' is that democracy 'has been one of the luxuries that their power has enabled [Western people] to afford.' But in view of widespread popular ignorance, the system has not been working too well. And the situation is likely to worsen in the future. For even in the United States, with its literate and well-educated population, the issues of politics are becoming too complex and too technical to be grasped even by the unusually well-informed, let alone by the masses. By Toynbee's analysis, the American people possess a political power commensurate with their supposed economic power; the problem is only that their unavoidable and increasing incapacity to understand the issues may lead them to wield their power uninformedly.[25]

It does not occur to Toynbee that there are many reasons to wonder about the precise extent of popular power in America, in view of the social and economic unrepresentativeness of the nation's political leaders and the relative imperviousness of the major parties that monopolize political power to the central needs and interests of the majority of the population.[26] As Toynbee himself has many times noted in his discussion of other national communities, the mere possession of the suffrage by no means assures the existence of democracy, however, 'democracy' may be construed.[27]

As with his discussions of the American aversion to Communism and of democracy, Toynbee has interesting things to say about worldwide attitudes towards the United States, but they are less than fully persuasive. He tells us that in 'travelling about the world [he has] got the impression that the [high] American standard of material living is not admired or envied by mankind at large.' If, according to Toynbee, America in the early 1960s was losing out to the Soviet Union in the battle for the hearts and minds of men and women, it was because America's affluence insulated it from 'the poor majority of the human race.' And the insulation was accentuated by race feeling. This allegedly pervasive American affluence was 'threatening America's security' as well as 'estranging America from her own ideals.' Far from enhancing the American image in the world, America's wealth alienated the world's masses who, in Toynbee's view, neither admired nor hungered after it. For, in his reading, the poor of Asia and Africa seek only 'the next meal for the family, ... some palm leaf thatching to shelter [them, and] a piece of cotton cloth to clothe [their] nakedness.' And little else.

In Toynbee's view, Americans must drastically change their ways if they hope to restore their popularity in the world. Their representatives abroad must in the future forgo the sybaritic pleasures they had grown so accustomed to, but they would be able to do so only if the mass of Americans on the 'home front,' finally decided to live more poorly. Their ideal would have to be St Francis of Assisi, 'the greatest soul that has appeared in our Western World so far since the Dark Ages.' Toynbee agrees with Tocqueville that Americans are materialistic. But, happily, all is not lost; they are not hopelessly so.[28]

Fortunately, the American people are also notoriously generous by temperament and by tradition. 'Give free rein to your American impulse to be generous,' he promises, and the United States may yet accomplish wonders, both in transforming itself for the better and in restoring its formerly high standing among the world's poor and downtrodden. The necessary shift in values and behaviour, while indeed possible and certainly necessary, will not be easy to accomplish. Americans will have to overcome two great obstacles, one of them, societal, the other characterological. They have come to crave luxuries because of Madison Avenue and its 'wants-manufacturing industry.' Toynbee is sanguine about the future – at least in this respect. He foresees a future American 'revolt against Madison Avenue' and all that it stands for. And Americans will have to overcome their unique homesickness, which to Toynbee is a 'conspicuous and distinctive handicap of Americans outside America.' Their insistence on 'carrying America with them,' wherever they might be stationed or visiting, leads them to stand out from native populations – in clothing, consumption, and general behaviour patterns. If Americans better understood both other people and America's own interests, they would burn down all PXs overseas and 'go native' – by dressing worse, eating less, and behaving more modestly than they do.[29] Toynbee the moralist shines through, in his prediction that future generations of Americans and Europeans 'will look back on this episode of Western history [that is, the preoccupation with luxuries] with astonishment mingled with disgust' and shame.[30]

Toynbee's argument on affluence and its untoward consequences raises as many questions as it answers. Not the least controversial of his perceptions is the suggestion that America's fabled material abundance is neither envied nor admired. Great numbers of post-Toynbee immigrants 'voting with their feet' hardly leave an impression of increasing indifference towards creature comforts. Nor has the American public given any discernible sign that it is prepared to abandon material for spiritual pleasures.

Toynbee as political historian of America demonstrates naïveté in dealing with the rhetoric of political leaders. He viewed the Marshall Plan as a great selfless giving and credited John F. Kennedy's lofty rhetoric in promulgating the Alliance for Progress as though these initiatives betokened an American dedication to solving the problems of 'the many who are poor.' Toynbee appears oblivious both to Secretary of State Marshall's blunt insistence that American capital reward only those who proved ideologically congenial and to much evidence attesting to the ideological and financial motives underlying America's insistence on a hemispheric alliance.[31]

Toynbee closes his discussion with an admonition to the United States that simultaneously attests to his high-mindedness as citizen of the world and his sometime tender-mindedness in appraising its affairs. If the United States continues to 'declare against social justice abroad,' he warns, 'she would, in effect, be proclaiming herself to be one of the enemies of the human race and,' he notes, 'we know what happens to these.' What indeed? Why, 'if the United States were to dedicate herself irrevocably to the cause of wealth and vested interests,' he believes 'history would sweep the United States out of the path of its onward march.'[32] One wonders whether the wish is the father to this thought. Perhaps more disconcerting than its lack of realism is the strange, if not sentimental, reading of historical evidence that underlies such a prediction.

In focusing, as I have been, on the weaknesses of and problems with Toynbee's observations on America, I fear that I have not sufficiently noted their originality. I have offered some chapter and verse on the deficiencies, inconsistencies, contradictions and excessive inference in his argument. I have said little about its virtues. For all its weaknesses, Toynbee's portrait of modern America illuminates significant but neglected characteristics of our ways and thoughts, and it does so because of its author's honesty, encyclopaedic range, and powers of analysis. My citizen's heart responds positively to Toynbee's trenchant critique of the disastrous foreign policy the United States has been pursuing over the past generation. But my historian's head, alas, must express disappointment at the lapses in method and judgment that permeate the renowned scholar's discussion of modern America. For all its flashes of insight, I find his response not fully adequate to the intellectual challenge.

NOTES

1 The citations for his allusions to the history of the United States reveal his reliance on uninspired secondary works and his evident high regard for some authors whom American historians of Toynbee's time hardly regarded as giants of historical scholarship. For a recent comprehensive catalogue of Toynbee's work, usefully categorized by nations and topics, see *A Bibliography of Arnold*

J. *Toynbee*, compiled by S. Fiona Morton (New York: Oxford University Press 1980).

2 My judgment is based on the evidence afforded by James T. Schleifer, *The Making of Tocqueville's Democracy in America* (Chapel Hill: University of North Carolina Press 1980) and my own reading of *Democracy in America* (part 1 originally published in 1835, part 2 in 1840) and of the many Tocqueville scholars who report his disdain for 'mere facts.' For a recent evaluation of *Democracy in America* that contains many references to the critical literature, see Edward Pessen, 'Tocqueville's Misreading of America, America's Misreading of Tocqueville,' *The Tocqueville Review/La Revue Tocqueville* 4 (spring-summer 1982): 5–22.

3 Matthew A. Fitsimmons, 'Toynbee's Approach to the History and Character of the United States,' in *The Intent of Toynbee's History*, ed. Edward T. Gargan (Chicago: Loyola University Press 1961), 146

4 My estimate is based on the comparative attention paid to the United States in volumes 1 through 12.

5 Toynbee, *A Study of History*, 12 vols. (London and New York: Oxford University Press 1934–61), 2: 295

6 Ulrich B. Phillips, *Life and Labor in the Old South* (Boston: Little, Brown & Co. 1929); Thomas P. Govan, 'Was the Old South Different?' *Journal of Southern History* 21 (1955): 447–55; Edward Pessen, 'How Different from Each Other Were the Antebellum North and South?' *American Historical Review* 85 (1980): 1119–49; and Forrest McDonald and Grady McWhiney, 'The South from Self-sufficiency to Peonage: An Interpretation,' ibid., 1095–118, which stresses the climatic and Celtic factors.

7 Toynbee, *Study*, 4: 290–1

8 Ibid., 10: 113–14

9 Toynbee, *America and the World Revolution* (New York: Oxford University Press 1962)

10 On Morgenthau's stance see his *In Defense of the National Interest: A Critical Examination of American Foreign Policy* (New York: Knopf 1951) and '"Another Great Debate": The National Interest of the United States,' *American Political Science Review* 46 (December 1952): 961–88.

11 Toynbee, *Study*, 12: 524

12 On the deceptiveness of the American Baruch Plan for international control of atomic power see Gregg Herken, *The Winning Weapon: The Atomic Bomb in the Cold War* (New York: Knopf 1980). For American determination to exploit their atomic monopoly to the hilt, both politically and militarily, see Martin

J. Sherwin, *A World Destroyed: The Atomic Bomb and the Grand Alliance* (New York: Knopf 1975).
13 Edward Pessen, *Jacksonian America: Society, Personality, and Politics*, rev. ed. (Urbana: University of Illinois Press 1985)
14 Toynbee, *America and the World Revolution*, 92–3
15 Ibid., 104–8
16 Ibid., 112
17 Ibid., 89
18 Ibid.
19 Ibid., 102
20 Ibid., 94–5
21 Ibid., 98–9
22 Ibid., 94
23 For a refutation of this Tocquevillean belief see Edward Pessen, 'The Egalitarian Myth and the American Social Reality: Wealth, Mobility, and Equality in the "Era of the Common Man,"' *American Historical Review* 76 (1971): 989–1034 (passim), and Pessen, *Riches, Class, and Power before the Civil War* (Lexington, Mass.: D.C. Heath 1973).
24 United States Bureau of the Census, *Historical Statistics of the United States*, 2 vols (Washington, DC, 1975), passim; Robert J. Lampman, *The Share of Top Wealth-Holders in National Wealth, 1922–1956* (Princeton: Princeton University Press 1962); Herman P. Miller, *Rich Man, Poor Man* (New York: Crowell 1962); and Gabriel Kolko, *Wealth and Power in America: An Analysis of Social Class and Income Distribution* (New York: Proeger 1965)
25 Toynbee, *America and the World Revolution*, 35–6
26 See the argument in Edward Pessen, 'Social Structure and Politics in American History,' *American Historical Review* 87 (1982): 1290–325, and Pessen, *The Log Cabin Myth: The Social Backgrounds of the Presidents* (New Haven: Yale University Press 1984).
27 Edward S. Herman and Frank Brodhead, *Demonstration Elections: United States' Staged Elections in the Dominican Republic, Vietnam, and El Salvador* (Boston: South End Press 1984)
28 Toynbee, *America and the World Revolution*, 115, 132–3, 142–3, 151
29 Ibid., 120–3, 132, 149
30 Ibid., 152
31 Ibid., 146, 210, 230. See too Ruth Leacock, 'Promoting Democracy: The United States and Brazil, 1964–68,' *Prologue: The Journal of the National Archives* 13 (1981): 76–99, and Clayton R. Koppes, 'The Good Neighbor

Policy and the Nationalization of Mexican Oil: A Reinterpretation,' *Journal of American History* 69 (1982): 62–82.
32 Toynbee, *America and the World Revolution*, 210

Toynbee and Jewish History
Frederick M. Schweitzer

To historians who have acquired a deep-going interest in Jewish history and those who, like myself, immerse themselves in the story of the Jewish people as a guide and resource for Christian- or Catholic-Jewish relations, Arnold Toynbee's *A Study of History* is a grave obstacle. For the study of Jewish history, and its suitable incorporation within the teaching of general or world history, Toynbee is a species of historiographical quicksand. In my own work, academic and interreligious, I have found that Jewish history is rich in relevance for Western civilization and Christian history, that the history of the Diaspora blends with that of the societies amidst whom Jews have lived in so numerous, dynamic, creative, and intimate ways that the historian is guilty of a serious default if he ignores the Jewish segment of his subject. In vain, however, will one search through Toynbee's twelve volumes to find any acknowledgment of Jewish contributions that were positive, precious, or creative. Other than those on the biblical prophets, all his Jewish entries are on the debit side of history's ledger: negative, deleterious, pernicious, studies in failure, moral degeneration, paralysis in 'fossilization,' and so on. Yet Israel's immortal prophets, consonant with a long tradition of Christian exegesis, Toynbee interprets as an aberration of Jewish religious development: they neither proceeded organically from what had preceded nor were they adhered to faithfully afterwards.

Apart from the merely secular tableau of history and getting the story straight, one has to be infinitely exacting in the presentation of Jewish history if one is to avoid the snares of anti-Semitic assumptions, whether in Christian or other guises, whether conscious or unconscious. At the very least, it is essential for historians to develop a particular theme of Jewish history at some length and with ample detail in order to provide their readers or students with a full-blooded understanding of the situation of the Jews at a given stage of history. Not to do so means that the skeleton of a few facts and scattered allusions will be clothed by students with the flesh of their own ideas about 'the Jews'; an author's ignorance, brevity, or silence means, or is likely to lead to, students falling back on stereotypes that are distilled out of the not-very-thin-air; such faults of omission and commission will perpetuate, strengthen, and – worst of all – legitimize those prejudices with which learners are, in varying measure, already imbued at home and in church, in school, or on the street. Given the insidious, Hydra-headed nature of Judaeophobia, it is incumbent upon historians to refute stereotype and prejudice by anticipation, in expectation of their students' antipathy which, in the great majority of instances, will be present, whether latent or blatant.

Almost every possible pitfall lying in wait for such scholars is epitomized by Toynbee's work; he is as remarkable for his ignorance of Jewish history (a matter of frequent comment by his reviewers) as he is for his oracular pronouncements of condemnation. There is no more striking irony, however, than that Jewish history illustrates better – more often and more fully – than any other civilization Toynbee's concept of 'challenge and response' as the driving forces of history; it is the same man, of course, who dismissed post-biblical Jewish history as a 'fossil' embedded in 'Syriac civilization.'[1] What a lively fossil! What a 'rambunctious fossil'! as Harry Orlinsky exclaimed.[2] If only briefly, it is necessary to recapitulate Toynbee's interpretation of Jewish antiquity, since, as in Christian historiography, his negative appraisal of that age dictates – as it is also a reflection of – his dismissal of two millennia of Jewish life as inert and his condemnation of Israel reborn as sterile and pernicious.

William F. Albright remarked in *From the Stone Age to Christianity* that 'though Toynbee seems to have overlooked the case of the Israelites between 1200 and 900 B.C., it would be difficult to find a better illustration of his principle of "Challenge-and-Response under the stimulus of blows." Under this stimulus the Israelites attained national unity in spite of the centrifugal forces operating to break up the confederation.'³ But nowhere does Toynbee relate anything about the period of the Judges, David, Solomon, and so forth. Nor does he invoke the example of the Babylonian captivity and the return under Cyrus as an illustration of his principle, although it coincides exactly with his paradigm of 'withdrawal' and 'return'; while his paragraph on the synagogue is fair, even favourable, there is no suggestion that it was an invention and an indication of Judaism's vitality, still less that it was to be the institutional exemplar and sine qua non of church and mosque.[4] Nor are we ever given an inkling of the startling fact that sometime in the last century BC or first century AD mandatory, free, elementary education flourished in Judaea, possibly the first instance in world history of a system of public education being established. Among many possible exemplifications of his thesis, Toynbee cites the Maccabean epic only to condemn it in the most resounding way. It is certainly not an oversight, as Orlinsky observed, that nowhere in his sprawling work does Toynbee 'adduce anything from Israel's rich and eventful history that would, at one and the same time, illustrate one of his principles and shed some glory on Israel.'[5]

A further problem arises from Toynbee's terminology, 'Syriac civilization,' in which Judaism was reduced to a 'fossil.' 'Syriac' would rightly apply only to an alphabet, language, and literature, rather than to a distinct civilization, Toynbee's yardstick for 'an intelligible field of study.' His use of the term reflects his inability to recognize Judaism as a 'civilization' or the ancient Jews as a 'society.' (It remains a puzzle how Toynbee could total up a list of 'civilizations' that includes the Christian, Moslem, Eskimo, Spartan, 'Far Western Christian' – read 'Irish' – but excludes the Judaic one.)[6] 'Syriac' is a contrivance enabling him to avoid employing such terms as Hebrew, Judaea, Israel, Jews, and so on, in a positive context. Many examples of this camouflage will be found in the *Study*: monotheism is 'the greatest achievement of the Syriac Society,'[7] Judaism has 'a Syriac inspiration,'[8] the Old Testament is 'an old-fashioned Syriac oracle,'[9] Judaism 'was a purely Syriac religion,'[10] and the immortal prophets of ancient Israel are 'the great creative period of Syriac history.'[11] In a passage characterizing the Maccabean revolt, it is insinuated upon the reader that one of the momentous chapters of Jewish history occurred not in Judaea, but in 'Coele Syria': 'The most fateful single event in all Hellenic history was the ideological and religious collision, in Coele Syria in the second century BC, between Hellenism and Judaism.'[12] The ultimate outcome of the conflict was, rather surprisingly for a fossil, that 'conquered Judaea took its Hellenic conquerors captive.'[13]

The plain historical fact of the matter is that there never was a Syriac society or civilization, and no historian worthy of his calling uses Toynbee's terminology; its manufacture by Toynbee reminds one of nothing so much as the fabrication of 'Aryanism' or 'the Aryan race,' that expression of the nineteenth-century mind's anti-Semitic proclivities and its wayward imagination in building historical interpretations that filled the sky of theory but never touched the ground of evidence.[14] Toynbee's learned language is such, and his evasions are so consistently persisted in, as to make his aspersions plausible to a lay reader, who will not deny him a profound objectivity any more than a tremendous erudition.

A large part of Toynbee's indictment of ancient Judaism hinges on what he calls 'the lapse of Judaism into militancy':[15] the Maccabees changed from 'violent-handed opponents of a persecuting Power [and] immediately became persecutors in their turn,' forcing the conversion to Judaism of non-Jews in reconquered areas, a development that Toynbee singles out as 'new and sinister'; apart from the issue of Jewish reaction to Antiochus IV Epiphanes' militancy and intolerance, one would think that forced conversion of the defeated might be preferable to the usual slaughter at the hands of the victors that prevailed in such circumstances. No reference is ever made to the invention by the Jews of voluntary conversion (until which one was simply and inescapably born into the religion of one's forbears), an idea or institution that was as unprecedented – and equally indispensable to Christianity and Islam – as that of the synagogue. We learn only that Maccabean 'expansion through persecution ... cost the Jewish religion the whole of its spiritual future.'[16] The sole Jewish invention appears to have been violence, persecution, forced conversion, 'ardent fanaticism,' 'savage denunciation,' and so forth, on which, as Abba Eban observed sardonically, Toynbee 'awarded [the Jews] the original copyright.'[17] Martyrdom was also a Jewish invention in that same Hellenistic age: that one could by one's death bear witness to one's faith and sanctify the name of God was more peculiar to Jews than 'violence,' and was – as one should not fail to note – part of that indispensable heritage taken up by Christianity and Islam.

Thus, according to Toynbee, the Maccabees launched Judaism off on the wrong path, that of a conventional power and territorial state, 'forfeiting any prospect that it may once have had of becoming ... a universal church,' that procrustean bed of Toynbee's imaginings into which he would force Jewish history.[18] According to Cecil Roth, 'generalization is even more difficult in Jewish than in general history,' whereas Toynbee suffered from historians' occupational hazards of parallelomania and analogyitis, so that much of his animus stems from the intractability of Jewish history to his formulations.[19] Thus, 'this was the disastrous aberration of exchanging their proper religious function for a political role,' and it indicated that Judaism had 'partially relapsed' from being one of the 'higher religions' – another of his procrustean concepts – back towards its 'primitive tribal' form.[20] The Jews persisted in their hope of 'an archaistic return' to a pre-Exilic state, since the 'etherialization' of Judaism effected by the prophets had been reversed in the 'ephemeral' political successes of the Maccabees.[21] 'Nor were the Jews cured of their crudely futuristic hope of a new mundane commonwealth' until it was battered out of them by force of Roman arms in AD 66–74, 115–17, and 132–5.[22] Yet, 'gradually taught by the repeated failure of this earthly quest ... the Jews made the further tremendous discovery of the Kingdom of God.'[23] The reader is heartened for a moment by this re-etherialization, especially when the historian rounds out his discussion of 'futurism' by noting the parallel responses of Rabbi Johanan ben Zakkai and the Christian church: both were non-violent, seemingly following 'the way of gentleness,' and both quietistically accepted the divine governance of the world and aspired to serve God's purposes, which 'can only be pursued in a spiritual field of super-mundane dimensions.'[24]

In the sequel to his analysis, however, Toynbee appears to be inconsistent: 'This spiritual reorientation as a discovery of the One True God' was persisted in by Christianity but forgotten, forfeited by Judaism.[25] The lead given by Zakkai was not followed. As a matter of fact, however, the rabbis in the generations after Zakkai greatly elaborated the teaching of the 'Noachide Covenant,' by which the gentiles were accorded a worthy place in the divine scheme of things if they adhered to the seven 'Noachide Commandments,' such as to maintain courts of justice, not to practise idolatry, blasphemy, murder, incest, theft, or 'to tear limbs from animals,' that is, not to give pain to God's creatures. This conception, which dates from the early first century AD and was canonized by inclusion in the Talmud, was to be further elaborated with regard to Christianity and Islam by such Jewish sages as Maimonides, Menaham Ha-Meiri, and Franz Rosenzweig, and is, for a religion making universal claims and at so early a stage in history, a remarkably tolerant attitude towards 'the other.' Contra Toynbee's ascription to Judaism of exclusiveness and 'militancy,' it could be argued that the Jews took out the first patent on tolerance.

In expositions that are plainly secular renderings of the hoary Christian theology of Judaism, we are told that 'the unfortunate change in the ethos of ... Judaism [to militancy] is revealed in the pathological exaggeration, in [its] petrified state, of the elements of ritual and legal observance.'[26] This is Toynbee's presentation of the familiar accusation of 'legalism,' as venerable as it is calumnious. One should note Christianity's indebtedness in the ritual of the mass and other liturgies to the order of services and readings in the synagogue, the music of the Temple, and so on, which is very great. But of this truth we hear nothing from Toynbee; rather that the Last Supper springs from the Hellenistic pagan mystery cults instead of the Passover meal.[27] We have, moreover, a charge of narcissism: 'The most notorious example of an ephemeral self,' Toynbee says, is the 'delusion' of being 'God's Chosen People.'[28] That the historian is declaring the Covenant to be sundered and forfeit in the manner of the Christian theology of Replacement or Supersession is brought home to the reader in Toynbee's assertion that this 'error of the Jews ... is exposed in the New Testament,' which he quotes extensively, seemingly as proof.[29] Thus Toynbee's reference to Matthew 25:25 about the talent 'perversely sterilized by hiding it in the earth' is the original version, Toynbee's rendering of it as fossildom is a simulacrum, not to say facsimile.

Toynbee himself confessed that he saw Judaism through the eyes of the Christian church and those of the German classical scholar and historian of early Christianity Eduard Meyer.[30] In what can only be called a historiographical disaster, he reproduces – and reinvigorates – every Christian stereotype about the Jews and Judaism. All his tremendous erudition in classical history, Byzantine history, Ottoman history, and what have you carries him back to three all-too-familiar, dog-eared, bloodstained ideas: (1) the prophets constituted the only creative age in Jewish history; (2) the spiritually and culturally fatal mistake of the Jews was their rejection of Christianity; and (3) that rejection has inflicted two millennia of fossildom and suffering on them. Accordingly, 'it is the supreme irony of Jewish history that the new ground captured for Judaism by the spear of [the Maccabees] did bring to birth ... a Galilean Jewish prophet whose message to his fellow man was the consummation of all previous Jewish religious experience, and that this inspired Jewish scion ... was then rejected and done to death by the Judaean leaders ... In thus deliberately refusing the opportunity that was offered to it of realizing its manifest destiny of flowering into Christianity ... Judaism not only stultified its spiritual past but forfeited its material future into the bargain.'[31] Thus Toynbee reiterates one secular-scholarly rendering after another of age-old Christian calumnies, effecting one cut after another of the historian's procrustean guillotine. Worse perhaps, he may be following many racist writers and Aryanizing exegetes of the nineteenth century. In the passage quoted and in the following one, Toynbee may be slyly intimating that Jesus the Galilean was not Jewish at all: under the heading 'The Stimulus of New Ground,' Toynbee writes that 'we find ... the Messiah of Jewry does come out of that obscure village in "Galilee of the Gentiles": an outlying piece of new ground which had been captured for Jewry by the Maccabees rather less than a century before the date of Jesus' birth,' which has an affinity, presumably, with the fact that 'the propagators of the new faith deliberately "turn to the Gentiles." '[32]

Toynbee's interpretation of the Pharisees (as hypocrites, supercilious, and men of the letter not of the spirit) is the same calumniation as in the New Testament. As he wrote in 1947 to a very close friend, 'Christ appeared, and they [the Pharisees] were caught out ... as heirs of the Promise, they are scrapped' – which is simply another rendering of 'fossilization.'[33] In volume twelve, *Reconsiderations* (1961), he did bring himself to say that 'the Pharisees' pacifism saved Judaism from perishing with the Zealots.' Pursuing the subject with such enlightened and eminent guides – discovered late in the day – as George Foote Moore and R. Travers Herford, Toynbee agrees that the Pharisees were the true heirs of the prophets, that Jesus was a Pharisee, that New Testament animadversions on them are 'unjust,' and even credits them with an exegesis of Scripture that 'kept Judaism alive,' quoting Herford approvingly that 'Torah means teaching ... Torah does not mean law and never did.'[34] Yet Toynbee's concept of Pharisaism remained excessively monolithic, and, in any event, his prior acceptance of the Gospels' denunciations of the Pharisees at face value never deserted him, as in this polemical asseveration: 'The sin of which I feel that we Westerners have to repent is Pharisaism.'[35] In the same vein is his accusation that Jesus was 'rejected and done to death by the leaders of the Jewry of his day,' for Toynbee follows the Gospel accounts of the trial and crucifixion literally, thus ignoring a long tradition of scholarship on the subject.[36] Whether through subliminal impulse or considered judgment, the motif of Jewish guilt for the crucifixion reappears: Jewish leaders were collaborators with the Roman power 'in order to compass the death of one of their own race'; the Jews persuaded 'the Roman authorities to put the founder of Christianity to death'; and so on.[37]

Not infrequently in history an enemy who is feared and hated will be demonized, that is, accused of being an ally of Satan, armed with the devil's superhuman power, engaged in his work of evil, destruction, temptation, demoralization, the ruin of souls, and so forth, through many permutations. In the sixteenth century Catholic and Protestant antagonists demonized each other, and all parties in turn demonized the Ottoman Turk enemy. The Gipsies were also demonized. Fundamental to the witchcraft craze of 1450 to 1700 was the demonization of women as paramours of Satan. Derived in part from the New Testament's references to the 'Antichrist' and 'Satan's synagogue,' the Jews too were demonized. Toynbee does not take up any of these subjects directly. Yet the devil theory of the Jews is buoyed up by his allusion to 'the demonic reaction of the Maccabees,' by his characterization of Jewish revolts against Roman domination as 'the Satanic Jewish *émeutes* of A.D. 66–70, 115–17 and 132–5,' by his reference to this classic minority's 'talismans' and 'magic' in surviving century after century against great odds, and by his characterization of the Zionists' 'demonic effort' in building up a Jewish homeland.[38] This demonization of the Jews, which has its origins in the fourth Gospel (John 8:43–7), is the most lethal weapon in the anti-Semitic arsenal, which, unfortunately, Toynbee does more to perpetuate than to condemn, employing the very idiom of demonological anti-Semitism.

Toynbee's trivialization of the Jewish past does not fail to re-intone the whole popular litany of the 'parasitic' Jews, the Shylocks of business, finance, and so on. Two stereotypes thrown together define 'the essence of Jewishness' in the Diaspora for Toynbee: 'a meticulous devotion to the Mosaic Law and a consummate virtuosity in commerce and finance,' which were fashioned into 'social talismans endowing the geographically scattered community with a magic capacity for survival.'[39] That an immensely diverse and creative line of Jewish thinkers – from Hillel to Martin Buber – contributed immeasurably to the 'essence' of Judaism we would never know from Toynbee's absolute silence about them. Instead, he fills the stage with the wizards of business and finance, 'and the spectacle of the wealth and power these aliens gained.'[40] But simply at the level of economic history, Toynbee greatly exaggerates the scale and significance of Jewish economic activity in early medieval Europe, and at a later time in east central Europe, in characterizing the economic transformation of those communities as 'Judaization' or 'modernization,' terms that he uses as synonymous.[41] To be sure, the Jewish role as economic pioneers, as primers of the economic pump in many countries of Europe in medieval and early modern times, was basic; yet it was born of need when the more conventional sources of livelihood were closed by Christian society's veto, and it entailed great risk. The idea that Jews 'dominated' the economy of any country at any time, 'monopolized' or were the sole sources of credit, 'controlled' this branch of trade or that line of industry, and so forth, are myths that Toynbee does more to propagate than to dispel. He also makes the track of Western persecution of Jews follow a too-exclusively-economic path. In comparing Spanish-Portuguese expulsions and massacres of Jews from 1391 to 1497 with Nazi genocide, he said: 'Both persecutions had been prompted by economic motives that had been given a less disreputable and less self-interested appearance by being cloaked under a shadow of idealism.'[42] That many centuries of Christian fulminations and reprobation of Jews had a bearing, either on the Iberian horrors or on the Holocaust, is an insight one will not find in this Christian or ex-Christian historian. Abba Eban commented in ironic humour that the 'legendary proficiency in commerce and finance' that looms so large in Toynbee's account is 'a characteristic which modern Israel has still failed to discover.'[43]

As Maurice Samuel and Elie Kedourie, among others, have noted, for Toynbee Jewish or Judaic was synonymous with everything evil in the modern world: Christianity went astray when it failed to heed 'Marcion's prophetically warning voice' – shades of the Nazi 'German Christians' who would also have de-Judaized Christianity.[44] He would out-Marcionize Marcion in eschewing Yahweh as a tribal god of war and vengeance and in seeing the New Testament as the revelation of a god of love. 'Why did Christianity, which appeared to have taken a decisive new departure from Judaism by recognizing that God is Love, readmit the incongruous Israelitish concept and service of "the jealous God" Yahweh?'[45] Which is to say, Toynbee carries us back to the long-discredited antithesis of Christianity as a religion of love, spirit, forgiveness, peace, and so forth, and Judaism as a religion of war and 'militancy,' carnal and material, given over to law and justice, jealous and unforgiving, and so on. 'In the past,' he rounds out his indictment, 'intolerance has gained the mastery where higher religions of Judaic origin had been in the field.'[46]

Not surprisingly, fanaticism and racism among Protestants – especially Dutch and Anglo-American Protestants – derived from their Hebraism and re-emphasis of the Old Testament. 'This has been a misfortune for Mankind, for the Protestant temper and attitude and conduct in regard to Race, as in many other vital issues, is inspired by the Old Testament [which is] very clear and very savage' on the subject. Toynbee assumes that, except for such factors as disproportionate numbers and the enervating climate, 'our British Israelites' would have exterminated the 'Canaanite' in India as they had in North America, and he implies that the slave trade and slavery were rendered possible by Protestantism, but only because it derived its ethic from the Old Testament, that is from Judaism.[47]

Marxism 'caught its spirit of violence from an archaic strain in Judasim,'[48] and Toynbee links together as malignant triplets Marxism, modern science, and 'post-Christian Western rationalism,' which last, he says, 'inherited from Christianity a Judaic fanaticism and intolerance': modern reason and science are identical twins, Marxism a 'half-brother by a Jewish Mother,' and all three are – here Toynbee avers his agreement with Martin Wight's formulations – 'parricidal offspring of Christianity.'[49] For three hundred years the West has been trying to purify itself of 'its ancestral Judaic fanaticism and intolerance,' but these have none the less reappeared 'in such ideologies as Communism, Fascism, and National Socialism.'

If Toynbee had said that a principal source of the relentless dynamism of Western civilization is its messianism, essentially Jewish in origin, one could accept his observation as a keen insight, but that is not what he is about. So one goes better to Norman Cohn's *Pursuit of the Millennium* for a meticulous account of a great many messianic movements, which were in varying degrees religious and secular in nature, and were derived from such sources as the Book of Daniel, the Book of Revelation, the Sibylline Books (Jewish), the Sibylline Oracles (Christian), and the twelfth-century Calabrian monk Joachim of Fiore. Joachim's was 'the most influential [apocalyptical eschatology] known to Europe until the appearance of Marxism,' according to Cohn. Most striking of all his examples is the so-called Revolutionary of the Upper Rhine, whose *Book of a Hundred Chapters*, c. 1510, 'is almost uncannily similar to the phantasies which were the core of' Nazism: agrarian primitivism, paganism, victimization by alien capitalists, Judaeophobia, a heaven-sent fuehrer, enormous massacres, and so on. Cohn argues that these movements are in significant ways precursors of twentieth-century revolutionary upheavals and totalitarianism: the 'parallels' and 'continuity' are 'incontestable.'[50] In his book on the 'Protocols of the Elders of Zion,' *Warrant for Genocide*, Cohn demonstrates how the Nazi phantasmagoria of a global Jewish plot to enslave, impoverish, and destroy descends from medieval obsessions. Both books are richly textured and complex, profoundly illuminating and suggestive, whereas by contrast Toynbee's foray into these subjects is simplistic and accusatory, the work of a terrible simplifier.[51]

One of Toynbee's most illuminating subjects was Russia's Byzantine heritage and his speculations on whether its Byzantine essence or Communist philosophy would ultimately prevail. 'But, whatever might happen, it seemed certain that, for a long time to come, the Russian spirit and outlook would continue to be Judaic since this Judaic ethos was common to the Byzantine and the Western tradition. Communism was ... patently Judaic in its ideology.' Is one to conclude that Toynbee's idea of Communism is not different from Hitler's 'an invention of the Jew,' 'Judaism with a tinsel of metaphysics'? Lest we be in any doubt about their affinities, Toynbee informs us that Communism, Fascism, and National Socialism are all ' "deviationist" Judaic religions.'[52]

Toynbee's list of the victims of the West's 'Judaic' aggressiveness is formidable (although unexpectedly Africa and Latin America are left off): the Russian and Orthodox Christian societies of east central Europe, the Moslem Arabic and Moslem Iranic societies, the Hindus, the Japanese and Far Eastern societies, and the Jews.[53] This last entry would appear to be an odd new twist to the old device of blaming the victim, and one can perhaps imagine a story à la Kafka in which the Spanish inquisitor, Nazi SS man, and Soviet KGB official taunt their victims with the explanation that all persecution is 'Judaic,' that everyone else who inflicts coercion and persecution is only partly blameable, since the evil, contagious example was set by the Jews. 'The irony of Jewish history,' Toynbee replied to a critic, 'surely is that the Jews have been the chief sufferers from a spirit which they themselves originally kindled.'[54]

On Zionism and Israel reborn Toynbee casts aside any attempt at empathy or objectivity. We learn not that Zionism is a main theological strand of Judaism as old as Abraham and the biblical marriage of the land of Israel and the children of Israel, but that Zionism goes against Judaism's nature and will be fatal for it; although it is hard to guess how anything can be fatal to something when it has been an unburied corpse for two millennia. Toynbee disconnects Zionism entirely from the ancient messianic impulse of Judaism, which, he insists, was 'finally' beaten out of the religion and people in the course of Roman suppression of the revolts of 66–74, 115–17, and 132–5; to him Zionism is but 'mimesis' of modern nationalism, and Israel almost a 'parody' of the modern national state, its prophet being neither Abraham nor Theodor Herzl but Machiavelli. Toynbee's loathing for the national state and all its works, together with his declamation that Zionism and a Jewish state have no religious sanction whatsoever in Jewish tradition or Scripture, placed Israel under a double condemnation and denied it any shred of legitimacy in his eyes.[55] He contrives to explain the Zionists' rejection of the British offer of East Africa or Kenya, not because it was not Zion and would violate Zionism's fundamental precept, but because the Zionists 'had succumbed ... [to] this Modern Western Nationalism which was inveterately archaistic.'[56] 'Archaism' is nearly as fatal a term in Toynbee's lexicon as 'fossil,' and it is one of his principal interpretive categories. He distinguished it from the idea of renaissance as a reversion to the past that is always dangerous, 'but it is most perilous of all when it is taken up by members of a community that is a fossil relic of a dead civilization.' Zionism was for Toynbee a quintessential example of archaism, since it embodied 'the aims and ethos of Joshua' and involved as well the revival of the, ex hypothesi, dead language, Hebrew.[57]

Britain's policies in implementing the Balfour Declaration (1917–48) he castigates as 'culpably wilful blindness' and he proceeds to interpret those policies in a power-political way that makes the power, influence, and wealth of international Jewry decisive, all of it following from the unstated assumption that the Jews are an all-powerful hidden hand, especially in the American government: Jews rose 'to a degree of economic and political power in American life at which the Jewish vote had become a force in the arena of American domestic politics for whose support the two party machines must eagerly compete.'[58]

In taking up the Middle East and Zionism Toynbee was violating the historian's canons of objectivity, since, as he acknowledged, he was 'a Western spokesman for the Arab cause,' which he portrayed in the most naïvely one-sided way, populating the Middle East with wholly right and righteous Arabs; moreover, throughout his long career as director of studies at Chatham House, 1925–55, he had 'a privileged access to the official world' of successive British governments, particularly to the Foreign Service, with the result that his interpretations of Arab affairs, Jewish history, and Zionism – especially as set forth in the annual *Survey of International Affairs*, which he edited and contributed to – gained a position tantamount to official standing.[59]

The Shoah (which with black slavery Toynbee judged to be the two great arch-crimes of Western civilization) combined a volcanic outbreak of 'Original Sin' with the technological means and organization of mass death. That Christian anti-Semitism and irrational racism had a decisive bearing on the Holocaust one would never guess from Toynbee, whose incessant moralizing does not extend so far. Jewish suffering at the hands of the Germans, causing six million deaths, he finds morally equal to – or less than – Arab suffering at the hands of the Israelis or Zionists, causing 684,000 exiles and refugees. He does not blanch at making a statement that can only be judged to be vile and obscene: 'But the Nazi Gentiles' fall was less tragic than the Zionist Jews'. On the morrow of a persecution in Europe in which they had been the victims of the worst atrocities ever known ... the Jews' immediate reaction ... was to become persecutors in their turn for the first time since A.D. 135 – and this at the first opportunity that had arisen for them to inflict [suffering] on other human beings who had done the Jews no injury.' (Toynbee here ignores the long history of Jewish-Moslem relations, the short history of Jewish-Palestinian relations under the Mandate, the career of the Mufti of Jerusalem, the numerous inter-war riots and massacres, the tremendous effort – not without result – of the Nazis in the Arab East, and the 800,000 Jewish refugees from Arab countries.) Their victims 'happened to be weaker than they were.' (Here he ignores the several powerful Arab states that invaded in 1948, vowing to drive the Jews 'into the sea.') None the less the Jews passed on 'some of the wrongs and sufferings that had been inflicted on [them] by their many successive Western Gentile persecutors during the intervening seventeen centuries.' (This is his peculiar idea of the phenomenology of 'vicarious victims.')[60] As for Israeli 'racism': they 'caught this psychic infection from their Nazi persecutors.'[61]

It is a measure of Toynbee's warped understanding of Zionism that he should judge the Jews to be more heinous than the Germans, for 'the Jews knew, from personal experience, what they were doing,' and presumably the Germans had not. And so we come to what must be the most bizarre moral judgment in *A Study of History*: 'On the Day of Judgment the gravest crime standing to the German National Socialists' account might be, not that they had exterminated a majority of the Western Jews, but that they had caused the surviving remnant of Jewry to stumble.'[62] As Abba Eban, who mocked the historian as 'the Attorney-General of the Almighty upon the Day of Judgment,' concluded sadly, Toynbee's denigrations of Judaism and his interpretation of Israel as reborn of 'a squalid and blood-thirsty conspiracy' delegitimize Israel and go far beyond 'a mere exercise of academic controversy.'[63] One wonders what Toynbee would have made of Chateaubriand's reflections on the Jews and Zion. That French Catholic nobleman visited Jerusalem not long after Napoleon's 1798 Egyptian expedition. The Jews had seen Jerusalem destroyed seventeen times, but nothing can 'discourage or prevent them from raising their eyes to Zion,' Chateaubriand noted, and he remarked how they, 'who in law and justice are the masters of Judaea,' persist in their belief and hope; how Persians, Greeks, Romans, and countless other powers have come and gone; but how 'one small nation, whose nativity preceded the birth of those great ones, still exists on its ancestral soil. If there is anything amongst the nations of the world marked with the stamp of the miraculous, this is that miracle.'[64] There is possibly more law of history than rhapsody in his peroration.

Toynbee's language is at its most invidious in describing the Israeli as a new type of Jew, out of the Book of Joshua and the pre-prophetic biblical books, 'part American farmer-technician and part Nazi *sicarius*' – meaning the Zealots who had rebelled against Rome. 'Not in Palestine, but in some no man's land,' would he have had them settle; they should not be citizens of a sovereign state or 'terrorists,' but 'martyrs' or 'peaceably abject non-Aryans.'[65] He would have them become 'quietists,' passive, non-violent, leaving it to God alone to restore Israel; Zionist self-help is 'impious' usurpation of God's prerogatives; all will be well if the Zionists 'leave the future of Palestine in God's hands.'[66]

In the earlier volumes of *A Study of History* Toynbee showed a degree of empathy for the Zionist movement, seeing in it a countervailing influence to assimilationism, for a Jew 'cannot cut off his Jewishness and cast it from him without self-mutilation'; but after the creation of Israel he regretted very much that Diaspora Jewry had not disappeared via the 'beneficent process of assimilation ... which offered the best hope of a solution of the Jewish problem'; we hear no more of his equation of 'emancipation-assimilation' with a kind of slavery.[67] He even suggested that for 'sixty generations' the Jews of the Diaspora had lived 'without disaster'![68] If there is to be no balm in Gilead, let the drama be played out in the Diaspora. In the end Toynbee conforms all too closely to the emancipationists' assumption over the last two centuries: let the Jews be emancipated, let them become French or German or whatever, and duly disappear by absorption – possibly as 'a Western bourgeois of Jewish religion' or, in Isaac Deutscher's phrase, the 'non-Jewish Jew'; as he conforms also to the age-old Christian solution of baptism-conversion and disappearance.[69]

In all this discoursing on the theme that Israel is inconsistent with Judaism Toynbee is simply reproducing age-old Christian historiography and historiosophy, rationalized and secularized, as he himself confessed in *Reconsiderations*. 'It is difficult for anyone brought up in the Christian tradition to make himself free from the official Christian ideology. He may have discarded Christian doctrine on every point; yet on this particular point he may find that he is still influenced by the traditional Christian view in his outlook on Jewish history ... I am conscious that my own outlook had been effected in this way.'[70] That he struggled earnestly to be fair appears in one of his many letters to a Benedictine friend: 'There is a lot in it about the Jews,' he confided while engaged on that twelfth volume. 'I wanted to make sure of doing them justice. It is extraordinarily hard, isn't it, for us to see them just in themselves, and not in relation to Christianity, which, in their view, is irrelevant to Judaism. But when one has had a Christian upbringing, it is difficult to see the Jews except through a Christian lens. This is irritating to them, and it does, I think, prevent one from seeing them straight.'[71] Yet despite such penetrating diagnosis, precious few reconsiderations, revisions, or corrections, much less 'seeing them straight,' ever followed, for as many reviewers commented, Toynbee's 'reconsiderations' wrought no 'changes.' And I am afraid that most historians, consciously or unconsciously, adhere to his central interpretive idea of the replacement of Judaism – 'digested,'[72] as Toynbee once invidiously expressed their relationship – by Christianity: such is the thread of theory on which we string those beads and pearls we call facts.

Toynbee did 'reconsider' his list of 'civilizations,' without, however, even broaching the issue whether there is a 'Judaic' one. The closest he came to doing so is in his excursus on 'a Jewish alternative model for civilizations'[73] as an organizing principle – along with the Hellenic and Sinic models – for the study of world history; the model from Jewish history is that of the diaspora, which is not unique to the Jews, as Toynbee notes. A more illuminating and less crabbedly prejudiced use of this idea will be found in Fernand Braudel's book on the age of Philip II, where he speaks of the Jews as constituting one of the 'civilizations of the diaspora type' and notes that 'there was quite undoubtedly a Jewish civilization ... an unquestionable civilization ... in its own right, a civilization full of vitality and movement, and certainly not inert or "fossilized," as Arnold Toynbee called it.'[74] But Toynbee was as impervious to Braudel's insights as he was to Chateaubriand's.

On the Pharisees, as noted previously, Toynbee reconsidered with some effect, but with no perceptible change in his evaluation of Judaism. On the more central issue of the 'fossil,' his reconsiderations did still more damage to historiography. 'My choice of this particular word may not have been a felicitous one ... But the fact is a fact, and the same name or other for describing it is needed.'[75] He was surprised that some readers – only Jews, he noted – found the term offensive, and he invites all the fossil people – Jews, Parsees, Armenians, Assyrians, and so on – to provide him with a better term. Until that crack of doom, he will rely on 'fossil,' even though 'a literal fossil is dead *ex hypothesi*' and his meaning is subject to that qualification! As for the ambiguity whether 'fossil' refers to the religion or the people: 'I do hold that Judaism, as well as Jewry, is a fossil both of the Syriac Civilization and Syriac religion.'[76]

Reconsiderations might better have been entitled *Reconfirmations*. 'On reconsideration I do not find that I have changed my view of Zionism'; '... in the Jewish Zionists I see disciples of the Nazis.'[77] The Judaic element in our civilization remains the source of evil: 'In my eyes the West is a perpetual aggressor. I trace the West's arrogance back to the Jewish notion of a "Chosen People."'[78] Toynbee does not trouble to understand the Jewish interpretation of election, chosenness, and covenant as matters, above all, of responsibility, if also of honour. The Jews were not chosen because they were morally superior to other peoples or because great and good deeds made them worthy of divine favour. For they were raised by God from the slough of Egyptian bondage in order to receive the Torah at Mt Sinai and – as a 'holy nation,' 'a people of priests' – to set an example of righteous conduct for all the nations who would thus come to know the one true God and accept his Torah. Rabbinic interpretation has consistently emphasized the sense of obligation, duty, and mission, even suggesting that God had first offered the burdensome gift to other peoples who had refused it. Accordingly, the Jewish understanding of chosenness is inconsistent with arrogance and exclusiveness, and it is a far cry from Toynbee's assumption that the Jews 'rested on their oars' and believed the Kingdom of God would be for themselves alone. Toynbee's false distinction between exclusivist Judaism and universalist Christianity is fundamental to his explanation of why the Jews did not accept Jesus. 'Oecumenicalism,' he declared, 'is positively antipathetic, and not merely foreign, to the Jewish tradition.'[79]

How imprisoned Toynbee remained in a Christian historiographical matrix is suggested by his resolution of the seeming Jewish dilemma of being caught between the incompatible allegiance to a universal

God and to a national community that must be preserved. The gentiles might 'take the initiative by snatching the treasure out of Jewish hands and running away with it ... There is only one solution ... The Jews must constitute themselves the One True God's missionaries to the rest of mankind ... The Jews have been wracked by this crux for 2,500 years up to date, and they still have to make the choice ... the Jews' own manifest destiny. This is still intact, for the Jews to embrace, if they will.'[80] Since the founding of Christianity or Islam, 'Jewish history ... is without significance except as a classic example of perversity on the part of a people that, of all peoples, ought to have known better.'[81] By accepting neither Jesus nor Mohammed, 'the Jews were failing to respond to the supreme challenge in their history, and were thereby putting themselves permanently in the wrong and on the shelf,'[82] where, no doubt, all fossils end up.

Toynbee pursues several alternating lines of approach to Jewish history and religion, shifting unaccountably from one to another exposition: of the difficulty or impossibility for a Christian or ex-Christian to be fair and objective in interpreting Judaism; of the necessity to see Judaism and Jewish history 'from the inside,' as do the Christian scholars Herford, Moore, and James Parkes; of a vehement reassertion of the old polemic springing from a Christian's or ex-Christian's antipathy for a Judaism that does not accept its 'mission, as it surely is,' to bear forth 'the vision of the character of the One True God.'[83] But always Toynbee's exposition is freighted with an unchecked anger over Jewish history's defiance of his categories and formulations of world history. Obsessively and tenaciously he insisted that the Jews choose what he thinks history demands of them: to worship the universal God of the prophets; to renounce the preservation of their national identity in the Diaspora; and to abandon the restoration of a Jewish homeland and state on its ancestral site of Zion. That the tension among these three strands is or could be creative, or that the three elements are intrinsic to Judaism and anything but 'incompatible' with each other,[84] Toynbee could never acknowledge. Such a conception was too inconsistent with his procrustean bed of historical interpretation, itself arising from Christian suppositions. To have assessed the Jews' own interpretation of their religion was quite beyond his knowledge, for he never steeped himself in rabbinics and had no direct acquaintance with the Talmud.

He was much too prone, as he put it, 'to streamline the pattern of history by getting rid of distinctions.'[85] It is astonishing what Toynbee leaves out of his historical account: of the vast subject of Jewish mysticism, Kabbalah, Hassidism – the subjects of Gershom Scholem's life's work – there is absolutely nothing; of the *Wissenschaft des Judentums* (the science of Judaism, that is, the scholarly study of Judaism and of Jewish history initiated in the nineteenth century), no mention; the revival of Hebrew is denigrated as 'archaistic,' and of Yiddish and the marvellous literature in it there is no mention; of Jewish creativity by the Maimonides, or secular Jewish creativity by the Einsteins, we hear nothing. Of the immensely exciting discovery of the treasure-trove of Dead Sea Scrolls, destructive of age-old stereotypes and suggestive of the prodigious variety and vitality of Jewish religious life between the Maccabees and Masada, Toynbee had nothing to say; he had apparently no interest. We get only a bit of what might be called a rounding out of Toynbee's 'social geology' of Jewish fossils. 'Less numerous and less notorious, but not less interesting to the student of history' are those Jews 'who have held their own by withdrawing into mountains and deserts where they have converted the primitive inhabitants to Judaism and have themselves reverted more or less to the primitive way of life.' These are the Jews in 'Fastnesses': Yemenite Jews (long since evacuated to Israel), the Falashas in Ethiopia (partly evacuated to Israel during the mid-1980s), the 'Mountain Jews' in the Caucasus, and those in the Crimea including the Karaites, some possible descendants of the Khazars, some with, some bereft of the Talmud, and so forth.[86]

The 'Jews in Fastnesses' are a 'variant form' of Jews in the Diaspora, those who 'have held their own by learning to endure the life of the ghetto,' among whom Toynbee submerges the Marranos or Crypto-Jews. As an example of a bit of glory, a unique study in endurance and fidelity – 'the most romantic tale in all history,' according to Cecil Roth – the Marranos, one would think, ought to have been 'not less interesting to the student of history' than 'the Jews in Fastnesses.' But they were not. Although Toynbee cites Roth's powerful *History of the Marranos* and judges the survival after four centuries of scattered, secret Jewish communities in rural Spain and Portugal to be 'amazing,' his references to them are confined to a couple of scattered telegraphic sentences and a pair of footnotes. Had he pursued the subject, as

Maurice Samuel suggested, Toynbee might have properly concluded that these minute, remote remnants of Jewry – who had practically lost the use of Hebrew, forgotten the Talmud, possessed only fragments of Jewish ritual and belief, and were petrified of the modern world – exhibited a form of social fossilization.[87] Thus Toynbee's ignorance of large chunks of Jewish history, his selectivity and lacunae, and disproportionate emphases, leave the reader baffled and make his work suspect.

Toynbee's last word on the Jews was, as it were, the same as his first utterance: he held out the prospect of 'a denationalized and defossilized Judaism' under a new prophet, who would inspire Jews 'to their universal mission wholeheartedly. The world has been waiting for this prophet for 2,500 years.'[88]

History à la Toynbee follows an all-too-familiar prescription: a full presentation of Jewish history to the Crucifixion, followed by the postbiblical blank, the age of the 'fossil' or a thousand years of 'usury' and other assorted stereotypes during which time Judaism, in the grip of the 'law,' is assumed to have remained 'unchanged' and to have become 'obsolete' and 'sterile,' until we come to modern money lending (the Rothschilds, and so on), anti-Semitism, and Zionism (which can be made into a cover by anti-Semites who urge that they are 'anti-Zionist' but 'not anti-Semitic'). Fossils have no rights except to be laid out in museums or relegated to history's slag heaps; certainly they have no spiritual value.

What significance Jewish history has after Toynbee is best evoked in Maurice Samuel's elegy. 'Here was Professor Toynbee, leading me to the conclusion that I should not be I, and my parents should not have been my parents, that the whole vast process that is continuing in my children, and that they plan to continue in theirs, is not a process but a paralysis. We are here, it seems, and we have been here these two thousand years, not because we know how to live, but because we do not know how to die; or rather because, dead without knowing it, we cannot perform the act of self-burial. What a ghastly mistake it has all been! The expulsions, the autos-da-fé, the wanderings, the laborious reconstructions in new and strange lands, the pious cultivation of books, the obstinate transmission of the foolish hope – all, all as senseless as the wash of the waves which accompanied my first reading of this illumination of our destiny. Now I did not know whom to pity more, the lifeless living or the deluded dead.'[89]

Toynbee is clearly subject to the great Heinrich Graetz's censure, voiced in an important programmatic essay, 'The Structure of Jewish History' (1846). To read his indictment today is a chilling reminder that in this respect the historical profession has changed little in nearly a century and a half: 'The Christian conception of history, as is well known, fully denies to Judaism any history, in the higher sense of the word, since the loss of its national independence ... It scarcely grants Judaism a few lines and believes to have discharged its obligations as soon as it refers, in a meager footnote,to a few disparate facts of Jewish history in the margin of world history. The stylus of the world historian races cursorily over the martyrdom of Jewish history ... The brisk activity of Jewish history, the immortal creations which Judaism brought to life behind the sealed gates of the ghetto, within the gloomy seclusion of its academy, how can these possibly find recognition and appreciation? ... This habit of lowering Judaism into the grave, of issuing Jewish history a death certificate is also quite convenient; one thereby avoids the difficulty which would loom before any strictly Christian construction of world history. Thus, all the more urgent is the demand on us to vindicate the right of Jewish history, to present its tenacious and indestructible character.'[90]

One can say that too much should not be made of Toynbee on the Jews, that professional historians either ignore his work altogether or condemn it as worthless, and so forth. But that is an evasion. The reading public is interested in Toynbee, a fact brought home to me recently by the request of one of my ablest students to tutor him in reading *A Study of History*.

Evidently, also, Toynbee's metaphor for denigrating Jewish existence is quite unoriginal. For 'fossil' and its synonyms were widely used epithets for nearly a century preceding Toynbee's reiteration of them, which, perhaps, helps to explain the resonance that his terminology and ideas have had for many readers. He might have been spared – and spared us – his learned caluminations had he pondered a marvellous novel published in 1876. George Eliot's hero in *Daniel Deronda* has it brought home to him that he knows practically nothing 'about modern Judaism or the inner Jewish history. The Chosen People have been commonly treated as a people chosen for the sake of somebody else.' Thus Daniel 'regarded Judaism as a sort of eccentric fossilized form, which an accomplished man might dispense with studying.' But then by his personal experience of living Jews, lingering outside and then inside synagogues during services, and reading books about Jews by Jews, there 'flashed on him the hitherto neglected reality that Judaism was something still throbbing in human lives, still making for them the only conceivable vesture of the world.' Thus Daniel underwent an 'awakening,' escaping from 'the supposition' that he held 'the right opinions' about a subject we take for granted, 'are careless about.'[91]

Toynbee remained 'careless,' however, following in the rut of the 'fossil' school, such as the biblical exegete Bruno Bauer, 'the Robespierre of theology.' In his essay of 1843 'On the Jewish Question' Bauer declared that the Jews were unfit for emancipation, that Judaism was a 'fossil.'[92] The 1840s, a critical decade for Jewish historiography, also saw the publication of Marx's well-known essay fulminating that there was no Jewish nationality or nation, that society had to be emancipated from the Jews by emancipating the Jews out of existence and into disappearance, that the Jews were preserved 'not in spite of history, but by history' – arguing in the manner of Baruch Spinoza that the Jews had been preserved largely under the pressure of Christian or gentile hostility.[93] That same decade saw Moses Hess's characterization of Jewish existence as a 'mummy,' not nearly so fatally petrified as a 'fossil,' however, and capable of reanimation like Ezekiel's dry bones; but only if a messianic prince charming should awaken the sleeping-beauty Jews to a national life in Palestine would they become a nation again and have a history again: 'The peoples believed dead ... in the consciousness of their historical task must assert their national rights.'[94]

More typical of scholarly judgment, so well disposed a person and profound a student of the historical sociology of religion as Max Weber could not break up the shibboleths. He too noted the statelessness of the Jews, saying that they had retreated from the clash and surge of world history to the quiet precincts within 'the Talmud's four cubits of the Law' and thus accepted 'a self-chosen situation as a pariah people.' This sophisticated version of blaming the victim is simply a restatement of the hoary notion about Judaism as stagnant and paralysed in the grip of the 'Law' as interpreted by the flagitious rabbis – again we end up with a fossil-like idea of Judaism.[95] It never seems to have occurred to non-Jewish students of the *halakhah* that – in a way parallel to and perhaps a model for the English common law, as J.J. Rabinowitz suggested – the rabbis of each generation reinterpreted and adapted the law flexibly and creatively to changing needs and circumstances in what has been called, by Amos Funkenstein, a 'historicizing hermeneutics,' (as fashioned by Maimonides, for example, in accounting for some of the ceremonial laws); the Talmud itself specifies that 'each generation has its interpreters and scribes.'[96]

Thus the way was opened to a dynamic understanding and creative interpretation of *halakhah*, so that prevailing Jewish legal practice was a far cry from the stereotype of a system of rigidly static law to which Jews adhered slavishly. In the course of the Maccabean revolt it was decided not to obey the Sabbath law, as it proved fatal in fighting the enemy. At a later period, after the Simon bar Kochba rising against Rome, it was decided that all except three laws – those forbidding murder, sexual perversion, and idolatry – could be set aside if adherence meant death. In the tenth century the law permitting polygamy was placed in abeyance (not repealed since the Torah is held to be God-given at Sinai and irrevocable). The Jewish way of life is expressed as obedience to God's will, communion with God through every human action, and the extension of the idea of right and wrong to all aspects of human conduct. Properly understood, Torah will be seen as a substitute for the state, the 'portable homeland' of Heinrich Heine's formulation. Toynbee, however, remained oblivious to Jewish perceptions of *halakhah* and he trotted out anew the old canard that the Jews, having abandoned their true missionary task, retreated inward to a paralytic life of 'pathologically meticulous observance' within the ever-more confining walls of the Mosaic Law.[97]

The nineteenth century saw the low point in estimating the worth and significance of Jewish history. Because the Jews were not a nation and did not have a state, they had no history; Jewish history had ended with the destruction of the Temple in AD 70; all that was left was a religion with a mission – so said some apologists as well as the historian Graetz – to bear ethical monotheism to mankind, an idea that Toynbee annexed as the axis of, not his historical, but his prophetic interpretation of Judaism. These negations were a very powerful idea in the nineteenth century, at once a reflection of the Christian belief that Jews were degraded and punished for the arch-crime of deicide, and thus dispersed, stateless, and historyless, as they were a reflection of the exalted idea of the state as apotheosized by the Hegelians and assumed to be the norm for every 'nation.' There is nothing of Hegel's glorifications in Toynbee, who saw the national state as destructive, as a time bomb ticking away to blow up civilization, and he looked to a form of world order to avert national collisions. Hence after 1948 he condemned the existence of a Jewish state. A different line of reasoning from his nineteenth-century predecessors, but the same judgment.

To what extreme denationalization had been carried is evidenced by Gabriel Riesser, a German-Jewish journalist, who urged in the 1840s that a Jew who preferred a non-existent state and nation in Palestine to Germany needed police protection, since he was obviously insane.[98] Such anti-Zionist ideas and stances were reflected in the interpretation of history by Jewish historians, especially those linked to Reform Judaism, such as Isaac M. Jost and Abraham Geiger, but not excluding Graetz. They played down the national and messianic elements in Judaism, and gave little or no attention to the persistence of the Jewish community in Jerusalem and Palestine. More particularly, Gershom Scholem, in his essay on the *Wissenschaft des Judentums*, 'The Science of Judaism – Then and Now,' criticized, if lovingly, what he decried as the *Wissenschaft* school's self-imposed 'system of censorship' and selectivity of the Jewish past that were apologetic in purpose. To win acceptance and to deserve emancipation, Judaism was depicted in the manner of Moses Mendelssohn, as merely an ethical code, rational, modern, consistent with the scientific outlook and swept clean of medieval cobwebs. In depicting Judaism as a religious idea rather than as 'a living organism,' the *Wissenschaft* group – too much under Christian influence, perhaps – 'spiritualized' Judaism; they were 'de-Judaizing' and 'de-actualizing' it. They thus left out many of the rich and vital aspects of Jewish history: the mystical and emotional as expressed in Kabbalah, messianism – much of Jewish history rightfully must be seen *sub specie messias* – Hassidism, and Zionism.[99] Such omissions and glossings-over appeared bitterly ironical later, since the price for emancipation and acceptance was pegged too high, namely, a complete assimilation to the point of disappearance that, as Professor Baron remarked, was 'preached alike by friends and foes [of the Jews] ever since the beginning of the Emancipation era.'[100] Well before the end of the nineteenth century more and more Jews were abandoning the primrose path of assimilation and were drawn to a renewed sense of Jewish identity, or were forced off that route by renewed anti-Semitic storms.

Clearly, then, Toynbee replicates and propagates the perennial ideology – whether in secular or theological guise – that negates Jewish religion, life, and history. It has been long and tenaciously dominant, and no one should deceive himself that he finally has sliced off the last of the Hydra's heads. Paradoxically, Norman Ravitch recently sought to rehabilitate Toynbee for 'an honesty and clarity rarely achieved elsewhere,' who, 'far from being insensitive to Jewish concerns, willingly admitted the permanent value of Jewish life and faith and even suggested that the splits between Judaism, Christianity, and Islam were unfortunate religious "schisms." '[101] He quotes Toynbee that 'Israel, Judah, the Jews, and Judaism did not play major parts in the history of mankind before they gave birth to the two "deviationist" Judaic world-religions. If Christianity and Islam had never been generated by Judaism's involuntary but undeniable paternity, Judaism would be surviving today in an environment of Hellenic "paganism," as Zoroastrianism does survive today in an environment of Hindu "paganism." We may guess that, in that event, the Jews' position in the world today would have been more like the actual position of the Parsees [who are also on Toynbee's list of "fossils"] than like the actual position of the Jews themselves. The Jews would have been more obscure than they now are, but they would also have been more comfortable. The Jews' present-day importance, celebrity, and discomfort all derive from the historic fact that they have involuntarily begotten two Judaic world-religions whose millions of adherents make the preposterous but redoubtable claim to have superseded the Jews, by the Jewish god Yahweh's dispensation, in the role of being this One True God's "Chosen People." '[102] Such statements, invidious and condescending as they tend to be, do not go very far to bear out Professor Ravitch's claims for Toynbee's sensitivity. Toynbee unwittingly provides us with the insight that almost all forms of anti-Semitism and Judaeophobia derive from and are simply the secular versions of Christian anti-Semitism, which has its starting-point in the Gospels. And Professor Ravitch is much more convincing when he acknowledges that, 'in the last analysis, Toynbee speaks for almost all Christians and ex-Christians when he finds the universalist vision of the Jewish prophets fulfilled in the Christian dispensation, with modern Judaism reduced to a narrow segregation of the biblical faith.'[103] That is a crippling bias.

In sum, Arnold Toynbee simply attacks Judaism and denigrates Jewish history, often lapsing into polemical language that he does not permit himself in addressing other subjects. Much of his reprobation is an unsparing reiteration of the ancient Christian theology and historiography of the Jews and Judaism. Their vitality and creativity are camouflaged under such rubrics as 'Syriac,' 'archaism,' 'fossil,' and 'scrapped,' or are ignored. Amidst his prejudice, ignorance of Jewish history, and lacunae, Jewish history suffers a historiographical disaster. And it really does not matter whether Toynbee himself was or was not anti-Semitic, because any anti-Semites who read *A Study of History* will feel confirmed in their beliefs and attitudes.[104] Yet as a participant observed when Toynbee came up at one of the weekly sessions of the discussion group I conduct in a Senior Centre: Toynbee is not the first, nor will he be the last of Judaism's detractors, but he too will be forgotten and Judaism and the Jewish people will live on.

NOTES

1 Toynbee, *A Study of History*, 12 vols (London and New York: Oxford University Press 1934–61), 1: 90–2; for works by and about Toynbee, see *A Bibliography of Arnold J. Toynbee*, compiled by S. Fiona Morton (New York: Oxford University Press 1980).
2 Orlinsky, 'On Toynbee's Use of the Term *Syriac* for One of His Societies,' in *In the Harvest of Time: Essays in Honor of Abba Hillel Silver*, ed. David J. Silver (New York: Macmillan 1963), 260
3 Albright, *From the Stone Age to Christianity*, 2d ed. (Baltimore: Johns Hopkins University Press 1946), 222
4 *Study*, 12: 499–500
5 Orlinsky, 'On Toynbee's Use of the Term *Syriac*,' 259
6 *Study*, 12: 546–7
7 Ibid., 2: 387
8 Ibid., 5: 369

9 Ibid., 1: 211
10 Ibid., 83
11 Ibid., 3: 140
12 Ibid., 12: 394
13 Ibid., 395
14 See Leon Poliakov, *The Aryan Myth: A History of Racist and National Ideas in Europe*, trans. Edmund Howard (New York: Basic Books 1971, 1974), passim.
15 *Study* 5: 657, n. 1
16 Ibid., 5: 657–8
17 Ibid., 4: 224; A. Eban, 'The Toynbee Heresy,' in *Toynbee and History*, ed. M.F. Ashley Montagu (Boston: Porter Sargent 1956), 324
18 *Study*, 5: 657
19 C. Roth in *The Cambridge Medieval History*, ed. H.M. Gwatkin and J.P. Whitney, 8 vols (New York: Macmillan 1924–36), 7: 648; E.R. Hardy, 'The Historical Validity of Toynbee's Approach to Universal Churches,' in *The Intent of Toynbee's History*, ed. Edward T. Gargan (Chicago: Loyola University Press 1961), 169
20 *Study*, 5: 125 and 126, n. 5
21 Ibid., 6: 120
22 Ibid., 122
23 Ibid., 124
24 Ibid., 128
25 Ibid., 129
26 Ibid., 5: 126, n. 5
27 Hardy, 'Historical Validity,' 172
28 *Study*, 4: 262; cf. J.L. Talmon, 'Uniqueness and Universality of Jewish History: A Mid-Century Revaluation,' in *Arguments and Doctrines*, ed. Arthur A. Cohen (New York: Harper & Row 1970), 127
29 *Study*, 4: 247, 262–3
30 Ibid., 7: 596. According to Pieter Geyl, 'Toynbee lives with the Bible, and its texts lie scattered thickly over his pages ... The idea inspiring him is Christianity ... God become man in Christ is to him the veritable sense of history ... His offer of salvation [is] through a return to the Christian religion ... Be converted or perish'; *Debates with Historians* (New York: Meridian 1958), 109, 114, 115, 159, 164.
31 *Study*, 5: 658
32 Ibid., 2: 73–4; cf. Nathan Rotenstreich, *The Recurring Pattern: Studies in*

Anti-Judaism in Modern Thought (London: Weidenfeld and Nicolson 1963), 109; and Eliezer Berkovits, *Judaism: Fossil or Ferment?* (New York: Philosophical Library 1956), 24–5, who remarks that Toynbee does not make Jesus an Aryan but that he de-Judaizes him.

33 *An Historian's Conscience: The Correspondence of Arnold J. Toynbee and Columba Cary-Elwes, Monk of Ampleforth*, ed. Christian B. Peper (Boston: Beacon Press 1986), 5 Oct. 1947, 202

34 *Study*, 12: 505–6

35 Quoted by Elie Kedourie, *The Chatham House Version* (New York: Praeger 1970), 460, n. 68; this was the last sentence of Toynbee's letter to the *Times Literary Supplement* 4 July 1954.

36 The idea that Jesus was a revolutionary insurgent against Rome and was punished as such by Roman authority appears as early as H.S. Reimarus at the very beginning of modern biblical exegesis. On this subject see Gerard S. Sloyan, *Jesus on Trial: The Development of the Passion Narratives and Their Historical and Ecumenical Significance*, ed. and intro. John Reumann (Philadelphia: Fortress Press 1973); S.G.F. Brandon, *Jesus and the Zealots: A Study of the Political Factor in Primitive Christianity* (Manchester: Manchester University Press 1967); Haim H. Cohn, *The Trial and Death of Jesus* (New York: Harper & Row 1971); Paul Winter, *On the Trial of Jesus*, rev. and ed. T.A. Burkill and Geza Vermes, 2d ed. (Berlin: de Gruyter 1974); and *Judaism* 20, no. 1 (winter 1971), for the symposium of eight articles from diverse perspectives on 'The Trial of Jesus in the Light of History.'

37 *Study*, 5: 544; 8: 283

38 Ibid., 6: 103; 5: 387; 8: 310, 309

39 Ibid., 8: 309–10

40 Ibid., 284

41 Ibid.

42 Ibid., 8: 288

43 Eban, 'The Toynbee Heresy,' 328

44 *Study*, 7: 438

45 Ibid., 439; according to Peper (ed.), *Historian's Conscience*, 462, n. 2, Toynbee had a consuming interest in Marcion with whom he 'wrestles' in his discussion of 'The Freedom of Human Souls That Is the Law of God,' *Study*, 9: 395–405; see Toynbee's letters of 22 Nov. 1965 and 25 Jan. 1972 in *Historian's Conscience*, 461–2, 537.

46 *Study*, 7: 438

47 Ibid., 1: 211; 212, n. 3; 211–5

48 Ibid., 5: 182
49 Ibid., 7: 474, n. 1; cf. his letter of 13 Apr. 1949; 'I am a through-and-through anti-rationalist,' in *Historian's Conscience*, 242.
50 Cohn, *The Pursuit of the Millennium: Revolutionary Millenarians and Mystical Anarchists of the Middle Ages*, rev. and expanded ed. (New York: Oxford University Press 1970), 108, 125, 285; cf. J.L. Talmon, 'Uniqueness and Universality,' 118–20, and especially the pithy insights of pp. 134–5.
51 Geyl, *Debates with Historians*, 198
52 *Study*, 12: 541–2
53 Ibid., 8: 405
54 Quoted by Frederick E. Robin, 'The Professor and the Fossil,' in Montagu (ed.), *Toynbee and History*, 318.
55 *Study*, 6: 123, and n. 5; 8: 300, 312; his predilection for the Ottoman *millet*, a depoliticized ethnic, religious, cultural community, probably reflects Toynbee's antipathy for the national state; cf. Talmon, 'Uniqueness and Universality,' 130–1; also Toynbee's letter at the time of the fall of France, 1940, 'The national state is over, and we are going to have a world state,' in *Historian's Conscience*, 67.
56 *Study*, 8: 301
57 Ibid., 5: 383–4; 6: 49ff., 70–1, 94–7; 8: 301
58 Ibid., 8: 304, 307
59 Kedourie, *Chatham House Version*, 377, 351–3; and *The Anglo-Arab Labyrinth: The McMahon-Husayn Correspondence and Its Interpreters 1914-39* (New York: Cambridge University Press, 1976), *passim*. Cf. Gordon Martel's essay attacking Toynbee's excessively one-sided and self-important pro-Arab stance, 'The Origins of the Chatham House Version,' in *National and International Politics in the Middle East: Essays in Honor of Elie Kedourie*, ed. Edward Ingram (London: Cass 1986), 66–83. According to Martel, Toynbee's condemnation of imperialism, nationalism and racism was a later conversion; until disillusioned by the First World War and the Versailles Peace Conference he had been an enthusiast of war, the British Empire, national self-determination à la President Wilson and Colonel Lawrence, and racism – affirming 'the soundness of race prejudice.' Martel emphasizes the importance of Toynbee's wartime service as an intelligence evaluator in the Foreign Office with responsibility for Turkey and the Middle East, for it was then that he adopted his extreme pro-Arab stance and 'painted a picture of a naturally peaceful and innocent Arabic society, explaining away some extreme movements like Wahabism and pan-Arabism as mere responses to the oppression and frag-

mentation imposed upon the Arabs' by the Turks and the European empires, in the light of which the Balfour Declaration became 'an exercise in imperialist double-dealing.' See also the exchange of letters between Toynbee and J.L. Talmon in *Encounter*, October 1967; reprinted in *The Israel-Arab Reader*, ed. Walter Laqueur (New York: Citadel 1968), 260–72.

60 *Study*, 8: 289. Toynbee fails to mention the juridical action that did most to legitimize Israel, the November 1947 UN resolution that provided for partition and sanctioned a Jewish state; such flouting of the fact that world public opinion supported the creation of Israel, J.L. Talmon called a methodology that 'amounts to untruth' ('Uniqueness and Universality,' 138); cf. the Martel essay cited above, n. 59.
61 *Study*, 8: 576, n. 2
62 Ibid., 290–1
63 'The Toynbee Heresy,' 335, 320
64 Quoted in Raphael Mahler, *A History of Modern Jewry, 1780–1815* (New York: Schocken 1971), 621–2.
65 *Study*, 8: 310–11
66 Ibid., 298–300
67 Ibid., 2: 253; 8: 293
68 Ibid., 6: 216
69 Ibid., 8: 293; Deutscher, *The Non-Jewish Jew and Other Essays*, ed. and intro. Tamara Deutscher (London: Oxford University Press 1968)
70 *Study*, 12: 478; a few years later he called himself 'an un-de-Christianized agnostic' in *Acquaintances* (London: Oxford University Press 1967), 146. See *Study*, 9: 634–5, where he calls himself 'a post-Christian Christian' and describes his summer 1936 dream wherein he saw himself grasping the foot of the crucifix over the high altar of the Abbey of Ampleforth and heard a voice urging '*amplexus expecta*' – cling and wait; his reference to himself as a 'philo-Catholic,' *Historian's Conscience*, 168; and the frequent mention of his 'Anglican upbringing at home and at school,' ibid., 19. H.R. Trevor-Roper concluded that Toynbee saw himself as Christ-like; see Martel, 'Origins of Chatham House Version,' 68.
71 *Historian's Conscience*, 404
72 Ibid., 199
73 *Study*, 12: 209–17
74 Braudel, *The Mediterranean and the Mediterranean World in the Age of Philip II*, trans. Sian Reynolds (New York: Harper & Row 1973), 803–4, 810 (original ed. Paris: Colin 1949)
75 *Study*, 12: 479

76 Ibid., 292–300, esp. 296
77 Ibid., 627, 628
78 Ibid., 627
79 Ibid., 4: 262–3; 5: 179, 387–93; cf. Berkovits, *Judaism*, 12, 75–6
80 *Study*, 12: 495–6
81 Ibid., 478
82 Ibid., 478
83 Ibid., 515; this penchant to play the prophet runs through his career and often swallowed up the historian, an indication of which appeared as early as 1914, when Clarendon Press rejected a manuscript as containing too much prophecy; Martel, 'Origins of the Chatham House Version,' 73
84 *Study*, 12: 488
85 Ibid., 196
86 Ibid., 2: 257, 402–11
87 Ibid., 244 and n. 2, 247–8 and n. 1; 4: 284–5; Samuel, *The Professor and the Fossil* (New York: Knopf 1956), 162
88 *Study*, 12: 517
89 Samuel, *Professor and the Fossil*, 38–9
90 Graetz, *The Structure of Jewish History and Other Essays*, trans., ed., and intro. Ismar Schorsch (New York: Jewish Theological Seminary of America 1975), 93–4
91 Eliot, *Daniel Deronda*, 2 vols (New York: Harper & Brothers 1876), 2: 371
92 Ismar Schorsch, 'Introduction,' to Graetz, *Structure of Jewish History*, 21
93 Marx, 'On the Jewish Question,' in *Writings of the Young Marx on Philosophy and Society*, ed. and trans. L.D. Easton and K.H. Guddat (New York: Doubleday Anchor 1967), 216–48; Spinoza, 'Of the Vocation of the Hebrews,' chap. 3 of *A Theologico-Political Treatise*, in *Chief Works of Benedict de Spinoza*, ed. R.H.M. Elwes, 2 vols (New York: Dover 1951), 1: 55–6
94 Lionel Kochan, *The Jew and His History* (New York: Schocken 1977), 3–4
95 Ibid., 5–6
96 Jacob J. Rabinowitz, 'The Influence of the Jewish Law on the Development of the Common Law,' in *The Jews: Their History, Culture, and Religion*, ed. Louis Finkelstein, 2 vols (New York: Harper 1949), chap. 16, pp. 823–53; Amos Funkenstein, 'Gesetz und Geschichte: Zur historisierenden Hermeneutik bei Moses Maimonides und Thomas von Aquin,' *Viator* 1 (1970): 147–78. Owing to its mode of 'inspired biblical exegesis,' the Qumran community was remarkable for its flexible adaptation of the law; see Lawrence H. Schiffman, *Sectarian Law in the Dead Sea Scrolls: Courts, Testimony and the*

Penal Code (Chico, Calif.: Scholars Press, Brown Judaic Studies 1983), 12, 14–17.
97 *Study*, 6: 113; cf. 126, n. 5
98 Walter Laqueur, *A History of Zionism* (New York: Holt, Rinehart & Winston 1972), 8
99 Scholem, *The Messianic Idea in Judaism and Other Essays* (New York: Schocken 1971), 304–13, esp. 304–7
100 Salo W. Baron, 'Modern Capitalism and Jewish Fate,' *History and Jewish Historians*, ed. Arthur Hertzberg and Leon Feldman (Philadelphia: Jewish Publication Society of America 1964), 47
101 Ravitch, 'The Problem of Christian Anti-Semitism,' *Commentary*, April 1982, 45
102 *Study*, 12: 479
103 'Problem of Christian Anti-Semitism,' 46
104 Commenting on Toynbee's exchange with Yaacov Herzog in a 1961 debate at McGill University, Montreal, Reinhold Niebuhr observed: 'I can't escape the feeling that, in spite of his best efforts, Toynbee has a deep-set prejudice against the Jews.' Toynbee himself professed shock and surprise at the uproar provoked by his equation of Nazism with the founding of Israel in 1948, explaining that in his pronouncements on Jewish history 'I feel I have given the Jewish people a bit of a shock treatment,' as though he were a psychiatrist concerned to heal Jewish pathologies (*Time*, 10 Feb. 1961, 38). Toynbee was an indefatigable world traveller, especially in the years of great fame after 1945; some of his most interesting writings are the travel-historical books about his journeys to North and South America, Eastern Europe and Soviet Russia, Turkey and the Middle East, Asia and Japan, and so on; but his wanderlust never carried him to Israel to see that country first-hand. That Toynbee never mellowed one can gauge from his letter to a Syrian general at the time of the Yom Kippur war, 1973: 'I send you my heartfelt wishes for an Arab victory'; quoted in William H. McNeill, *Arnold J. Toynbee: A Life* (New York and Oxford: Oxford University Press 1989), 248.

Toynbee Amended and Updated

Theodore H. Von Laue

Reconsideration of Arnold Toynbee compels us to advance from our scholarly interest in him to our own need as historians and human beings to come to grips with our historical condition. Whatever Toynbee's shortcomings, his ambition was to understand the world of which he was part, in the largest contexts of time and space. Let us follow his example and subordinate all our intellectual pursuits to that crucial end; our survival, as Toynbee recognized, may well depend on it. Inspired by Toynbee, these pages will expand his insights as a means of coming to a clearer understanding of our twentieth century, the most momentous in all human existence. We will take – surely with his blessings – the immortal Toynbee beyond his mortal self.

To begin with a disciple's tribute to the immortal qualities of Toynbee's work: as a historian of immense mental energy and far-reaching sensibilities, trained by an unusually deep immersion in the intellectual and spiritual resources of Western civilization, he set out to fathom the wholeness of civilizations as the basic collective environment for human existence and as the only intelligible unit for historical analysis. Meaningful historical analysis, he teaches, has to be set into the largest applicable contexts. Only by viewing historical events within the full framework of the factors influencing them can we gain the understanding necessary for a sense of control over human destiny.

Next, Toynbee deserves praise for his insistence that in the totality of cultural experience religion plays a central role. He himself confessed that he had 'found his vocation in a call from God to feel after Him and find Him.'[1] With this sensibility he was aware of religion as a unique community-enhancing force at the core of all functioning civilizations, a metaphysically founded prescription for a socializing self-discipline. That discipline – we might extend Toynbee's thoughts – structures the raw physical energy in the human subconscious – call it soul, if you will – for the purpose of constructively tying individuals into a larger group. Being absolutely essential for collective survival, that community-building prescription has traditionally been held sacred. In this manner religion has shaped – and still shapes in secularized form – the human subconscious far below human awareness, below all rational thought or deliberate behaviour. The openness of mind required for understanding our world therefore demands, apart from all other skills, a refined religious and moral awareness, though not necessarily in conventional terms.

Finally, Toynbee commands our admiration as a thinking human being who never separated his roles as a scholar, citizen, and religious seeker. He was a true existentialist historian, a 'complete historian,' who approached the record of human existence from a central awareness that drew on all his faculties and sensibilities. Any lesser, more fragmented approach to history demeans historians and diminishes their human effectiveness. Historians should view history and life through the undivided force of their concentrated psychosomatic vitality as – in Toynbee's language – through a call from God.

For these qualities Toynbee still towers above the historical profession, an inspired historian determined to assess the human condition in a newly unified and still unexplored world. In the unprecedented age of global interdependence we crave a commanding sense of control over our destiny that ties our inward selves to a world too suddenly and incomprehensibly enlarged. If, in retrospect, Toynbee's view of the world appears too narrow and his genius diminished by the limits imposed by his times and origins, his work still indicates the direction in which we must move. Drawing then on Toynbee's writings, especially those contained in *The World and the West* (1956), and inspired by his boldness, this essay will venture into the largest perspectives of our existence by reassessing – all too incompletely – Toynbee's voluminous conclusions about the present century with which he was too closely associated for proper insight.

Applying Toynbee's sense of direction to our times by examining the flaws in his work, we find at the outset a troublesome shift in his perspectives, of which it seems he was not fully aware. He began before the First World War with a British Whig's view of the world, a Church of England religious orientation, and a classicist's approach to ancient Greece and Rome as a guide to non-Western civilizations, at the historic moment when his cultural assumptions met their first check. 'Born into the age of the Late Victorian optimism and encountering the First World War in early manhood,'[2] he said, he was struck by the existentialist question: Why do civilizations die? Will Western civilization, his own, also die? His *Study of History* constitutes a monumental inquiry into the rise and fall of twenty-odd cultural mansions, tracing the dynamics of their evolution essentially to internal factors.

After the end of the Second World War Toynbee found himself in a different world, a unified world in which the surviving cultural mansions turned out to have coexisted, since AD 1500 he said,[3] under a common roof. Consequently in 1947, while still sticking to his cultural conditioning and earlier insights, he urged an advance from the 'antediluvian Western traditional historical outlook' (which still permeates his *Study of History*) to a global perspective.[4] Obviously, what mattered in the new setting were not the internal dynamics of isolated or self-propelled cultural entities but the dynamics of their world-wide interaction. Toynbee himself recognized the logic of the change when he subsequently explored the 'Encounters between Civilizations,'[5] though without ever recognizing the full challenge posed by the change of framework.

In other words, born into an interdependent global world, Toynbee planned and wrote *A Study of History* from a perspective outdated from the start. Not civilizations separately, but their common framework, the interdependent world, constituted the sole intelligible unit for a true historical understanding of the present world and the fate of Western civilization. That framework was far larger and more complex than Toynbee realized.

Moreover, the world under the long-established common roof that Toynbee had first recognized in 1947 no longer contained non-Western civilizations as self-contained integrated units. All of them had been discultured and recultured to various degrees. They survive now – if it is survival – in an acute state of cultural chaos or disorientation, which contrasts sharply with the continued – or at least residual – cultural sovereignty of the West. Under the common roof, civilizations as defined by Toynbee – even Western civilization – can certainly no longer be considered intelligible units of historical analysis. They have been downgraded into ineffectual and ever more shadowy subunits. Under the common roof of an interdependent world the effective subunits are the states and polities from which Toynbee wanted to liberate historical analysis, subunits often at war with each other, although belonging to the same religious or cultural tradition. In the twentieth century, it would seem, world events have been determined by the encounter not between civilizations but between states ever more intensively shaped in their political culture by their competitive interaction in the global state system.

Under these conditions top priority for any comprehensive and meaningful historical analysis clearly must be given to the nature of the global framework in which all the states interact. In the face of the challenge Toynbee essentially remained a nineteenth-century Englishman who heroically tried to rise to a larger view, but still looked at Europe, the West, let alone the non-Western world, through insular eyes.

For an updated Toynbeean view of twentieth-century reality under the common roof, we must first distance ourselves from Toynbee's spiritualizing and self-indulgent Whiggish benignity. A product of British power at its peak he never fathomed the fullness of that power, no matter how poignantly he commented on power politics (the powerful are notoriously dimwitted in recognizing the scope of their power). Like most historians writing about Western civilization from the inside, he played down both the role of raw power in Western history and the inhumanity accompanying it. Such bowdlerization of Western history constitutes a fact limiting our perception of that inhumanity: power, like sex, seemingly does not exist when it is not mentioned. In any comprehensive analysis, however, it needs to be given its due place. The arms race existed from the beginning of the European state system; it culminated in the atomic bomb, a product of Western civilization. And with all the undeniable advances in humanitarianism,

Western civilization did not overcome war. On the contrary, as Toynbee himself sensed, it built up war to frightening proportions.

More important yet is the factor of raw power in the relations between Western and non-Western civilizations, both while the latter still enjoyed a measure of sovereignty (that is, to the end of the nineteenth century) and after their subsequent subversion. Toynbee admittedly used strong language in describing the Western impact on the world. It was 'so powerful and so pervasive,' he wrote, 'that it turned the lives of all its victims upside down and inside out – affecting the behaviour, outlook, feeling, and beliefs of individual men, women, and children in an intimate way, touching chords in human souls that are not touched by mere external material factors.'[6] Yet approaching non-Western cultures bookishly, as he did ancient Greece and Rome, he never left his own cultural envelope despite his many travels; he never got experientially to the other side. Consequently, he never comprehended the destructive dynamics of the Western impact on non-Western societies in a world increasingly crowded under one roof.

For contrast, let us look at another Englishman a generation before Toynbee – at Lord Lytton as viceroy of India, who had a clearer insight into the impact of the West. As early as 1878 he admitted that British rule meant, under 'that supreme law – the safety of the state,' the forcible imposition of a foreign and uncongenial system 'scarcely if at all intelligible to the greater number of those for whose benefit it is maintained.' Recognizing that English history had long outgrown the contexts of Western civilization, he summed up the essence of British imperialism in a statement still impressive by its profundity: 'It is a fact which there is no disguising ... and also one which cannot be too constantly or too anxiously recognized that ... we have placed and must permanently maintain ourselves at the head of a gradual but gigantic revolution – the greatest and most momentous social, moral, and religious, as well as political revolution which, perhaps, the world has ever witnessed.'[7]

We note the significant points: Lord Lytton's emphasis on the incompatibility of Western and non-Western cultures; on the fact that British culture was imposed by naked force, for the safety of the state; and that such imposition was part of a competition for power in the world in which Britain was determined to stay in the lead. Viewed in this light – realistically – the Westernization of the world meant a profound brutalizing process of reculturation under external compulsion. Following Lord Lytton's observation and re-examining the process of Western expansion, we can therefore properly speak of the world revolution of Westernization, the original revolution compared with which the other twentieth-century revolutions, the anti-Western revolutions of Communism and Fascism, were mere counter-revolutions, as explained below.

That world revolution of Westernization[8] created, as a radically novel fact in all human existence, the common roof that, according to Toynbee, had existed since the sixteenth century. A common roof solid enough to merit the name, however, was pulled over the world only at the eve of the twentieth century, after the chief European powers and the United States, taking advantage of their new rapid communications technology, had occupied and established control over 85 per cent of the world's land surface and all the oceans as well. Under that roof and under the prompting of that mighty revolution there rose the interdependent global state system of the late twentieth century, a framework more ruthlessly power-minded than the old European state system, and more anarchic.

The Europeans had competed with each other within the bounds of a reasonably common civilization. In the world of global interdependence, however, we find a bewildering association of cultures evolved over millennia under starkly different conditions, operating with sharply unequal resources – all compressed into intense competition over wealth and power under rules laid down by the West. Compelled against their will to adapt themselves to Western ways, the run of non-Western peoples has infused global politics with unprecedented bitterness. In the face of mounting political, economic, and ecological crises the revolution of Westernization continues from the past into the future, now commonly referred to simply as modernization and conducted by non-Westerners themselves.

One of the biggest escalations in that revolution of Westernization occurred late in Toynbee's life and therefore did not make much impression on him: the process of decolonization that universalized the basic Western unit of effective socio-political organization, the nation-state. The nation-state has made permanent the pressures of modernization, without regard to indigenous tradition and often in murderous conflict with it. The Westernized non-Western state absorbed basic aspects of Western culture: a keen alertness to all power relationships and to the instruments that create power, including the large-scale organizations that go with statehood; plus the latest weapons, the agencies and skills that create those weapons (including science, technology, and higher education); and prestige items like a high standard of living and conspicuous consumption that confer victory in what Thorstein Veblen has called invidious comparison. To this day power furnishes the universals that uphold the global roof. And no aspect of power is more crucial than the capacity to foist cultural change on others while remaining unchanged oneself.

That modernizing reculturation, we should keep in mind without Whiggish flinching, was – and is – always conducted with a keen eye to power, world power no less. Contemporary Westerners, like Lord Lytton before them, generally dwell on the positive aspects of their global influence. The West has brought freedom, human rights, a sense of human control over nature, and a vast material advance to all humanity. What is conveniently overlooked, even by Toynbee's disciples, is the fact that the Westerners have also taught a monstrous appetite for world power. They have dominated the world, culturally even more than territorially, providing an impressive illustration of the benefits, both material and psychological, to be derived from such majesty. Seen through critical non-Western eyes Western expansionism has been a key factor in the evolution of Western civilization with all its attractions, including government by consensus.

How different by comparison is the experience of non-Westerners at the receiving end of the Western world revolution! Prompted by the competitive global pursuit of wealth and power non-Western states now enforce the permanent revolution of Westernization within their own boundaries. Toynbee hardly came to grips with the problems of 'development,' how to transfer the manifold externals of Western power to culturally unprepared and uncomprehending peoples. Admittedly, he commented on the miseries of the non-Western intelligentsia without, however, being able to fathom their role as power-hungry agents of Westernization waging a cultural war against indigenous tradition (often in the name of that tradition). From Toynbee's days to the present the world revolution of Westernization has been unceasingly at work between different strata of non-Western populations and within non-Western individuals down to their souls, sometimes with terrifying results. And local folk, however competent in managing their own affairs in the past, are now hopelessly disadvantaged; salvation lies in access to the universals of power, in Westernizing modernization.

What has stung sharpest in the West's revolutionary impact was the subversion not only of local pride and culture, but also of local governments, not once but a hundred times, as long as their helplessness was revealed in war or peace. Was it a wonder that eager imitators aimed at power first and foremost? The capacity to imprint one's own culture upon the world was triumphantly flaunted before their eyes not only in their daily lives but also in the political ideologies trumpeted from the West, say in Lord Lytton's praise of Britain's imperial mission or Woodrow Wilson's crusade to make the world safe for democracy. Were the others to submit to a permanent inferiority?

Take a specific case from Toynbee's own lifetime that he never understood: the sudden imposition after the First World War of the externals of Western democracy upon the peoples of central and eastern Europe. Here the alien ideals and institutions, together with the latest technologies of communication, created a new type of politics: illiberal mass politics, for which the Western model provided no guidelines. Newly enfranchised voters, inexperienced, excitable, opinionated, were caught up in the disorientation following an unsatisfactory or lost war, caught up also in the conflict, both practical and metaphysical, between indigenous tradition and the influx of Western practices, and fired to boot by the new globalism of the world war and its heady propaganda. Under these conditions the transferable formal aspects of Western democracy like constitutional government or civil liberties never had a chance; instead they created opportunities for ambitious newcomers eager to build up a world empire in the manner of the victors in the late war.

Thus, viewed in a globally adjusted Toynbeean perspective, both Communist and Fascist leaders echoed the Western trumpeters of wealth and power they had heard from afar; the scope of their ambition was not of their own making. Put differently, both Communism and Fascism (in both Italy and Germany) were counter-revolutions trying to limit Western subversion by imitating the voracious political expansionism of the model countries that had humiliated them and by copying their instruments of power as best their indigenous resources permitted. Thus the modern dictators themselves were agents of Westernizing reculturation – through non-Western means of compulsion.

This observation calls for a brief comment on the dynamics of the cultural challenge-and-response mechanism within the global system, another dimension hardly explored by Toynbee. The essence of the jumbled efforts by Communist and Fascist leaders to create from the disoriented human raw material at their disposal a political culture capable of standing up to the Western challenge was expressed in a simple formula by Lenin as early as 1902. 'What is to a great extent automatic in a politically free country must [in our country] be done deliberately and systematically by [our] organization.'[9] What is commonly called totalitarianism was a form of Westernizing substitutionism. It replaced the Western practice of voluntary co-operation subliminally conditioned over centuries – the invisible formative agents that cannot be transported across cultural boundaries – by deliberate and rationally devised controls reinforced by terror. Where the customs of social co-operation were fairly well developed, as in Germany, totalitarianism assumed a relatively moderate form; in rebellious pre-industrial Russia it was bound to be extreme.[10] Until very recently such substitutionism, often dressed up as socialism or communism, was very much in vogue. It seemed to be the only method of overcoming the humiliations of underdevelopment in a world ruled by Western standards of wealth and power.

Looking at the world through British eyes and living too close to two world wars fought against Germany, the key challenger of the West in his time, Toynbee never turned a compassionate eye on Germany. As regards Russia, a more remote power threat, he was more sympathetic, recognizing the influence of the West in shaping Russian history; Soviet communism he depoliticized, failing to probe into the bloody details of the externally enforced reculturation undertaken by Lenin and Stalin. As for the non-Western world, he sometimes thought of Westernization in terms of mere 'cocacolanization' – 'the penetrative power of a strand or cultural radiation is usually in inverse ratio to the strand's cultural value'[11]; only superficialities left their mark. In reality, we should say, what penetrated most deeply and instantly was the capacity to inflict mortal defeat by destroying indigenous authority.

Everywhere things fell apart after the Europeans – or the West – won in the battles that followed the crucial encounter. Toynbee's ethnocentricity never allowed him to comprehend the awful truth emerging from the fact that the world had become a single unit of interaction: *the ultimate responsibility, moral and otherwise, for the horror of the anti-Western counter-revolutions as well as for the mayhem in the contemporary 'developing' countries, squarely belongs to the West itself.*

Thus – to extend briefly these perspectives – the West also bears responsibility for the chief experiment of militant anti-Western Westernization, the Soviet Union. That country represents the mirror image of the West's ambition to reshape the world in its own image – a mirror image distorted by the tensions of the Western impact upon backward peoples in a vast and inhospitable continent. In Eurasia the Western impact has been at work for centuries, and even more tragically than Toynbee realized. The pride-power interaction between the Western challenge and the indigenous response has reached its dramatic culmination in the present super power rivalry that may yet destroy all humanity – largely through Western ignorance of the political and cultural processes in the encounter between civilizations. A lasting relaxation of controls in the Soviet system and a reduction of hostility between the super powers can come only through a Western recognition of the West's subversive role in world affairs and of the West's moral responsibility for the anti-Western counter-revolutions with all their outrages.

This viewpoint raises another – and even more controversial – issue of Toynbee's treatment of the encounter between civilizations. Despite his good intentions, he never escaped the cognitive imperialism of analysing other civilizations by the light of his own, never realizing that people of different cultural conditioning are experientially incapable of understanding each other. Cultures (in whatever form, including political cultures) are essentially incompatible entities, lacking common denominators for meaningful comparison except in terms of the universals of power – raw power in crucial encounters.

The global universals of power allow comparisons of the kind expressed in the global hierarchy of 'advanced,' 'developing,' and 'least developed.' But in the deeper recesses of the collective unconscious, as well as in the assumptions locally accompanying the global universals, incomparability prevails, just as different languages are mutually incomprehensible. Thus far – and certainly in Toynbee's case – inter-cultural comparison has proceeded imperialistically, through the medium of Western sensibilities and Western experience. What we need for true inter-cultural understanding is insight into the problem of crossing to the other side, of seeing the others as they see themselves. Toynbee's impressive sensibilities did not carry him far enough; he rather followed the common practice of transubstantiating bits of alien culture into components of his own, as had always been done by classicists in regard to ancient Greece and Rome.

The chief difficulty in crossing over to the other side mentally, analytically, and – above all – experientially lies in the fact that the bulk of cultural substance lies hidden in the subconscious, taken for granted by the insiders and therefore left unarticulated (except in subtle hints and allusions inaccessible to foreigners). How under these conditions can there be meaningful inter-cultural comparison except imperialistically in terms of the gut reactions of power: whose views of reality, whose values, shall prevail? For the purposes of cross-cultural analysis the working concepts of most social scientists and historians, including 'freedom,' 'individualism,' and 'rationalism,' are culture-bound and therefore useless (or worse, especially in the American treatment of the USSR).

What matters is not only Toynbee's awareness that heart and mind give different signals, but also an insight that hearts are tuned differently and minds have separate structures in different cultures. Far more than Toynbee realized, we still live in a pluralist world steeped in cultural relativism; even in our Westernized world the West has not become the measure of all things. The universals of power do not touch the soul, nor do they explain the dynamics of the anti-Western counter-revolutions. While under the global roof the visible superstructures grow ever more uniform, the cellars preserve essential parts of the original cultures. However disoriented and confused, they still remain secluded separate worlds (which accounts for the fragility of the whole edifice).

Yet does not historical understanding in Toynbee's sense demand that with ears and eyes wide open we cross over to the other side, even if it is into an enemy's camp? That we must transcend our cultural limitations and penetrate to the cellars of human, political, or cultural motivation? In the tightly packed global community power-oriented political cultures embodied in states clash with each other in mutual incomprehension, with often terrifying consequences. For the sake of peace and survival – for the sake of Toynbee's moral convictions – we need an all-inclusive historical understanding that, starting from a compassionate cultural relativism, rises above all cultural barriers – a big job not yet attempted by anyone.

What then – to go on to the ultimate Toynbeean concern – of the West in this fragile Westernized world? Is it still a separate entity? The chief distinction between the World and the West, it would seem, still lies in the fact that the West has preserved its sovereign cultural integrity. It has universalized itself while forcing all other civilizations to reculture themselves rather against their inclination. It still possesses the monopoly of that capacity.

Building on Toynbee's awareness of the importance of religion, one should say then that the West, with the help of its intensely ascetic religious heritage glorifying the mortification of the flesh through Christ crucified had made the greatest progress towards the cultural skills of large-scale organization needed for an age of global interdependence. There exists, by a rule of thumb, a single equation between the effective size of a community and the necessary ascetic self-denial reaching down to the core of libidinous sexuality: the larger the community, the smaller the individual and the greater the individual's imprisonment in restraints that have to be sublimated into a sense of freedom and individual autonomy. The command 'Love Thy Neighbour' is relatively easy to obey in a small group; a loving adjustment to millions of neighbours requires an infinite range of subtle curbs internalized so deep as not to enter into conscious awareness.

Only the West has developed the capacity for integrating selfish individuals into reasonably voluntary co-operation under large-scale organizations – organizations culminating in the consensus-based nation-state counting tens if not hundreds of millions of docile citizens. By comparison, the members of other civilizations (such as they now are or have been – Japan excepted) are far less ascetic in their conduct, more selfish and anarchic, the framework of their effective socialization in the past often no larger than the family, lineage, or clan. The vast and impersonal associations that make up the modern nation-state were alien to the majority of humanity until the mid-twentieth century; they cannot manage them now. Operating large organizations is a cultural skill of the utmost importance; only the Japanese possess the essential ingredients. While the others are reluctantly learning, the West, now immersed in a Westernized world, still claims the cultural assets of mastering large-scale co-operation; it can set the pace of the transition from statehood to global organization.

In that world – to look in conclusion at the future, Toynbee style – Westernization has turned into modernization and the encounter between civilizations into power competition within a global state system. Through its incessant politico-cultural interaction that system, like the European state system before it, enjoins a constant competitive mobilization upon all its members. The future, therefore, is determined not so much by the minor ups and downs of individual polities as by the evolution of the system as a whole. What are its prospects?

The interdependent global state system has been characterized as an anarchic community; the community-building forces are balanced against the community-destroying forces in an age when humanity walks the knife's edge between survival and a nuclear holocaust. The community-building forces derive their strength from the realities and opportunities of interdependence. The present volume of human life on earth can be sustained only by the present level of peaceful worldwide co-operation. Any increase in numbers or improvement in the standard of living calls for even more intensive co-operation. The ultimate goal of peaceful globalism beckoning in the distance is not only the avoidance of nuclear conflict but also the establishment of a reasonable equilibrium between population and the resources of the world's ecosystem, requiring a virtually universal practice of extreme ascetic individual self-discipline. There is no lack of instruments for accomplishing these goals, from the UN and its agencies down to the host of transnational organizations, all of them counting on support from a far-sighted, globally minded, and rational world-wide constituency. Does that constituency exist in sufficient strength?

The forces of anarchy include the diversity of geographical conditions and of human capacity for voluntary large-scale co-operation, the differences between rich and poor, as well as the rivalry between the super powers in setting a superior model for human evolution. In addition, the very nature of the tightly compacted global community promotes anarchy. In the first place, the vast volume of detail to be handled in the transactions of peaceful interdependence constitutes an intolerable burden on human energy, considering the pressures on the poor for making ends meet on the ground floors of life, the demands of the knowledge explosion upon the experts, and the busy self-indulgence of the rich. Who can keep up with the avalanche of information needed for effective globalism? No specialists, no governments are in control of their responsibilities; the world has grown over our heads. Who under these circumstances is not tempted to shrink back into self-indulgent indifference?

More important, the inescapable openness of all polities to the goods, ideas, and values swirling around the globe is promoting a profoundly restrictive moral relativism. All traditional identities – even in the West itself – are threatened; all creeds, all ideologies, all convictions, all absolutes disprove each other by their coexistence. What then is right, apart from the external universals of power? Regarding ultimate truths, the Westernized world is a Tower of Babel. In the face of that reality people everywhere are hardening their views, falling back on traditional identities, on their roots, their nationalism, thereby undermining peaceful co-operation and contracting their awareness. Or they become mindless technicians, as though science and technology existed in a societal vacuum.[12] Worse, in their metaphysical insecurity they are apt to resort to violence as the ultimate (and self-defeating) guarantee of security; hence the unceasing escalation in the arms race. A common basement of world-wide metaphysics, a soul-anchored sense of global community, obviously does not exist.

At this point we turn to Toynbee's vision of a new epiphany. Obviously, what is needed for human survival is a creed providing the heightened ascetic self-discipline required for the integration of individuals, not only among tens or hundreds of millions but also among five and more billion neighbours with greatly divergent capacities and outlooks. Are the conditions ready? Toynbee was impressed by the advance of the strict monotheism of the Jews to the even more demanding de-ethnicized universalism of the early Christian church. It was a momentous step, providing a transcendence-oriented metaphysical base not only for the late Rome Empire but also for the universal Catholic church and, in secularized form, for the nation-state.

Is such a spiritual quantum jump possible in the present world? We possess no counterpart of the Roman Empire, in its day a world-state offering civic security for its citizens and sufficient cultural cohesion for the spread of a transcendent universalism; our Westernized world has not reached that measure of unity. And where do we see evidence of the soul-enlarging ascetic universalism that enables individuals to adjust their conduct to the global overload? Where is the superior, more globally minded internal or external proletariat? In the United States, as in much of the West generally, the dominant trend of the moment seems to run in the opposite direction, towards a shrinkage of civic awareness.

A quantum jump into a more ascetically enlarged sense of social responsibility, as Toynbee realized, has historically occurred only as a result of major catastrophe in the body politic. What form will such a catastrophe take in our interdependent world, in our nuclear age? Weighing the community-building, transcendence-promoting factors in the global world against the anarchy-promoting factors, a contemporary disillusioned Toynbeean might see the latter pulling us down towards a dark future. What lies ahead is certainly not a *civitas sanctorum*. Will it be the nuclear holocaust?

In that grim perspective the only consolation, a liberating one in the existentialist historical perspective, is that we can know the forces at work in the new age of globalism; we can achieve an enlarged sense of command over our destiny. Our lives are not worth living – if we are to survive at all – unless examined with the most refined sensibilities and in the largest contexts. As long as there is an open-eyed historical analysis probing into *all* factors shaping the human destiny, there is a glimmer of immortal Toynbeean hope.[13]

NOTES

1 Toynbee, *The Study of History*, 12 vols (London and New York: Oxford University Press 1934–61), 10: 1
2 Quoted from *Civilization on Trial and The World and The West* (Cleveland and New York: Meridian Books 1958), 348
3 Ibid., 65

4 Ibid., 64
5 Ibid., chapter 11
6 Ibid., 189
7 Lord Lytton, quoted in A.J. Thornton, *Doctrines of Imperialism* (New York: Wiley 1965), 178
8 This theme is more fully developed in the author's book *The World Revolution of Westernization: The 20th Century in Global Perspective* (New York: Oxford University Press 1987).
9 Lenin, *What Is To Be Done?* in *The Lenin Anthology*, ed. R.C. Tucker (New York: W.W. Norton and Co. 1975), 83
10 A further explanation of the author's view of Soviet totalitarianism may be found in his article 'Stalin in Focus,' *Slavic Review* 42, no. 3 (summer 1983), 373–89.
11 Toynbee, *Civilization on Trial*, 278–9
12 Because of limitations of space this essay cannot treat the role of technology in the modern world. For a Toynbeean discussion of the subject see the author's article 'Technology, Society, and Freedom in the Tower of Babel,' *Technology in Society* 5 (1983), 119–38.
13 The prerequisites for world-wide peaceful co-operation ('the liberating discipline of globalism') are outlined in the last chapter of the author's book *The World Revolution of Westernization*.

Working with Toynbee:
A Personal Reminiscence

Jane Caplan

I was in some trepidation while I was on my way to Arnold Toynbee's office in St James's Square. Within the next few minutes, I should be in the presence of one of the most eminent men now alive in Britain. I took the lift, rang the bell, and went in, and I was quickly reassured. Arnold Toynbee's presence was not at all alarming ...

Those who know Toynbee's writings well may suspect that they have read these lines somewhere before, and they are right. My opening sentences are adapted from Toynbee's own memoir of his first meeting with the celebrated historian and statesman Lord Bryce, in 1915. At the time, Toynbee was a young man working for the Foreign Office during the war, and he had been seconded by HMG to act as Bryce's amanuensis in the drafting of a Blue Book on the treatment of the Armenians in the Ottoman Empire (an entry, as he soon realized, in the annals of propaganda rather than of scholarship or truth). Toynbee's mixed sense of fascination and hesitation at the prospect of meeting in person this almost legendary figure paralleled my own feelings over half a century later: 'I knew ... that Bryce the famous historian was only one of this many-sided personality's facets ... When I had first read *The Holy Roman Empire*, Lord Bryce had, for me, been an already historic figure; he had seemed to belong to a receding Victorian past; and now here I was having to present myself to him as [his] amanuensis ... How was I to live up to the part for which I had been cast?'[1]

I came across this account only after I had started working for Toynbee in 1970, when he was eighty-one and I twenty-five. No doubt

Bryce had had a more public life than Toynbee, and certainly Toynbee at twenty-five had a more erudite knowledge of Bryce as a scholar than I had of Toynbee by the same age. But when I read his words they seemed to collapse together in time the shared experience of two young people brought face to face not just with men of unusual reputation and distinction, but with history itself.

I do not know whether, when Toynbee in his own old age wrote down his memories of Bryce, he consciously reflected on his own passage through time. But rereading them, I notice his observation that Bryce 'had not grown old in any but the irrelevant chronological sense.' As a comment on an old man's still unflagging curiosity, this was equally true for Toynbee in his eighties, and was also partly the reason for my meeting him: he was still hard at work, and we were to collaborate on a new revision and abridgment of *A Study of History*.[2] In *Experiences* Toynbee invokes curiosity as one of three 'dynamos' that powered his urge to work, the others being conscience and anxiety.[3] In this trinity of puritan virtues, he claimed anxiety as his primary impulse; but this is often a private motivation, invisible unless disclosed. Curiosity is surely the attribute most of us would apply to Toynbee, the one that is proclaimed by both the scope and the detail of his life's work. It was certainly as characteristic of him at eighty as it had been half a century earlier, when he had set himself an agenda of research for his lifetime.

The concept of a lifetime agenda of work was something that struck me very forcefully, perhaps because it epitomized the austere self-discipline that crowned Toynbee's other 'old-fashioned' virtues. The capacity to grasp one's own future as a whole – and then, indeed, to live it – seemed quite extraordinary and inimitable. Clearly, it *was* an old-fashioned virtue, part of Toynbee's particular cultural background; but it was also the legacy of his experience of the First World War. This experience was not one of combat but of survival – the gift of an accident of ill-health that apparently precluded his being conscripted in 1914.[4] Toynbee's writings are strewn with references to this exemption from the premature death that extinguished so many of his school and college friends between 1914 and 1918, foreclosing the promise of their own life agendas. This sense of his own survival and others' loss was an equally persistent motif in his conversation: it was something he lived all the time, just as he worked in a study lined with sepia photographs of the dead friends of his youth. Although Toynbee had set himself his agenda before the war broke out, it was the war that lent a permanent urgency to its completion, as he converted his sense of chance and demerit to one of compulsive duty.[5]

By the mid-1960s, however, Toynbee had literally completed his agenda, and found himself free to turn to 'Any Other Business.' He was too old to draw up a new agenda, but he would also never emancipate himself from the habit of work, and he felt more distressed than redeemed by the fulfilment of his fifty-year project. The years between 1966 and his death at the age of eighty-six in 1975 were to become a decade of non-agenda items, amounting in the end to an astonishing harvest of some fifteen books, including major historical works such as his biography of Constantine Porphyrogenitus, a further bout of Hellenic studies in *The Greeks and Their Heritages*, and his synthetic world history *Mankind and Mother Earth*. Among these non-agenda items was a series of lavishly illustrated volumes for the London fine art publishers Thames and Hudson, including *Crucible of Christianity* (1969), and it was in this context that the decision was made in 1970 to publish a new abridgment of *A Study of History*, thoroughly revised and generously illustrated.

The original ten-volume *Study* – eleven with the subsequent *Reconsiderations* – totalled several million words of text. It was now to be reduced to 250,000 words by Toynbee, working in collaboration with an assistant, and it was in this position that I came to know him. At the time I had just left Oxford with an unfinished doctoral dissertation. I was uncertain what I wanted to do, except that I knew I no longer felt comfortable as a full-time student (this was one measure of my distance from the young Toynbee, with his lifetime agenda). I was therefore intrigued by the prospect of such an unusual and unexpected commission, especially given my background in the rather traditionalist training of the Oxford history school and my recent experience in narrow monographic research. My first meeting with Toynbee was thus not on secondment from 'HMG' but in the suppliant status of a candidate for employment. I was interviewed, as I recall, in a windowless room in Chatham House and across an immense empty table – but perhaps that distance is a metaphor inserted by imagination rather than memory. At any rate, after some delay the job was mine, and I began work in the autumn of 1970.

The project was planned to last about a year, and the object was to prepare an abridgment that differed significantly from the version previously edited by Somervell.[6] The earlier abridgment had faithfully reproduced every turn of the original argument, but at the cost of sacrificing the detail of historical exposition and example. Somervell's abridgment had captured the range of the original, but was perhaps more attractive to the student of Toynbee's thought than to that elusive category, the general reader. The new version set out to capture that readership, rejecting the miniaturization of the entire canvas in favour of a more selective epitome. Some parts of the original would be jettisoned wholesale – for example, virtually the whole of volume six, in which Toynbee had developed his heavily criticized concept of 'withdrawal and return.' By this means space was made for the retention of selected historical examples in much of their original detail, thus restoring the depth and interest of 'real history' in the book.

When I joined the project, Toynbee had already worked out the scheme of abridgment, and had completed his own revision of part one of the new edition: a 50,000-word version of passages from volumes one and two, amalgamated with parts of *Reconsiderations*. My task was to reduce by two-thirds the remaining selections from the original, which totalled almost 700,000 words. If my commission had been merely to write a summary of this, it would have been an unusual and interesting task, but somewhat mechanical. In fact, something rather different was demanded: an abridgment that reproduced Toynbee's style, as a writer no less than as a thinker, and that brought the original up to date in terms of new evidence and recent history. Toynbee's own work on the new version guaranteed that it would represent his own ideas, changed and unchanged. What was left to me was to reconstruct the remaining text in Toynbee the author's own style: a challenge that was as fascinating as it was unexpected.

As I write about this work for the first time since it was concluded over fifteen years ago, I find myself almost automatically falling back into Toynbee's style, with its long balanced sentences and carefully measured syntax. As he explains in one of his reminiscences, Toynbee felt more at home in the classical languages than in English.[7] He wrote English almost as a foreign language, allowing it to reproduce the cadences of Greek or Latin; he found it easier to express his innermost thoughts in those languages, rather than in English. And as an unkind but accurate critic wrote, Toynbee was someone who never used two adjectives where three would do. At one point during our collaboration, I suggested that I was actually reproducing an older style of writing that Toynbee himself had substantially modified and lightened in his more recent work. At any rate, I must say that without comparing the published version with these corrected drafts, or indeed with the original, I am no longer able to say with certainty which are 'my' sections and which Toynbee's. But perhaps these differences are more obvious to the alert reader.

The working procedure we established for the project was quite straightforward. I drafted new versions chapter by chapter, and mailed them to him. He would return them with his amendments, comments, queries; and from time to time, perhaps once a month, we would meet in his rambling Kensington flat to review our progress and discuss outstanding questions. Updating the text required a certain amount of research as well as rewriting. It was easy enough to modernize the terminology, for example by abandoning some of Toynbee's more recondite coinages – thus his 'General War of 1914–1918' reappeared in its more familiar form as 'First World War' throughout. Equally, there was little difficulty in bringing a narrative up to date or inserting an apt contemporary example; indeed, there was a certain pleasure in thinking up something apposite and congruent. In the new part four, the 'idolization of ephemeral military techniques' epitomized in the story of David and Goliath was illustrated by a then-topical reference to America's reliance on massive aerial fire-power against peasant guerrilla fighters in Vietnam. Similarly, the EEC bureaucracy made its way into the discussions of the civil services of universal states.

More fundamental and problematic, however, were the alterations and modifications that resulted from recent historical research, and from shifts in historiographical perspective over the years since the original *Study* had been conceived. For example, Toynbee's discussion of nomadic society as an 'arrested civilization' had to be substantially revised in the light of recent research into the history of climates, of animal and crop domestication, and of demographic history. Even more fundamental a change was the decision to include Africa as a civilization, on the grounds that it fitted both Toynbee's ethical and others' material definitions of the term.[8] This decision not only highlighted some of the problems of revision, but also questioned once again the premises of the whole Toynbeean schema.

The responsibility of researching African history fell mainly on me, and was an activity of a quite different order from that of merely checking recent research in subjects already discussed in the original, or of chasing up new and more accessible references. It was implausible to suppose that I or anyone else could in effect impersonate Toynbee himself in the act of generating such a major new component of the *Study* as an additional civilization: my role was something that questioned the entire intellectual basis on which the project had originally been constructed. Toynbee's ethical concept of civilization defined it as 'an endeavour to create a state of society in which the whole of Mankind will be able to live together in harmony, as members of a single, all-inclusive family.'[9] Whether this is true of what we called the African civilization I do not know; indeed, it is also questionable whether it is true of all the other civilizations identified by Toynbee. The example of Africa betrays the extent to which his essentially Helleno-Sinic model of civilization represents more than the ideal type he proposed it as.[10] It suggests a profound incompatibility between his spiritual convictions on the one hand, and his practical ecumenism on the other.

Of course, it was not my task to reconstruct the architectonics of the Toynbeean system. The new edition remained fully a version of his own particular vision, and whether it was improved or not by the collaboration is something that readers and critics must judge. But in the course of our collaboration many changes were made, not all of them at Toynbee's own behest. It is less surprising to me now, with a certain amount of my own work behind me, that he could view his writing with some detachment. But at the time I was struck by his willingness to concede argument rather than defend what he had written. It is, I think, a matter of public record that he had been surprised and disappointed at the generally unfavourable response to the publication of the post-war volumes of the *Study*. Pieter Geyl's pugnacity had especially pained him – he used to describe Geyl as having tried to pick a fight that he, Toynbee, had no desire to wage. In revising the *Study*, he made it clear that he had no wish to reopen these hostilities. It was on these grounds that, for example, the concept of withdrawal and return had been dropped from the revision: it was something that had originally attracted particular critical scepticism.

During our work together, Toynbee accepted or rejected my suggestions not according to their compatibility with the original plan of the *Study*, nor I think in terms of a categorically fixed vision, except in the most general sense. Rather, as he repeatedly emphasized to me, this was to be a version of his work that was above all accessible to a wide readership, whose interest one could say Toynbee sought over and above that of the professional historical community by which he had already been once rejected. Disinclined as he was to court fresh controversy, Toynbee was nevertheless keen to continue developing and propagating his ideas, as the books of his old age testify. If I say that some of the impulse for this attitude was automatic, I imply no disrespect for his motives, nor do I claim insight into all of them, by any means: despite his volumes of memoirs and self-analysis, there was a core of privacy that remained utterly hidden, at least to me. At any rate, his approach to our project sometimes made my work rather difficult. It was often hard for me to draw concrete conclusions about his intentions from our discussions, because on the whole he did not reject an idea categorically, but rather sidled around it, adding something, taking something away, and generally coaxing out a new configuration of thought from the stock of his old.

By the end of the project, we had rewritten and revised a considerable proportion of the *Study*'s central components – among them, universal churches, China, and the purpose and meaning of history and its study. In the course of it, we had barely disputed a single positive point of interpretation – partly, of course, because I had usually reserved my own opinions, such as they were, and tried to work through Toynbee's mind.[11] Yet the fact that this act of impersonation turned out to be so oddly feasible was not, I think, so much a tribute to my ability to enter his mind as it was a witness to the elasticity of the book's original conception. It was pliable enough to undergo all kinds of rearrangement. As the anonymous reviewer of the new version in the *Times Literary Supplement* noted, Toynbee was distinguished by his unshakeable self-confidence – more, I would add, than by dogmatism or rigid unteachability. I found him a curious amalgam of modesty and pretension, a paradox paralleled in my sense of him as being both deeply private in many areas and almost naïvely self-revealing in others. A humane and generous man in many respects, he conveyed a commitment to truths so vast and abstract that in a way there was no need for him to defend them, as one might defend a more partial or lesser thesis. Perhaps that sense of a sublime confidence was what chiefly antagonized his many critics.

As a historian, I do not myself share Toynbee's spiritual interpretation of history. Both at the time of the project and now, my perspectives remain materialist, premised on the primacy of social determination above spiritual agency – though perhaps with enough of a post-Hegelian tinge to bring about a certain sympathy with Toynbee's search for structure, even if not with its realization. In a different context, and at a different age, I might have found our collaboration impossible. The profoundly anti-rationalist current that flows through his work is certainly disturbing, and it can hardly be denied that he made some deeply mistaken judgments about history and about his own time. The convention among historians who taught my generation was to dismiss him as marginal or anachronistic, or both. Yet perhaps that judgment is less secure from the vantage-point of the 1980s. True, Toynbee may never be redeemed as a philosopher of history; but as a thinker who chose, perhaps mistakenly, to cast his ideas into the form of historical studies, his insistent demotion of Western 'sociocentrism' must surely be valued. On a personal note, I have never regretted the two years I spent working with him, exposed to all the convolutions and contradictions of his capacious historical vision. After the narrowness of the Oxford history school in the 1960s, channelled further into the thin rivulet of my doctoral research, to work on the *Study* was the most glorious expansion a young historian could imagine. It was an opportunity to roam, on salary, through the recorded history of the world, directed by an overseer of intellect and imagination: a perfect combination of freedom and discipline, of authority and irresponsibility. What more of an education could one ask for?

NOTES

1 Toynbee, *Acquaintances* (London: Oxford University Press 1967), 149ff.
2 Toynbee, *A Study of History*, new edition revised and abridged by the author and Jane Caplan (London: Oxford University Press 1972)

3 Toynbee, *Experiences* (New York and London: Oxford University Press 1969), 87–91
4 Ibid., 38–9
5 Ibid., 104; chap. 7 and 8, *passim*
6 *A Study of History*, abridgment by D.C. Somervell (New York and London: Oxford University Press 1947, 1957)
7 *Study*, 12 : 587–90
8 *Study* (new ed.), 44–71
9 Ibid., 44
10 One of the points in the original *Study* that critics had much difficulty in swallowing was the assertion that Toynbee's method was strictly empirical, that he had 'found' rather than constructed his object of knowledge, the civilization. The issue was side-stepped in the revised version by the device of recasting his method as a search for a model – a Weberian ideal type, in effect; cf. chap. 6: 'The Comparative Study of Civilizations.'
11 It was characteristic of Toynbee's generosity and intellectual courtesy that he insisted on referring to the project as a collaboration from the start. If it was a partnership of this kind, it was clear that Toynbee remained the senior partner throughout, and that my contributions were always to be filtered through his authorship. I think he came to rely on me to sort out a lot of the procedural work and to act as a testing-ground for his ideas; he needed someone who could, mechanically, create a shorter book, but also someone who could criticize the contents. I enjoyed both roles, but can claim only the former as my contribution to the finished book.

Contributors

THOMAS W. AFRICA, professor of history at the State University of New York, Binghamton, has written *Phylarchus and the Spartan Revolution, Science and the State in Greece and Rome*, and *The Immense Majesty: A History of Rome and the Roman Empire*, among other works.

JANE CAPLAN was Toynbee's assistant in the early 1970s, and worked with him to write the one-volume edition of *A Study of History*. She is now professor of history at Bryn Mawr College, and author of *Government without Administration: State and Civil Service in Weimar and Nazi Germany*.

C.T. MCINTIRE, professor of history at Trinity College, University of Toronto, has published *England against the Papacy, 1858–1861, God, History, and Historians, History and Historical Understanding*, and other books.

WILLIAM H. MCNEILL, is Distinguished Service Professor of History (emeritus) at the University of Chicago. Among his many books are *The Rise of the West, A World History, Plagues and People*, and *The Pursuit of Power*.

CHRISTIAN B. PEPER, a friend of Toynbee's, is the editor of *An Historian's Conscience*, Toynbee's correspondence during almost forty years with Father Columba of Ampleforth Abbey. He is senior lawyer of the firm Peper, Martin, Jensen, Maichel and Hetlage in St Louis, Missouri.

MARVIN PERRY is the author of *Arnold Toynbee and the Crisis of the West* and *Western*

Civilization: Ideas, Politics, and Society, and associate professor of history at Baruch College, the City University of New York.

EDWARD PESSEN, Distinguished Professor of History at Baruch College and the Graduate Center of the City University of New York, is author of *Most Uncommon Jacksonians, Riches, Class, and Power before the Civil War, Jacksonian America, Three Centuries of Social Mobility in America, The Log Cabin Myth: The Social Backgrounds of the Presidents*, and many other works.

BERNICE GLATZER ROSENTHAL, the author of *Dmitri Sergevich Merezhkovsky and the Silver Age, A Revolution of the Spirit* (co-author and co-editor with Martha Bohachevsky-Chomiak), and *Nietzsche in Russia*, is professor of history at Fordham University.

FREDERICK M. SCHWEITZER is professor of history at Manhattan College, and has published *A History of the Jews since the First Century A.D.* and *Dictionary of the Renaissance*.

ROLAND N. STROMBERG, Professor Emeritus of History at the University of Wisconsin, Milwaukee, wrote *Arnold J. Toynbee: Historian for an Age in Crisis, European Intellectual History since 1789, Redemption by War: The Intellectuals and World War I*, and other books.

THEODORE H. VON LAUE, Frances and Jacob Hiatt Professor Emeritus of European History at Clark University, is the author of *Leopold Ranke: The Formative Years, Sergei Witte and the Industrialization of Russia, Why Lenin? Why Stalin?, The World Revolution of Westernization*, and other books.

W. WARREN WAGAR, Distinguished Teaching Professor of History at the State University of New York, Binghamton, has published *H.G. Wells and the World State, The City of Man: Prophecies of a World Civilization in Twentieth Century Thought, Good Tidings: The Belief in Progress from Darwin to Marcuse*, and other works.

www.ingramcontent.com/pod-product-compliance
Lightning Source LLC
Chambersburg PA
CBHW071154070526
44584CB00019B/2784